AF889496

SERVICE SECTOR AND GLOBALISATION

SERVICE SECTOR AND GLOBALISATION

TALWAR SABANNA
Karnatak University, KRC P.G. Centre
Belgaum, Karnataka (India)

SERIALS PUBLICATIONS
NEW DELHI

© Talwar Sabanna

First Published - 2008

ISBN : 978-81-8387-140-2

All rights reserved with the Publisher, including the right to translate or reproduce this book or parts thereof except for brief quotations in critical articles or reviews.

Published by

SERIALS PUBLICATIONS
4830/24, Ansari Road, Darya Ganj
New Delhi-110002
Phone : 23245225
Fax : 91-11-23272135
E-mail: serials@satyam.net.in

CONTENTS

	Preface		*vii*
1.	Nimbus Four Twenty and India–A Deathnell to Social Sector Contracting the IPRs	*Nimbur B.N. & Madari D.M.*	1
2.	Intellectual Property Rights: Gear up India to Meet the Challeges and Opporunities	*S. K. Karimulla & A. Ranga Reddy*	11
3.	Precision Farming: Importance and Relevance to Indian Agriculture	*Siva Jyothsna V. Sudhakar Goud R. & Kamalakar Reday A.*	21
4.	Social Sector in Globalised Economy Workers' Perspective	*Sham Bahadur Katuwal*	27
5.	Health Care Infrastructure in the Context of Globalisation in India	*J. B. Komaraiah & Rinky Sharma*	57
6.	India's Power Sector-Potential, Performance and Prospects	*Kiran Kumar P., Jayasheela & Basil Hans V.*	79
7.	Banks and Rural Development.	*B. Siddappa*	97
8.	Problems and Prospects of India's Tourism Industry under Globalize Regime-an Exploratory Study	*Akash S.B. & Kamble H.Y.*	103
9.	Banking Sector under Globalisation	*Sumathy Venkatesan*	117
10.	The Economics of Domestic Violence Against Women	*N. Dharmaraj & J. Cyril Kanmony*	123
11.	Intellectual Property Rights and Economic Development	*S. N. Yogish*	131
12.	Impact of Financial Sector Reforms in Banking Services–A Study in Kerala	*Benson Kunjukunju & Varghese Antony*	139
13.	Agriculture-India's Backbone Industry and its Plight in the Wake of Globalisation	*Pushpa P.*	159

14.	Sustainable Fishery Resource Development in Maharashtra	*P. S. Kamble & Vidya Chougule*	185
15.	Primary Education and Infrastructure in India: Progress and Problems	*Harisha N., Jayasheela & V. Basil Hans*	191
16.	Health for all in India and Human Distress	*W. N. Salve*	205
17.	Problems and Prospects of Dairy Co-operatives in India	*P. S. Kamble, A. S. Suryavanshi & Lalita Jagtap*	215
18.	Problems and Prospects of Escoms in Power Distribution	*B. Siddappa*	233
19.	Education and Telecommunication	*S. N. Yogish*	239
20.	The Law on Industrial Designs	*M. S. Sowmya & N. S. Sreenivasulu*	247
21.	GATs and India's Education Sector-Issues and Options	*Showkat Ali Magalmani, Jayasheela & V. Basil Hans*	259
22.	Water-shed Development-An Emerging Area of Voluntary Work in India	*V.S. Adigal*	279
23.	Application and Procedure under the Patent Act	*Kuljit Kaur*	295

PREFACE

The waves of reform affect the economy in three stages. The head, i.e., government has to reform firs of all governance so that other reforms follow suit; hence government becomes the first to feel the waves of reforms to start with. Once reforms in basic governance are completed, it will facilitate the smooth functioning of sectoral reforms in many quantifiable ways. It is in this wave period that the social, environmental reforms are completed and a holistic development epoch ushers in. For some, the order could be reversed. But there cannot be a second opinion on the simultaneous launch of the different reforms and their combined impact, provided the resources and their management is utilized toward that end. Many a country has experienced the fruits of reforms in varying degrees, but the moot question is, are we really in the reform age? In all these things education has played an important role and hence the reforms have the tendency to affect the quality of education.

The experience on reforms in India has been a parody of introversion and suspicion, both internal and extern. There was practically lack of innovativeness in ushering in an appropriate governance system in tune with the requirements of various groups of citizens. Thus the colonial with the requirements of various groups of citizens. Thus the colonial system of administration continued with little changes. It may appear as a negative reform accomplished. Reasons could be aplenty for its continuance but such a system did not bring in a new character policy and economy as against the preceding regime. With this background the present book intends to provide a great forum for debate and interaction about IPR and Social Sector.

NIMBUS FOUR TWENTY AND INDIA– A DEATHNELL TO SOCIAL SECTOR CONTRACTING THE IPRs

Nimbur B.N. & Madari D.M.**

INTRODUCTION

The preamble of the constitution is explicit to mention that "India is a Democratic, Sovereign and Republic." This has stood steadfast from its inception in 1950 to 2005. However in 2006 and in the James Bond year 007, it appears that there has been an encroachment on the sovereignty of the country and as a result the society has been taken for a ride. Therefore, in the phobia of globalization, the interest of the Indian society should not be lost sight off. The attempt being placed before the Supreme Court remains a matter of subjudice and stands hegemony for days and months. In the meantime the Nimbus stands free and firm to play its game of four-twenty with the vast Indian society. It is really a serious matter of national interest and challenge to the sovereignty of the country, not only should the present monopolistic international hegemony Nimbus issue should be kept in mind. But also the future IPRs contracting[1] should not miss the national bus. There are immense cardinal and ordinal losses to the Indian social sector.

Given this, the present article attempts to discuss the implications of international terrestrial telecasting IPRs contracts reached by the Prasar Bharati of India with the Nimbus International Communication Company (Co.).

I

THE BACKGROUND

Since the advent of globalization with the birth of World Trade Organization (WTO), the international commodity trade agreements have not been reached. There are trade groups belonging to the countries of

* Professor, and Lecturer, Deptt. of Economics, Gulbarga University, Gulbarga-585106 and Karnataka State Women's University, Bijapur-586101.

different continents. However, the developing and like minded countries including India as a leader have taken a serious stand for implementing the idea of free trade. A number of meetings have been held in this context. The failure of Doha round of talks have brought the negotiations almost to a stand still. Further a number of intra continental trade groups have been forging ahead so as to bring about free trade among themselves. The SAARC, Asian Common Market, For East Asian Common Market, Afro Asian Common Market are some of the conducive institutions have been emerging slowly but steadily[2]. The giants like Japan, China, Africa and even Russia have been sharing a platform in the direction of introducing negotiated free trade. Whereas the countries of European Union, and the country like America have put forth the argument for free trade suitable to them which is detrimental to the developing countries including that of Brazil, Sweden, Slovakia and others.

Whereas side by the free trade agreements relating to International Intellectual Property Rights (IPRs), Trade Related Intellectual Property Rights (TRIPs) and International Investment Related Rights (TRIMs) have been advanced in the recent past. As a token of these, many countries have brought about patents and copyrights in addition to laws relating to TRIPs and TRIMs. The patents[3], copyrights cover important national products and TRIPs and TRIMs have been aimed to safeguard the rights of national in the international arena. For example, India has introduced patent and copyright act relating to TRIPs as early as in the year 2002-03. However, during the year 2003-04 a law to contract IPRs in the information and communication sector. Further these contracts are applicable to many aspects of the social sector such as health, education, sports, culture, Information and Technology and Bio-Technology (ITBT) etc.

II

NIMBUS–420

It may be recalled that India desirous of going global and realizing its limitations in the area of communicational technology decided to make a contract with a technologically strong international communication company of USA the Nimbus. The Nimbus company being too large has the monopoly in the field of communications in the international arena. The company with its financial strength has not only reached various channels but also the channels of various countries and continents. Furthermore, it has in the recent past introduced its own channel known as Neo-telecast in a number of countries. The company has the privilege of being received the IPR contract even with the Government of United States. The company had acquired the sole right to telecast a world Soccer Cup held at USA in the recent past. India realizing its international strength and potential thought of making a periodic contract for terrestrial right to live telecast national and international events as a sole authority which provides the company an authority or the right to appropriate the Ad revenues. In the year 2003-04, India made a contract with Prasar Bharati to undertake the terrestrial live telecast of national and international events through its restricted domestic channels of various countries. However, in the year 2006-07, the contract made between Prasar Bharati and Nimbus came to a point of breach of contract. The negotiated settlement failed because the Nimbus company thought of losing Ad revenues originating from live telecast of recently held international cricket matches in India. The one day international cricket match with West Indies was not telecast on Prasar Bharati or any national and international channels except its own channel the Neo. However, for the second match out of the four with West Indies, the company agreed to share the live telecasting but with an important rider. By accepting this rider, the company introduced two India's which the Prasar Bharati CEO called as Taji (fresh) and basi (unfresh) delayed. Under the renewed sumoto action of the Nimbus the company decided to give live telecast with a gap of seven minutes, which continued on national Doordarshan (DD) for seven matches i.e. three matches with West Indies and four series with Srilanka. It is but common sense to understand that the advertisement revenues are fixed on the basis of the durational units i.e. seconds. If the telecast is given live with a delay of seven minutes would mean a delay by *420 seconds*. Instead of the match, the brief of what has been happening from the beginning was shown in terms of scores on D.D. news channel. Thus the crores of India sports lovers were to be content with this type of inconvenience caused by Nimbus company. Therefore Nimbus Company may be brought under Article 420 of the India IPC. The sole purpose of the Nimbus was that of mind your business.

III

CHALLENGE TO THE LAW OF LAND

No doubt that India is a vast country, it is also a second largest populous country in the world. Further, more than these due to the strong spiritual, philosophic and humble cultural background, the country has produced people of a altogether different quality in many respects than that of the people of other nations. It is a noteworthy by nook and corners of the people of this country, besides the legislators and law abiding citizens. The Parliament of India enacted the Prasar Bharati bill and go it approved by the parliament of the country which *inter alia* provides autonomy to this institution[4]. Consequent upon its network and start various channels of its own. Needless to mention the fact that the information and communication Act provides opportunity for various private commercial channels on which the Prasar Bharati has no rights whatsoever.

However, becoming an autonomous and governmental representative body, the Prasar Bharati to become independent and self sustainable in terms of its operations has been given the right to introduce the important national channels. Among them, the national Channel-I is considered to be most important and vital for the entire DD networking and its other channels As such, the right to award contract to national and international terrestrial communication companies to telecast important national and international events on Channel-I and provide contractual revenues to the Prasar Bharati. The awardees can do so by collecting revenues by means of advertising products and services or even sponsor the advertisements for which the awardees can collect as much money as it feels by means of sub-contractings. There are differing rates for different time units and number of displays in a given period of time. These will be noted in details in the next section.

The Nimbus Company was awarded the contract for telecasting national and international events for a fixed period with fixed amount in the form of contractual rental to the Doordarshan. But the company decided to breach this contract with Prasar Bharati. This breach not only directly challenged the authority of the Prasar Bharati but also indirectly the supremacy of the law of the land. The people were denied the opportunity of not seeing the live telecast of one international cricket match. In order to prevail upon the Nimbus, the meetings with CEO of Nimbus did not yield results. However, fearing the action from the government to the extent of sumoto termination of the contract with Prasar Bharati and make it null and void, the Nimbus eased its stand and introduced 420 seconds delayed live telecast. Not satisfied with this, without resorting to the final sturn decision, the government promulgated an ordinace[5] in this context. But the Nimbus turning to become humble not only as continued its 420 activity but also has sort refuge with Supreme Court of India. The matter is yet under subjudice and hearing has been posted in the month of March 2007.

IV

LOSS OF MONOPOLISTIC REVENUE

The main motive of the Nimbus which could be understood by its this type of act in the context of a post contractarian society[6] like India is the fear of revenue loss and the loss of monopolistic power of terrestrial. Telecasting IPR contract entered into with Prasar Bharati and Ministry of Information and Broadcasting. However, the communication Ministry has not only did not take any step to disturb the international information highway but even did not open its mouth. It remained tight lipped which is highly praise worthy. Whereas, Mr. Priyaranjan Das Munshi, the Hon'ble Minister for Information and Broadcasting (including telecasting) went to the extent of making a public pronouncement that the Prasar Bharati will share only 27 and 27 per cent of total revenues and balance amount of 73 per cent will go to the Nimbus corporation. However, there is no respite from the company. The probable total earnings for the telecast of one day international cricket match for a period of seven and half hours live telecast on Doordarshan (DD) and consequent revenue loss to the Nimbus has been worked out on the basis of approximations announced by Prasar Bharati from time to time regarding the number of seconds display and chargeable advertisement amount has been attempted below.

Table 1
Revenue Earnings for Doordarshan

Item	*In Seconds*		*Advertisement Charges (Rs. in Lakhs)*
Total Telecasting Time	27000		
Hourly Interval	1800		
Approximate Total Second for Advertisement displays	9000		
The Range of Advertisement Amount Fixed	(a)	1-10	0.50
	(b)	1-20	0.75
	(c)	1-30	1.00
	(d)	1-60	1.50

Note: Revenue Earnings data is approximate calculations.

It has to be noted that the Ministry and Nimbus have hoped that there will be a revenue earnings up to the extent of Rs. 1200 crore of which 27 per cent will have to go to Prasar Bharati. Therefore, we have not made any exercise of the amount fixed for units of seconds and number of displays that a product or service which are brought in between the live telecast of a match. Therefore, the original contract of Nimbus with

Prasar Bharati remains alive and untouched. The Government also has kept in mind the international phenomenon of liberalization and globalization in mind. Under these circumstances, the Nimbus activity of 420 clearly fits into the IPC 420 of the country. It should be subject to the imposition of appropriate amount of penalty for the damage that it has made to the Indian DD viewers of delayed seven international matches hitherto held in the country.

V

DAMAGES TO THE SOCIAL SECTOR

Indeed it is very difficult to make the correct assessment of the damage that has been inflicted by Nimbus on the post contractarian globalised and vibrant Indian society. It is difficult for measurement if a cardinal yardstick is adopted. However the Indian trade and commerce sector largely based on the mass visual media for their enhancement have suffered to some extent a quantifiable loss. In this too, it is highly problematic to measure as to the loss incurred by each product and the services that the sector renders and the amount of loss that has been caused by Nimbus. Similarly, cardinal loss for the social sector are beyond the reach of any human scale or meter for quantification. But, nonetheless the ordinal loss to the social sector could be identified and may be put into black and white in a way one imagines.

Before bringing out the social sector damages of the Nimbus Act, it may be noted that as per the TRIPS agreement, the Agreement on Trade Related aspects of Intellectual Property Rights, including Trade in Counterfeit goods contained in Annex IC of the Marrakesh Agreement establishing the WTO was signed in Marrakesh[7], Morocco on 15th April 1994. In accordance with the TRIPs agreement, countries are free to determine the 'appropriate method' for implementing the agreement within their own legal system and practice[8].

The agreement reaffirms the well-established principle of 'national treatment', which means that the nationals of any country member of the agreement are to be treated in the same way as nationals of the country where protection is granted[9]. It also extends to IPRs the 'most-favoured-nation clause', i.e. the obligation to extend, with some limited exceptions, to any member the advantages granted to any other member or members[10]. These principles are meant to end discrimination, both between foreigners and national and between nationals of different countries, which arises when IPRs are granted only to the nationals of the country.

TRIPs agreement allows member countries to provide for the international exhaustion of rights[11] and therefore, to admit parallel imports if they so wish. This principle can be crucial for the protection of consumers' interests and for ensuring access to industrial or agricultural inputs at competitive prices.

The TRIPs agreement embodies an important principle by which the member countries are empowered to formulate or amend their laws and regulation and thus to adopt measures to protect public health and nutrition, and to promote the public interest in sectors of vital importance to their socio-economic and technological development, provided that such measures are consistent with the provisions of this agreement[12].

It also empowers the member countries to take appropriate measures that may be needed to prevent the abuse of IPRs by right holders or the resort to practices which unreasonably restrain trade or adversely affect the international transfer of technology[13]. These provisions facilitate legislating limitations to exclusive rights, as well as the enactment of legislative provisions concerning the compulsory licensing of certain IPRs. In particular, the grounds mentioned are relevant for the granting of compulsory licenses in the pharmaceutical field in order to keep prices at a reasonable level or to ensure access to particular medicines by the population. However, the TRIPs agreement itself sets out conditions which could reduce the scope to grant compulsory licenses[14].

Thus it is evident that the Nimbus has breached the IPR agreement with India. As a result, in the first place, because of 420 minutes of delayed telecast introduced two types of viewers in the Indian society. It is important to note that the delayed receivers were at a loss of information. They also suffered from the mental hiccup that the news channel gave a summary of the 420 seconds direct telecast view of the match.

The large number of youth in the country keen to see and learn many things besides the cricket were lost to a greater extent. The contract made by Prasar Bharati with members became a subject of great hatredness in the society in general and the sports loving section of the youth in particular. Thirdly, the other social damage is the disgust that people could realize regarding the cultural technological advertisements which were telecast with less clarity and provided less enthusiasm to make further advancement. Lastly, the serious damage is that it is the first kind of IPR breach that India could openly sense the ill effects originating from the contracts with respect to IPRs and a unforgettable lesson for the people and the government[15].

VI

A FUTURISTIC VIEW

It is very crucial for the government and people of the country that our desire to be globalised and be a party to WTO and its agreements relating to TRIPs have if not honoured by other international organizations could put India into very seriously disadvantage position. There are a number of other areas where India has a great potential for development and has a unique place in the domain of plant medicines and plant related drugs which can cure dreaded diseases with very simplicity and with very vary nominal costs[16].

Similarly the tropical country has very diverse geographic capabilities in terms of variety of foods, plants and medicinal practices. If these are not brought under proper IPR network India stands as a great looser. It has been brought to the attention of the Indian scientists that the high quality basmati rice has been genetically transformed by some advanced countries and have been claiming their patent right for its sale in India itself.

Thus, there are various aspects of TRIPs covering production and social sectors which call for a proper handling with respect to WTO–TRIPs. For example, the copyright of some ingenuous literary and scientific works of Indians have very remarkable place. They have to be protected. The Indians have been considered as an intelligent race in terms of Science and Technology. There are some distinct industrial designs, layout designs, geographical indications, trade marks, topographies of integrated circuits, trade secrets and the control of anti-competitive practices in contractual licenses. Therefore, the future is very wise and bright for the globalizing India and it has the distinction of having highest per cent of young talented and technically equipped per cent of population which has to be reckoned with not only in India but also compared to large number of developed and developing countries.

VII

CONCLUSION

The establishment of WTO and the desire to have free trade among members of WTO has met with serious hurdles and blocks between developed and developing countries. In particular, the subsidies given to farmers in USA and European Union (EU) have become the hot bed for discussion. However, there are yet some ray of hopes that the dialogue between countries of the world may take place in 2007 and may pave the way for free trade as per the objectives of WTO.

Similarly, there are some agreements relating to TRIPs and TRIMs under the umbrella of WTO. The IPRs and their protection has been very important agreement. As per the Marrakesh agreement reached in Morocco, the contracting under IPRs are subject to laws of the land of the contracting parties. The Nimbus International Communication Company was awarded contract with Prasar Bharati for international telecasting right with regard to some important international events. However the Nimbus corporation breached the contract by delayed telecast of cricket matches by seven minutes which is nothing but 420 seconds gap. This coincides with the Indian Penal Code 420 on which the government can take necessary legal action. Accordingly, Government of India, the President signed an ordinance to correct the behaviour of the Nimbus. The matter is with the Supreme Court of India. The company has damaged the feelings and sentiments of the people and hurt the sport loving community of youth. Similarly, there are many social sector IPRs which should be subject to scrutiny before reaching an agreement or contract. The monetary loss is one part but social damages are the others. Future IPRs should take cognizance of the act of Nimbus with India.

REFERENCES

Kumar Nagesh (2003), "IPRs, Technology and Economic Development: Experiences of Asian Countries", *Economic and Political Weekly,* pp. 209-225.

Stetanie Weigman, Research on Intellectual Law in an *International Context*, LLRX.Com.

Ramanna Anitha (2002), "Policy Implications of India's Patent Reforms" Patent Applications in the Post–1995 Era, *Economic and Political Weekly,* pp. 2065-2075.

Vaidya Vandana (2006), "IPRs–A Boon to Indian Companies", Available at *Legal Service India.com* accessed on March 18.

President of India Signed an Ordinance to Restore the Terrestrial Right Entirely with Prasar Bharati and declare the contract with Nimbus as Null and Void in the month of January 2007.

See Buchanan James (1973), "The Democracy in Deficit". The Choice Between Anarch and Leviathan–*The Legacy Left by Lord Keynes*.

See Marakkaesh (1994), "Agreement on establishing the WTO" with Special Reference to TRIPs, meeting held in Marrakesh, Morocco in 15th April.

Article 1 of the TRIPs Agreement.

Article 3 of the TRIPs Agreement.

Article 4 of the TRIPs Agreement.

Article 6 of the TRIPs Agreement.

Article 8(1) of the TRIPs Agreement.

Article 38(2) of the TRIPs Agreement.

Article 31 of the TRIPs Agreement.

Dhavan Rajeev (2004), "The Patent Controversy", *The Hindu*, Delhi.

Link Exchange (2006), "IPRs in India".

INTELLECTUAL PROPERTY RIGHTS: GEAR UP INDIA TO MEET THE CHALLENGES AND OPPORTUNITIES

S.K. Karimulla & A. Ranga Reddy***

INTRODUCTION

The paper highlights the entry, existence, competition and complementarily of Intellectual Property Rights (IPRs) in India.

One of the most controversial outcomes of the Uruguay Round (UR) is the Agreement on Trade Related Intellectual Property Rights (TRIPRs). IPRs along with TRIMs and services were called the new issues negotiated in the UR.

Protection of Intellectual Property Rights has become a throny issue of wide and serious debate, with the formation of the General Agreement on TRIPRs under World Trade Organisation. It is feared that IPRs regime is largely against indigenous communities in developing countries and would escalate bio-piracy in the name of Science and Development. Indian Government wants a balanced view on IPR, adding that phenomenal technological advancement was a double edged weapon which posed serious challenges along with opportunity[1]. IPRs agreement put numerous burdens on the developing countries-raising cost consumer products such as medicines and hindering innovation and technology upgrading[2].

DEFINITION

IPRs may be defined as "information with commercial value". IPRs have been characterised as a composite of "ideas, inventions and creative expression" plus the public willingness to bestow the status of property. IPRs are nine categories: patent, trademarks, copy rights, geographic indications, undisclosed information (such as trade secrets) industrial

* Ph.D Researcher in Economics.
** Professor, Department of Economics, Sri Venkateswara University, Tirupati-517502.

designs, industrial designs, integrated circuits, micro-organism and plant variety protection[3]. Special (*Sui generis*) form of protection have also emerged to address specific needs of knowledge, products in the case of plant breeder's rights and the protection of layout designs of integrated circuits.

OBJECTIVES

The following are main objectives:

(a) To Encourage and Reward Creative Work: Protection of copy right and related rights is to encourage and reward creative work.

(b) To Encourage Innovation: They are designed to provide protection for the results of investment in the development of new technology.

(c) To Promote Fair Competition: To protect distinctive signs and other IPRs aims to stimulate and ensure fair comptition among producers.

(d) To Help Consumer Protection: To protect distinctive signs and other IPRs aims to stimulate and ensure fair competition among producers.

(e) To facilitate Transfer of Technology: To facilitate foreign technology in the form of FDI, joint ventures and licensing. There should be a balance in between legitimate interests of right holders and of users.

BENEFITS

Stronger IPRs protection may encourage investment, both foreign and domestic. Stronger implementation of IPRs could be expected to give a boost to R & D in countries like India, whose intellectual capital potential may be expected to grow in great width and depth. IPR system provides a great opportunity to developing countries to benefit from protection of indigenous property rights and traditional knowledge. Developing countries hold approximately 90 per cent of world biological resources, which are particularly important in the development of new pharmaceuticals. Mechanisms of sharing the proceeds from commercialising genetic resources can be written into the IPR law[4].

DISADVANTAGES

The developing countries are very poor and are ill equipped for significant R & D. Industrial countries are the major producers of technology and developing countries heavily depend on imports of technology. Probably,

IPRs turn out to be generally, more beneficial to industrial countries than to developing countries. Developed countries enormously benefit from the benefits of higher prices resulting from the market power provided by IPRs, at the expense of developing countries. Industrial countries gain huge amounts of net transfer from TRIPRs, developing countries including India, are expected to experience net outwards transfers on account of TRIPRs. A strong IPRs regime without adequate safeguards to protect interests of weaker sections can create very serious problems in developing countries. Exorbitant prices will make patented essential drugs beyond the reach of common man.

Developing countries don't have adequate institutional mechanism and resources to properly administer IPRs regime. For example, a proper competition law (made in India) and its efficient enforcement are required to combat the potential anti-competitive abuse of IPRs. While in many industrial countries such abuses are dealt with by general Competition Law.

Unless developing countries rapidly establish adequate competition frame works and regulatory institutions that also address monopoly abuse of IPRs, it is possible that increasing IPR protection could result in welfare losses from monopoly behaviour. This country preserves 6 per cent of world's flowering plant species, 14 per cent of world's birds, one third of the world's identified plant species numbering over 45,000 and over 5 per cent of the 81,000 species of wild animals (The World Bank 1996). Biological resources immensely contribute to agriculture; at least 166 species of crop plants and 320 species of wild relatives of cultivated crops originate in India. 90 per cent of medicinal plants are harvested. Under IPRs it may endanger species as forest authorities are not allowing people.

EXPERIENCES AND PRACTICES

Studies have shown that a realistically designed IPRs system becomes beneficial after a country has attained a certain level of technological development and R & D capability. It is observed that although ensuring a core level of IPR protection may increase developing country access to foreign technologies by safeguarding returns for foreign technology producers, excessively strong IPRs can inhibit the diffusion of knowledge. In developing countries, knowledge is built more through access, imitation and diffusion of foreign technologies rather than only local research. Japan introduced patents in the early 20th century after reviewing IPR systems in Europe and the United States. Malaysia and Koreas', growth in industrial sectors took place under weak IPR regimes, and later periods governments emphasized incentives for innovation in IPRs as sophisticated local technology sectors developed.

Developing countries can avoid patenting life forms and can apply special provisions under TRIPRs to exempt public goods from IPR protection. They can expand IPR scope to protect genetic resources, traditional knowledge and folklore, as is promoted by the World Intellectual Property Organisation. Free trade in IPR protected goods ensures competition in product markets, reduces prices, and enhances consumer access to new technologies. But trade in IPR protected products may restrict access to new technologies for developing countries. TRIPs neither endorses nor prohibits parallel imports.

PATENTS

A patent is a legal protection granted for an invention that is new, non-obvious and useful. The patent grants the patent holder the exclusive right to make user or sell the patented products or process. The main purpose of the patent is to benefit the society patents, by providing an opportunity to recoup the cost of invention and to make profit out of the invention, encourage research and development and thereby contribute to the well being of the society. An invention, to be patentable, must satisfy three conditions–it is new, it is useful to the society, it is non-obvious to a person possessed of average skill in the art. Exclusion of an invention from patentability for commercial exploitation is permitted if it is necessary to protect public order or morality, including to protect human, animal or plant life or health or to avoid serious prejudice to the environment.

INDIAN PATENT LAW

East India Co., was introduced patent law in 18th century. Formal patent protection was enacted as patent Act, 1911. The patents Act, 1970 amended and consolidated the law. Being a member in World Trade Organisation, India was accepted to follow it with effect from January 1, 2005. The Indian Patents Act 1970, as amended and effective from Jan. 1, 2005 as follows–eligibility, procedures and conditions for grant of patents, grounds for revocation of patents, matters related to working of the patent and compulsory licensing and Rights of government regarding patented products. The amendment expanded the scope of patentability to all fields of Technology including food, drugs and pharmaceutical and agri-chemicals[5].

ITEMS NOT PATENT

Inventions which are frivolous or contrary to public interest; method of agriculture or horticulture; any process of treatment of human beings or animals; plants and animals; a mathematical or business method or a computer program *per se* or algorithms; the mere discovery of a scientific principles or the formulation of an abstract theory or discovery of any living thing or non-living substance occurring in nature; a mere scheme or rule or method of performing mental act or method of playing game; a presentation of information; topography of integrated circuits; an invention which, in effect, is traditional knowledge or which is an aggregation or duplication of known properties of traditionally known components.

PATENT PRODUCT AND PERIOD

The amended Act provides for grant of product patent. Previously, for food, pharmaceutical and chemical products only process patent was granted in India. This meant that any body was free to manufacture the same or similar product by a process different from the patent one. For Food, Pharmaceutical and Chemical products, previously the patent period was 14 years. Now patents are granted for all products for a period of 20 years from the date of application. Patents are granted merely to enable patentee to enjoy a monopoly but to encourage inventions and to secure that the inventions are worked in India on a commercial scale. The benefit of patent invention would be available at affordable price to the public.

The critics fear that adoption of product patent will enable to multinational drug firms to exploit the Indian consumers. The patent protection period of 20 years is too long a period. Five to seven years may be reasonable period.

By participating in the international system of IPR protection, India, with its vast pool of scientific and technological personnel, and well-established expertise in medical treatment and health care, has unlocked vast opportunities in both exports and outsourcing and has the potential to become a global hub in the area of Research and Development based on clinical research.

BIODIVERSITY AND TRADITIONAL KNOWLEDGE

The Doha Ministerial declaration emphasized the importance of traditional knowledge (TK). It instructed the Council for Trade-Related Aspects of Intellectual Property Rights (TRIPRs) "to examine, *inter alia,* the relationship between the TRIPRs Agreement and the Convention on Biological Diversity, the protection of traditional knowledge and folklore, and other relevant new developments raised by members Traditional knowledge is essential to the food security and health of millions of people in the developing world. In many countries, traditional medicines provide the only affordable treatment available to poor people. Moreover in developing countries upto 80 per cent of the population depend on traditional medicines to help and meet their healthcare needs. However, it is only recently that the international community has started giving recognition to traditional knowledge.

Some of the patents are even based on Geographical Indications (GIs) from developing countries; for instance, patent on Basmati rice from India and jasmine rice from Thailand. After a patent on Basmati rice lines and grains granted by USPTO to M/s Rice Tee Inc., USA on September 2nd, 1997, India contested this patent. In a long litigation of almost five years, ultimately the title of the patent was changed in year 2002. The products list could include goods such as Indian saris. Oriental carpets specialty Teas such as Darjeeling (India), Cheeses such as parmigiano Reggiano (Italy), Jamon de Huelva (Spanish Ham), art paper (China), porcelain from Limoges (France)[6].

GEOGRAPHICAL INDICATIONS

Geographical Indication (GI) is defined as an indication which identifies a good as originating in the territory of a member country of the WTO or a region or locality in that territory where a given quality, reputation or other characteristics of a product is essentiality attributable to geographical origin. Often it was an indication of source of the product, like Swiss Watches, German Lens, Florida Oranges, and was the "appellation of origin"[7].

A GI certificate will mean that only the rice grown in India will quality to be called as "thus conferring legal protection to the product and safeguarding its unauthorised use by other countries or producers besides eliminating unfair competition for the benefit of genuine producers and consumers. Basmati is a major export earner for India with exports touching 11,20,000 tones in 2005, registering a growth of about 45 per cent over the previous years. In value terms, exports rose to $596 million in 2005 from $432 million the previous year.

The application field with geographical Indications Registry in August 2004 by Heritage Foundation, a trust based in Karnal, Haryana for registering basmati as a GI is found to be flawed in terms of representation of basmati growers/ farmers on the trust[8]. Europe Union alone has granted so far more than 5,000 different GI's.

India's ancient use of Haldi (Turmeric) was sought to be patented under the American law in 1995. Luckily for India, Dr. R.A. Mashelkar, Former Director General, Council of Scientific and Industrial Research Challenged it. The U.S. patent office acknowledged its mistake and cancelled the patent on "Haldi". An American Company has been granted a patent right for Neem as a pesticide.

IPRs ON INDIAN ECONOMY

India felt IPRs had disastrous effects especially more on two vital areas i.e., pharmaceuticals and agriculture. Both these areas affect the well being of the people. A dangerous provision has been introduced in patent protection and this relates to changing the philosophy of the patent regime whereby products imported or locally produced, will be covered under patent protection without any discrimination. This implies that the patent regime not only tries to establish import monopoly.

Pranab Mukerjee, former Minister for Commerce stated that India does not recognize patents in the field of drugs, food products and chemicals, has been allowed a transition period of 10 years for establishing a product patent regime for such items. Government retains the right to institute price control on drugs. Many intellectuals may not accept it. India is plagued by mass poverty and high unemployment, which is needed life saving drugs and other basic medicines should be available at affordable and low price. This can be achieved by control over drugs of prices at global level. The government has to continue with the drug price control and keep medical treatment at lower level, reach to the poor. Already, the situation has been changing in this direction with the growing trend of privatization in health. Stronger IPRs can increase the price of input and consequently denial of life saving medicines to the poor[9]. The Government of India has been under constant attack that the *Sui generis* (Plant Breeder Rights) system is against the interest of the farmers and would act as an impediment to the development of new plant varieties.

IP ON SEEDS AND MONOPOLISATION OF LIFE

The inherent right of the farmers to save and exchange seeds is under threat. The proposed plant variety protection act fails to protect the rights of the small and marginal farmers. The patents (second) Amendment Act 1999 provides for patenting on life and promotes biopiracy of our indigenous knowledge and resources.

The plant variety, protection act is being amended to allow corporate IPRs on farmers varieties. This made the farmers were become custodians and steward of biodiversity and its knowledge. IPRs on biodiversity as evidenced in Canada, the US and other countries where they are in place, increase the cost of seed for the farmers leading them deeper into debt.

The Biodiversity act is better as a Biopiracy Act, as it takes away the rights of our communities and indigenous healers to use biological resources for their livelihood and survival. The importance of IPRs to agri-chemical and agri-business corporations revolves round the fundamental issue of control. Seed is the first link in the food chain. Whoever controls the seed, controls the food supply. Therefore Monsanto spent over $8.5 billion acquiring seed and bio-tech companies Dupont spent over $ 9.4 billion to acquire pioneer Hi-Bred, the worlds largest seed company and Dow chemical brought Cargill seeds north America in Mid September 2000. Today, the farmers saved seed and state run seed programmes are worth around $ 22 billion which is almost equal to the $ 123 billion total commercial seed market worldwide. Thus the Gene Giants are developing new mechanisms such as the genetic Engineering technology to enforce their corporate monopolies. Biological control by corporate lead to enslavement's of agriculture. In 1999, at least 43 patents were issued relating to genetic trait control technology. Patent and IRPs regime as system of monopoly control will further aggravate the severe crisis the farmers facing. The TRIPRs regime of WTO will therefore create conditions for a deepening of the economic crisis for the farming community in India. Therefore, Indian Government and Multinationals have to share equally the responsibilities and liabilities to balance the production of seed and distribution, we must develop our indigenous *Sui generis* system to protect farmers seed sovereignty.

Traditional rights of the farmers to freely conserve, develop use share, exchange their seeds are fundamental rights, which cannot be alienated by any IPR law. To defend the rights of the small farmers and for the food security of people there should be a call for exclusion of seeds, life and life forms from TRIPRs/ WTO. In fact, farmers representatives should be adequately represented in the commission on Agriculture on commodities and prices[10].

BIOPIRACY FROM INDIA

Large number of patents were grounded over genetic resources without the consent of the indigenous people, who possess Indigenous Environment Knowledge (IEK) over the resources in India. Aswaganda traditional ayurvedic system of medicine of India has been patented to

Reliv International Inc. for Dietary supplement for nutritionally promoting healthy joint function. Karela, Jamun and Bringal have already been patented to non resident Indians. Patent has also been granted to Cromark Research Inc. US on Karela, Jamun and Gumar for herbal diabetic properties to reduce sugar. India's herbal products like Amla, Vasab, Saptrangi and baelbel have been granted patent by the US patent and trade marks office for their derivatives. Pepper, ginger, mustard, bitter gourd, soapnut, gooseberry black berry, cumin–India's traditional herbs, plants and fruits have all been Patented. In this economic hijack, the corporations were gained people and nature loose.

The use of bio-resources including turmeric, Neem, basmati has been inscribed in an Ancient Sanskrit Text and it has been the long standing art and common knowledge and practiced for thousands of years by India's indigenous community. Some of the popular/ journals like *Down to Earth and Honey Bee* are also exposing the apathy of local communities usage of bio-resources in their respective regions[11].

Maintenance of biodiversity register at the national level comprising documented indigenous knowledge is the need of the hour. The future economic development making use of a variety of diversity resources such as genes and plant varieties etc. is impossible without prior consent of the holders of IPRs on such resources. It is difficult to sustain the balanced and equitable multi-lateral trade based on the principle of shared access. Finally, patent regime would put farmers to depend upon multinational corporations for seeds to food and health of a nation.

CONCLUSION

Introduction of Intellectual property rights by World Trade Organization in Indian Agriculture would bring many reforms both advantages and disadvantages. New knowledge is patented is good, but developing countries have not produced it. They have to depend on developed countries. Transfer of technology can change the developing countries economies, but developing countries also be ready to change their mindset for exporting it. With robust optimism developing countries should facilitate to modernise their "knowledge centres" to generate innovations and inventions in order to copy foreign technology. Our indigenous flora and fauna are to be protected and sustained and keep multinationals as competitive and complementary. Under IPRs regime, many products prices many rise, but state has to take firm steps to produce and keep them affordable to the poorest of the poor. Nonetheless, India has to gear up it's economy to face challenges and took it as an opportunity to make India as a developed country in 2020 through IPRs.

REFERENCES

Correspondent (2004), "Govt. for New Norms to Protect" IPRs, *Hindustan Times.*

Martin Khor (2006), "Impasse at the WTO: A Development Prospective", *Economic and Political Weekly,* p. 4659.

Shaik Saleem (2006), "Business Environment", *Pearson Education*, New Delhi, p. 502.

Francis Cherunilam (2006), "International Economics", Tata McGraw-Hill Publishing Co. Ltd., New Delhi, p. 598.

Planning Commission (2005), "Mid-Term Appraisal of 10th Five Year Plan 2002-07", p. 396.

Research and Information System (2003), "World Trade and Development Report 2003", *Cancum and Beyond, Academic Foundation*, New Delhi, p. 94.

Dr. S. Nagaraj (2006), "Several Policy Initiatives in Place", *The Hindu Survey of Indian Agriculture,* p. 49.

P. Manoj (2006), "Bid for Patent for Basmati Rice Hits a Hurdle", *The Hindu,* p. 10.

Joseph Stiglitz (2002), "Globalization and its Discontents", Penguin Books, New Delhi, p. 245.

Vandana Shiva and Kunwar Jalees (2006), "Seeds of Suicide", *Navdanya*, New Delhi, pp. 252-259.

C., Nanjundaiah and S. Rajendran (2004), "Intellectual Property Rights and Protection of Indigenous Environmental Knowledge of Indigenous Community", *National Seminar on Institutional Policy Options for Sustainable Agricultural Development, Pre Conference Volume,* April 10-11, Dept. of Economics, Osmania University, p. 419.

PRECISION FARMING: IMPORTANCE AND RELEVANCE TO INDIAN AGRICULTURE

*V. Siva Jyothsna**, *R. Sudhakar Goud*** &
*A. Kamalakar Reddy****

INTRODUCTION

Precision farming refers to the exactness and implies accuracy in any aspect of production. It is application of technologies and principles to manage temporal and spatial variability associated with all aspects of agricultural production for the purpose of improving crop performance and environmental quality.

Precision Farming is one of the most scientific and modern approaches to sustainable agriculture. In developing countries like India, where the land-person ratio is rapidly declining, the only means of meeting the needs is through increased productivity without detriment to environment and sustainability. Precision farming aims at sustainability of agricultural industry. It is information based, technology enabled and decision focused to enhance productivity and reduce ecological degradation.

The main components of precision farming are:

- Geographical Information System (GIS)
- Global Position System (GPS)
- Remote Sensing
- Variable Rate technology and
- Yield monitors

The objective of precision farming is managing variability with in the field so as to maximize the economic returns and minimize the environmental problems.

* Project Associate, NIRD, Hyderabad.
** Project Associate, NIRD, Hyderabad.
*** Professor of Geography, Osmania University, Hyderabad.

The basic steps of precision farming are:

- Assessing the variation
- Managing the variation and
- Evaluation

The existing technologies enable us in understanding the variability across the field area and the same can be managed by giving site–specific recommendations. Finally evaluation must be an integral part of any Precision farming system.

In developed countries like USA and Europe, Precision farming is popularly practiced due to large holdings and they are implementing it at a profitable rate.

In those countries, a farmer will have a GPS guided tractor, which gives the exact location of the tractor within the filed. It sends the signal to the computer in the tractor, which has a GIS, storing the soil nutrients requirement map in it. The GIS, in consultation with a decision support system, decides what is the exact requirement of the fertilizer for that location. This is all done in fraction of minute before the tractor moves further.

But this type of farming is something like a fiction movie for the Indian farmer in present situations. So there is need to develop our own method of practicing the principles of Precision farming.

We can follow the Precision farming with the available technologies at farmer level. The basic steps of Precision farming are, identifying the variability, managing the same and evaluating it. In the very first step itself remote sensing plays an important role (Moran et al.-1999).

- In first approach, the multispectral images can be used for anomaly detection. The anomalies can be in the form of disease/pest/weed growth or water stress etc. This is possible through reflectance measurements in the visible portion of the spectrum.
- The next approach is based on correlating variations in spectral response to specific variables such as soil properties or crop yield. Soil physical properties like soil water, organic matter and soil texture can be correlated to spectral reflectanc Vegetation spectral response has also been used to infer other soil conditions.
- The third approach is to integrate biophysical parameters (such as leaf area index or temperature) derived from high–resolution

satellite based remote sensing data with physical crop growth modeling towards an operational decision support system for precision farming.

Moran et al. (1995) utilized remotely sensed estimates of Leaf Area Index (LAI) and evapotraspiration as inputs to a simple Alfalfa growth model. To derive biophysical parameter, the remote sensing system needs to have high spectral resolution covering the whole range of optical and thermal region.

But there are many limitations for the use of remote sensing for mapping which needs lot of preprocessing and post processing analysis. Keeping in view the agricultural scenario in developing countries like India the remote sensing technology should be,

- Available at low costs (Rs 100/acre/year i.e., for all the three seasons)
- Processing time should be less (1 or 2 days)
- High spiral (2m/hac.) spectral (10-20 nm) and temporal (5-6 dates per season) resolutions are needed
- The analytical products should be with in the reach of local agricultural expert's knowledge.

Fulfilling the above conditions is a little difficult considering the present Indian conditions.

The reasons for the limited implementation of Precision farming in India are:

- Highly fragmented holdings
- Cost/benefit aspects
- High heterogeneous nature of cropping systems
- Vast gap in technology transfer from lab to field.

Out of these the two major hurdles for implementing PF are small land holding and cost. In India more than 57.8 % of operational holdings has size less than 1hact. With this field size and the farming being mostly subsistent farming, it is difficult to adopt technologies of Precision farming at individual field level.

ACTION PLAN

We can define our own method of practicing Precision farming with the existing available technologies. For identifying the variability across a small field we can follow soil-sampling techniques, which are already in practice. Soil cores taken from the random locations in the sampling are combined and sent to a laboratory. Crop advisors make fertilizer application recommendations from the soil test information for the field. Grid sampling uses the same principles of soil samples collected in a systematic grid also have location information that allows the data to be mapped. Grid soil samples are analysed in the laboratory and an interpretation of crop nutrient needs is made for each soil sample. Then the fertilizer application map is plotted using the entire set of soil samples. Accordingly the farmer is advised to apply the nutrients across the field over the entire crop growth period.

The other important aspects we should look at are, the water conservation, ground water prospects, Slope and the current land use patterns.

Ground water, the most important natural resource i.e. widely used in agricultural production amounts nearly 80% of the total irrigated area. A detailed ground water map should be prepared using already existing maps and remote sensing techniques. This should be fed as a database in GIS environment and water conservation measures should be proposed in the areas where there is ground water depletion. We can use multi spectral satellite data of 5.8 mts. resolution from IRS P6 LISS 4 image.

Slope maps are needed as water conservation process. These we can derive from soil toposheets at 1:25000 scale. Based on this information soil, groundwater, slope and current land use, the farmer should be advised by the experts about the alternate cropping. This should be done once in each season.

A production system is proposed with different cropping pattern that suits to the site and situation. Finally site specific and crop specific recommendations are suggested to improve crop performance and environmental quality.

Mobile soil testing laboratories with a lab expert and an agronomist with GIS knowledge can advise the amount of nutrients inputs based on soil test analysis report. A single visit per one crop season is sufficient before the crop is taken up. And like wise, a mobile advisory unit with an entomologist, pathologist and a physiologist can be arranged once in fortnight. The Govt. has to should encourage this kind of network. This should be approached in an extensive manner just like PULSE POLIO program to make crop plants and environment grow healthy.

The farmer also should co-operate with the Govt. at a bare minimum cost of Rs. 30 per acre per season. Water conservation measures should be implemented simultaneously through the same network to meet future water demands.

FUTURE PROSPECTS

This type of management can easily be implemented for Precision farming with a GPS driven tractor with GIS, variable rate applicator and yield monitor in India in the near future.

REFERENCES

Floyd F. Sabin's (1996), *Remote Sensing Principles and Interpretation.*

Gowrisankar, D. and Adiga, S. (2001), *Remote Sensing in Agricultural Applications: An overview. In: Proc., The First National Conference on Agro-Informatics (NCAI),* INSAIT. Dharwad, pp. 9-14.

Inoue, Y., Moran M.S. and Tomita A. (1999), *Remote Sensing of Canopy Variables for Model Prediction of Growth and Yield–FAPAR, Nitrogen Status and Spectral Reflectance in Rice Canopies, In: Proc, International Symposium–World Food Security and Crop Production Technologies for Tommorrow,* pp. 292-293.

Moran M.S., Inoue Y. and Barnes E. M. (1997), *Opportunities and Limitations for Image–Based Remote Sensing in Precision Crop Management, Remote Sensing of Environment,* 61: pp. 319-346.

Moran M.S., R.D. Jackson, T.R. Clarke, J.Qi, F. Cabot, K. J. Thome and B. L. Markham (1995), *Reflectance Factor Retireval from Landsat TM and SPOT HRV Data for Bright and Dark Targets, Remote Sensing of Environment,* 52, pp. 218-230.

Moran M.S., Clarke, T.R., Inoue, Y. and Vidal A. (1994), *Estimating Crop Water Deficit Using the Relation Between Surface-air Temperature and Spectral Vegetation Index, Remote Sensing of Environment,* 49: pp. 246-263.

Navalgund R.R. (1991), *Remote Sensing Applications in Agriculture: Indian Experience in Space and Agriculture Management, Special Current Event Session, International Aeronautical Federation, 42nd IAF Congress,* Montreal, Canada.

NRSA and AIS & LUS (1986), *Utility and Relative Efficiency of Various Remote Sensing Techniques in Soil New Data and Abstraction,* Chitradurga RS Project, Karnataka, India, Project Report.

Venkataratnam, L. (2001), *Remote Sensing and GIS in Agricultural Resources Management, In: Proc, The First National Conference on Agro-Informatics (NCAI),* INSAIT. Dharwad, pp: 20-29.

SOCIAL SECTOR IN GLOBALISED ECONOMY: WORKERS' PERSPECTIVE

*Shyam Bahadur Katuwal**

INTRODUCTION

Today, globalisation has become a buzzword among the people in the both developed and developing countries. It implies the integration of national economies with the world economy. By its horizon of application, globalisation can be observed from economic, social, cultural, political, technological, environmental, and even from the military aspects of human life. By the mechanism of opening economies to private sector with a view to attract capital and with the deep trade linkages with outer world in the wake of the globalisation process, it offers many opportunities and challenges in every spheres of life. The main attraction towards globalisation is to increase efficiency through competition and ensure growth through integration of national economy with the world trading system.

Globalisation has multiplier effect on human life raising both apprehensions and expectations on them. In this context, the crucial challenge is to ensure that all the sectors of society including workers have equally benefited from the prosperity obtained through global interaction and technological innovation. Since globalisation is a moving phenomenon and cannot be stopped, the real issue is to harmonize domestic policies that help countries adapt to the realities of change. It is argued that the countries that lag behind integration have to pay a higher opportunity cost to gain from globalisation.

Thus, the focus of this paper is to analyse the social aspects of the globalisation process in order to assess that how far the weaker section of the society in the developing countries like Nepal are benefited from the process of globalisation. In this regard, the some selected macro socio-economic parameters at the starting phase of globalisation process and

* Lecturer Faculty of Management, TU, Post Graduate Campus, Biratnagar, Nepal.

the latest period of globalisation are compared to identify the impact of globalisation. The growth data of service sector are used from secondary sources to pave with the importance of service sector in Nepalese economy.

CONCEPT AND CONTEXT

For many people, globalisation is an economic interaction among countries. Globalisation, as a phenomenon of the free flow of knowledge, goods, and services throughout the world presenting competitive business environment by the means of privatisation, liberalisation, denationalization, marketization, deregulations and debureaucraticzation policies, has affected every sphere of human life including the producer of goods and services and their consumers. In its full sense of implication, brings multidimensional impacts to the society-challenges and prosperity.

Globalisation has been defined in many contexts. Redding (1999:19) defines globalisation as the increasing integration between the markets for goods, services, and capital. Further, Visser and Van Dijk (2006) say, "Globalisation may be defined as a process of geographical up-scaling and increasing density of integration of final product and factor markets".

In the words of Scholte (2005:11), it refers to a trend and process, namely, the growth of trans-planetary connections between people. Globalisation involves the reduction of barriers to trans-world contacts. By this, he further says, "people become more able—physically, legally, culturally and psychologically—to engage with each other in one world". In this regard, components of globalisation are not only the economic but also the information, service, ideology, technology, and culture affecting human life in society.

The international system of the twenty-first century would be characterized by a seeming contradiction and fragmentation, on the one hand, and growing globalisation, on the other (Kissinger, 1994: 806). This process of globalisation is considered as "the process of consolidating wealth and power by the rapid integrating and structuring of national economies into one global economic order through trade liberalisation, privatisation, and deregulation. The aim is to remove the obstacles to the global movement of capital and production of goods that have accumulated in advanced, industrial capitalist countries. It is characterized by the accumulation of surplus capital in the form of private profit, the presence of monopolies, concentrating and centralising capital; the merging of finance and capital; the dividing of world into markets; the global movement of and speculation in capital and collusion with and using national and international institutions to consolidate power.

"It is also closely associated with" dramatic disparities in wealth and income within and between nations; intensification of exploitation and oppression of labour; use of high electronic technology; widespread influence of mass media; changes in means of transport; revolution in bio-technology and multinational corporations supported by new supranational institutions" (Women's International League for Peace and Freedom, 1997: 5-6).

In its economic dimensions, globalisation refers to the increasing degree of economic interaction among countries, reflected especially by rising shares of world output that are traded internationally and by rapidly expanding international capital flows(Berry, 2005:11). Although globalisation is a process towards growing economic integration of goods, services, and capital market, its benefits do not come automatically but require good policies–especially "stable macro economic policies, open trade regimes, and flexible product and factor markets supported by effective 'exit' policies for non-competitive industries" (IMF, 1997: 81-96).

Thus, the term globalisation is different in meaning, context, and application with the terms internationalisation, multinational, regionalisation, and liberalisation. Therefore, it is necessary here to be clear about the distinctions between these terms before discussing about the globalisation.

GLOBALISATION AND INTERNATIONALISATION

Most of the definitions denote globalisation as a borderless activity of economic, government and communities. In the words of O' Brien (1992:5), international are the activities that take place between different countries. It means the trade occurs outside the broader of a country but not within its boundary of a nation.

GLOBALISATION AND MULTINATIONAL

Multinational stands for the activities taking place in more than one country. However, global is a more advanced stage of integration between countries of the world. It combines both elements of international and multinational. In its true sense of implication, globalisation does not recognise any internal borders for the activities. Because of this fact, the country remains irrelevant when it comes to global activities.

GLOBALISATION AND REGIONALISATION

Regionalisation is the process of economic integration of economies of countries in a given region. It paves the way for multilateral trade liberalisation. Globalisation is an extension of regionalization process because it helps to reduce borders between countries and regionalization.

GLOBALISATION AND LIBERALISATION

Liberalisation is the process of providing freedom to the parties concerned to forward their activities without any control form government and other invisible regulatory hands. In liberalisation, activities perform and act upon the market-forces. Liberalisation is an important step in expediting the process of globalisation by the means of reducing trade barriers. Liberalisation is the reductions in government intervention in markets, partly with respect to international interaction—the policy decisions just referred to—but also more generally, as with labour markets, domestic financial markets and so on (Berry, 2005:1). It involves giving product and factor markets greater responsibility in the resource allocation in an economy. Marketisation, denationalisation, privatisation, deregulation etc are other such economic policies that link globalisation and liberalisation together as one.

GLOBALISATION: AN ARGUMENT

Since globalisation is a dynamic and signifies changes in our lives, various arguments have emerged in its support and against. The basic philosophy of globalisation is to provide sufficient scope for the specialisation and free movement of goods, services, capital, and technology throughout the world by keeping them open for all. By this, it is anticipated that the process of globalisation will create opportunities for jobs and economic growth as business opportunity increases with the reduction of trade barriers, use of advanced technology and specialisation, and the decentralization of production to take the advantage location specific resources. The other awaiting benefits of globalisation are efficient allocation of resources, equitable distribution of income, macroeconomic stability in the countries tied in the globalisation process. For many people, globalisation is the source of prosperities, opportunities, and benefits (Bhagwati, 2004). It is more than a 'rising density of economic integration between countries and economies' (Wade 2003: 567).

However, it is widely criticized as unbalanced and unequal process of distributing benefits to the hands of a minority of people and of countries, leaving many excluded and real disadvantageous to some (Rodgers, 2005: 47). Unemployment and insecurity pose further challenges that demand appropriate and effective economic policies and structural reforms become necessary to allow market to function properly. Opponents have put challenges against it rationality in economic activities saying that the impact of globalisation on developing and developed countries differed.

GLOBALISATION AND INCOME DISTRIBUTION

The study of IMF (2000:1) showed that the per capita level of production increased dramatically since the start of the twentieth century. The problem is that the distribution in countries is more skewed that at the beginning of the twentieth century. Brittan (1998:8) argued that despite of some positive impact on the developments of some developing countries globalisation could not reduce the greater poverty and risks of marginalization in the developing countries rather it led to an increase in the wealth of developed countries. However, Hak-Min (1999:2) believed that the distribution of income between developed and developing countries has become less skewed by indicating that globalisation in the integrated world economy has lead to industrial growth in a limited number of developed countries.

Studies suggest that it is wrong to argue that globalisation caused low and unequal distribution of income in developing countries. (Masson, 2001:7) in his study concluded that the thirty developed nations that actively took part in the process of globalisation grew by 3.5% in the eighties and 5 % in the nineties. The countries that did not actively take part in the process of globalisation did not realize any or just marginal growth rates after 1980. The countries that opened their economies grew at a faster rate that the developing countries.

Although the increased global GDP growth per capital reached almost five times during in the 20th century, the study of IMF (2000:2) also has observed an unequal and unstable economic growth during the period. The highest growth observed in the second half of the century due to the increased in trade and the process of financial liberalisation. But it could remain on an average of less than 1 % in the interwar period (1913–1950) with the countries adopting a more inward looking policy stance by increasing tariffs. Thus, this finding clearly indicates that increase in the trade volume with liberalised trade and financial policy could help globalisation process positively impact in GDP growth.

By the analysis of aforesaid studies, we can conclude that despite economic growth globalisation did not correct the skewed distribution of income between developed and developing countries. In this regard, we can suggest that the boundless participation of developing countries in the process of globalisation could improve the situation of skewed distribution of income. So that program and policies that facilitate for easy entry, attract, and continue the participation of developing countries in the verge of globalisation process should be introduced without any hesitation to eliminate gap of developing and developed countries.

GLOBALISATION AND ECONOMIC GROWTH OR ECONOMIC DEVELOPMENT

Here is a question that whether economic growth could be an indicator to denote economic development? Social development of low-income countries in the world is also possible without increased economic growth by active participation in process of globalisation. The study of IMF (2000:5) shows that several low-income countries (e.g. Sri Lanka) have inspiring social development indicators, without their active sharing to increase economic growth by globalisation. That means skewed distribution of income in favour of developing countries caused by globalisation could not hamper the economic development in these countries.

According to Goldsmith, (1996:26) only GDP per capita cannot be considered as the good indicator of measuring economic development of a country. He further indicated that if wider measure of economic development, like the social conditions in countries is compared, the situation regarding economic development is better than only comparing the relative level of income.

Human development indicator is another indicator to denote economic development of a country. According to Crafts (2000: 6), the development situation is also more positive if measured by the Human Development Indicators Developed by the United Nations based on education level and life expectancy.

Thus, Craft referred in his study that the low-income countries, despite their persistent low-income level, have improved HDIs due to the improvements in medical technology and the resultant improved living standards and thereby the increased living standards lead to a better life expectation. This finding of Craft clearly indicates the differences in the levels of the Human development indicators and the income gap.

Whatsoever are the arguments in favour of the fact 'globalisation lead to skewed distribution of income between developing and developed countries', the integration of national economy of developing country like Nepal with export driving policies can get many benefits from the process of globalisation. Keeping every thing aloof, it can contribute to increase world production, levels of trade, economic growth, standard of living, and economic development (See Quattara, 1997:177 and Todaro, 1985:123).

GLOBALISATION AND MACROECONOMIC POLICY

Globalisation has also been criticized from the angle of macroeconomic policy. In criticism, it is argued that globalisation through the affect on macroeconomic policy hampers the financial stability in nations. Excessive short-term capital flows due to globalisation makes monetary policy execution complicated. Short-term capital outflows pays negative impact on the capital account of the balance of payments and the outflow of capital diminishes the money supply in the country leading to increased interest rates. In both cases of short tem capital flow and outflow, the interest rate policy of the central bank would be influenced negatively. The private sector is also equally hampered by the globalisation. By capital flows, the private sector cannot increase wages and prices without considering the impact on its international competitiveness.

For this, the IMF (2000:8) argues that globalisation does not affect negatively on the economic policy of the country, but acts as discipline for the monetary and fiscal authorities in countries. It is also argued that globalisation will not necessarily hamper governments in the execution of fiscal policy (IMF, 2000:8). According to the IMF, the goal of fiscal and monetary policy is sustainable growth, low inflation, and social development.

PROCESS OF GLOBALISATION IN NEPAL

The incident of poverty in Nepal is very high with about one-third of population (30.85 percent) living below the poverty line (CBS, 2004). Agriculture is the foundation of the economy, providing a livelihood for two-third (66 percent) of the 23.15 million population of Nepal (CBS, 2003: 353) and accounting for 39.2% of GDP, gradually shifting from agriculture to the industrial and service sectors. The small but growing industrial and service sectors contribute about 22.2 percent and 38.6 percent to the GDP respectively (NPC, 2006). Nepal, being one of the least developed countries of the world, is far behind in the level of social and human development. The Human Development Report 2006, based on the Human Development Index has placed Nepal in the 138th position (HDI=0.527), out of the total 177 countries included in the report (UNDP, 2006).

In this backdrop, the Structural Adjustment Programs (SAP) introduced in 1985 with the changes of monetary and fiscal programs has tuned Nepalese economy from state-owned concept of economic activities to private, open, liberal, and market-oriented concept. In real sense, being influence from the entry of neighboring countries into the liberalised economic policy to exploit benefits of globalisation and inefficiency of public enterprises, Nepal has also put the step towards this direction by adapting economic stabilization program under the standby-credit facilities of IMF in December 1985.

Later on in 1986/87, the Structural Adjustment Program (SAP) was implemented in the support of the World Bank with the main objectives of attaining the macroeconomic balances and raise GDP growth rate on sustainable basis. Raising internal revenue mobilisation through tax reforms, containing prices through improving supply situation, abducting import restrictions, etc were prepared to make the program successful.

In the meantime, the Structural Adjustment Program (Facility) (SAP-I) was also implemented with the support of the IMF in 1987, to change the transition from economic stabilisation to more rapid form of development on a sustainable basis. Major program of this facility was to improve macroeconomic management by the activities of enhancing government revenues and public savings, liberalising industrial, trade, and exchange rates policies, limiting the growth of less essential expenditures, increasing investment levels, improving the management of PEs and initiating privatisation process.

As a result of the implementation of this reform program, there was a growth in economic and investment levels, inflation rate decelerated, macroeconomic management improved and considerable progress was felt in reducing trade restrictions, liberalising import and providing incentives to exports (ILO,2004:16).

Being encouraged from the economic reform programs of 1987, other consecutive reform programs were adopted in order to enhance economic growth through increased private participation in economic activities. For this, private sector initiating liberalised pattern of economic, industrial, monetary, financial, and capital markets, trade and investment, agricultural and other social and economic sectors were initiated in the different phases of economic stabilisation and adjustment programs. The second Structural Adjustment Program (SAP-II) complimented by the IMF Structural Adjustment Facility (SAF) arrangement in the FY 1989/90 is the last reform program before the restoration of democracy in Nepal. Prior to this, the Open General License System (OGLS) was introduced in 1987 to liberalise the trade sector instead of the licensing mechanism adapted since 1985. However, this system could not sufficiently facilitate the trade and enter the country into the stir of globalisation process. In overall basis, the liberalisation policy could not be implemented successfully during the period of 1980s and thus, the role of state remained pervasive and the approach to reform was incremental during the decade (ibid: 17).

Nevertheless, the real sense of economic liberalisation started only after the restoration of democracy in 1990 with an attempt to globalise the national economy, industry, trade, investment, foreign exchange, financial sectors by the means of deregulation, delicensing, and privatisation. Enactment of the Privatisation Act 1991 is its first attempt to reduce the burden on the government and release government resources to other sectors and encourage private sector involvement.

With its objective of national development through the private participation, the democratic government for the first time in 1992 negotiated a new Enhanced Structural Adjustment Facility (ESAF) arrangement with the IMF with a view to expedites the economic reform programs in almost all sectors of the economy. Consequently, the new Trade Policy 1992 came into existence with a view to eradicate almost all constrains in trade that hinder liberalisation and globalisation process in the country. Under this policy, imports of raw materials, consumer goods, industrial machinery, and services were made free from the requirement of government permission. Adoption of open current account system, restructuring financial institution and changes in banking system and monetary policies including loans in foreign currency and flexible foreign exchange rate system and abandonment of invoice valuation process, changes in the tariff rate, duty-draw-back scheme and one window system were the major attraction of this policy for international traders. Though some of them are to be completed yet, full convertibility to Nepalese currency, payment by telex transfer system, institutional arrangement for trade facility, introduction of bonded-ware house, initiation of the multi-modal facility and dry port and other necessary measures in the field of trade promotion supported the growth of trade.

To attract foreign investment and increase private participation in the national economy development, even in the infrastructural sector, the Industrial Enterprise Act, 1992 and Foreign Investment Act and Technology Transfer Act, 1992 were also enacted along with announcement of open, liberal and market oriented Industrial Policy 1992.

Overall, the performance in the macroeconomic sector remained unsatisfactory during the adjustment period. During the period, the economy is suffered from chronic imbalances, growing resource gaps, and heavy dependence on foreign aid. Inflation reached the double-digit line. The most of the Indian boarder side industries were closed. Very little has been accomplished in efficiency management of public enterprises, productivity in agriculture, mobilisation of domestic resources and attracting foreign private investments. (Dahal, 2005:107). In specific, more than 40 percent of the small scale industries were closed (Kansakar, 1996: 157); corporations except Nepal Rastra Bank could earn mere 1 percent profit and inefficiency, corruption, politicisation and overstaffing of corporations (K.C. 1997) are some bitter facts in economy during the period.

Other unsatisfactory performances of liberalisation include confinement of the annual growth rate of GDP to 2.5 per cent, 1.4 percent decrease of average industrial production index, and widening the fiscal deficit (9 per cent of GDP) due to gap between revenue collection and public expenditure. Increase in the size of foreign debt up to 50 per cent of GDP by mounting share of debt servicing of regular expenditure is also the indication of unsatisfactory performances of liberalisation during the period (Dahal: ibid). He has further pointed that devaluation of Nepalese currency and increase in the price of public goods and services without corresponding increase in the income and wages of people indicate that the neo-liberal policies not only led to the exploitation of Nepalese citizen, customers, workers and environment but also a symptom that the levers of globalisation in Nepal failed to break the monopolistic control of big business houses on the supply of many essential goods but also the social economy maintained by the families and communities.

However, by all these actions for economic reform and considering the globalisation as the panacea to solve all kinds of socio- economic problems, Nepal has entered into the huge verge of globalisation with many hopes of development and prosperity. Its entry in the globalisation process has become strong from the period when Nepal has obtained the status of full member in the WTO on 23 April 2004.

SERVICE SECTOR IN NEPAL

In the early thinking of classical economy, service was considered as an unproductive attempt. Therefore, that it was not covered in the branches of economies. But around the period of the great depression in 1930s, economists like Fisher and Clark acknowledged the importance and relevancy of service sector by divided the economy into three sectors, primary (agriculture), secondary (manufacturing), and tertiary (services). Economists, with foresee of the importance of services in the economies of the future, further sub-classified the service sector into three parts consisting of quasi-domestic services (food and lodging-whether performed in the home or not); business service; and other (including, recreation, health care and education). The structural change, growth, and heterogeneity of service sector in the post-industrial societies attracted the economists to see service sector from different angles. The services earlier provided within the manufacturing sector became possible to hire from specialized agencies outside the manufacturing sector. Consequently, the demand for primary product would increase less than proportionately with rising income, and the composition of demand shift from secondary products towards tertiary products as suggested in Engle's curve. Thus, now the service industry seems to have won its independence from goods. With the advent of technology, the orientation of service industries shifted from labour-intensive to technology-intensive/ technology-sophisticated industries in the global trade specially in transportation, financial services, banking, insurance, retail and wholesale trade, telecommunications, health care and professional and personal services.

Rendering the heterogenic economic influence of the service sector in our life, classifying and defining service has never been easy. Bell (1973) analysed the service-oriented postindustrial society from a sociological aspect. By its heterogenic nature, service sector been classified into the following categories (Inman, 1985):

(a) Stagnation personal services, where the quality is highly correlated with the labour time spent, e.g. haircutting, teaching, life artistic performance.

(b) Progressive impersonal services, where the dependence on electronic technology is immense. There is no contact between the producer and consumers. The technology and productivity growth in this sector is very high, e.g., telecommunication and multimedia.

(c) Asymptomatically stagnant impersonal services, where productivity growth is self-extinguishing, e.g., broadcasting, computation, and R&D.

The service sector is the fastest growing sector of the economy by creating ever-growing number of employment. It reflects the raising share in the international trade. The growth in service industries serves as an essential index of countries development. That means progress and prosperity would originate from the service sector. In the world scenario, service sector reflects the raising of international trade in the world output.

GLOBALISATION ON SERVICE SECTOR IN NEPAL

On the positive side of globalisation in Nepal is the growth in service sector activities. Official expenditure has increased, especially in public health and education during the process of globalisation with a view to increase social status of people. The share of social sector in the total expenditure is found always increased from 1984/85 onwards, except the decrease of 1.5 per cent in 2004/05 as compared to the previous year. However, in comparison to the overall growth rate of government expenditure, the policies of liberalisation have also caused deduction in social expenditure in recent past.

The faster growth can be observed in security related expenditure with the subsequently slower growth in the education and health expenditure (social sector) and serious decrease in the economic service expenditure (Table 1). In total expenditure, the security related spending has mounted to 17.3 percent in 2004/05 from 9.2 per cent in 1994/95 whereas service sector raised only by 2.4-point per cent during the period and the economic services drastically decreased to 17.3 per cent in 2004/05 from 36 percent in 1994/95. The decline in economic service expenditure is due to the slower increase in spending on economic services like irrigation, transportation, electricity etc.

The slower growth rate of service related expenditure are attributed due to the raising share of debt servicing (payment of principal and interest on domestic and foreign debt) and increase in security expenditure in total expenditure to manage internal insecurity caused by Maoist insurgency.

Table 1
Share of Social Sector in Total Expenditure (in %)

Heading / FY	*1984-85*	*1994-95*	*1999-00*	*2001-02*	*2003-04*	*2004-05*
General Administration	4.7	4.3	4.2	5.5	4.9	5.0
Police	3.4	4.1	4.9	7.5	7.1	7.3
Defense	6.0	5.1	5.3	7.3	9.5	10.0
Social service	22.8	27.3	31.3	31.1	31.2	29.7
Economic service	45.5	35.7	31.5	24.2	20.8	17.3
Principal and Interest Payment	8.1	15.6	15.1	15.2	19.0	19.7
Miscellaneous	9.5	7.9	7.6	9.1	7.4	10.9
Total	100	100	100	100	100	100

Source: Economic Survey, MOF (Various Issues).

Expansion of Social Services

Another positive impact of globalisation is the considerable increase in the number of tourist arrivals, hotel facilities, transportation facilities, communication services, health facilities, educational institutions, banking, finance, and insurance services, and growth of NGOs, with cumulative positive impact on employment and income generation in these sectors.

Table 2
Extension of Different Social Services

Year	*No. of Tourists Arrival*	*No. of Hotels*	*+Extension of Roads (in KM)*	*Distribution of Telephone Lines*	*+Hospital Beds*
1989	239945	159	6611	45457	4329
1990	254885	168	7036	57320	4572
1991	292995	192	8328	65298	4570
1992	334353	203	8851	68886	4798
1993	293567	214	9293	72033	4848
1994	326531	394	9664	77317	4848
1995	363395	520	10724	82774	3604
1996	393613	632	11237	112645	3604
1997	421857	706	11714	153782	3904
1998	463684	739	13223	181302	4189
1999	491504	785	13709	221863	4955
2000	463646	848	15308	255777	5190
2001	361237	888	15702	288036	5250
2002	275466	943	16834	327673	5250
2003	338132	966	16947	371816	5250
2004	385297	996	17182	408417	5250
2005	375398	1006	17279	433631	6796

+Fiscal Year (data indicates the mid July of the respective year).
Source: Economic Survey, MOF (Various Issues) and record of line organisations.

As the data presented in the Table 2, these entire sector have been grown considerably during the process of globalisation. Tourism is the important sector of GDP contribution and foreign currency earning in Nepal. Although the number of hotels and beds available in country has been increasing, the analysis of tourist arrival reveals that the numbers of tourist entering into Nepal started to decrease from December 1999 onwards. It is just because of internal insecurity situation. It is a great challenge for Nepal to revive the peace and security and thereby to attract tourist and earn foreign currency.

Despite of the facilities of air, railway, and trolley bus services, the road transportation has been always preferred in Nepalese plans. Consequently, the total road network (black topped, graveled, and fair weather) by end of the FY 2004/05 reached to 17279 km. with the increase of 10668 km. of road length from the mid July 1989 to Mid July 2005.

After liberalisation, telecommunication is the most improved area in Nepal. Nepal Telecommunication Authority is the sole authority to issue telephone service license for basic, cellular mobile, email/internet, V-sat services, Video-conferencing service, local data network service, Fax mail service and so on. Nepal Telecom Ltd. is the largest organisation to provide telecommunication services in Nepal. By the end of the FY 2004/05, it has provided 433631 lines telephone service through 218 telephone exchanges throughout the country. The distribution of telephone lines has been increasing year by years. Beside it, customers have also been benefited from the phone lines based on CDMA technology and email and internet services. In private sector, United Telecom Ltd., Spice Nepal in collaboration with United Telecom Ltd., and STM Telecom Sanchar Pvt. Ltd. are also providing telephone services in different places of the country. Other means of communication and information, like radio broadcasting, TV broadcasting, newspaper publishing, and postal and private courier services have also been increased tremendously in private sector due to liberalisation policy of the government in Nepal.

Hospital facilities have also been increased during the period. In overall, the number of hospital beds has been increased from 4329 in 1988/1989 to 6796 in 2004/05, with the total increment of 2467 beds during the period. The number of all kinds of skilled health manpower has also increased by 62899 persons from 1988/1989 and reached to 90847 persons in 2004/05 (MOF, 2006).

Banking and financial sector are the most liberalised sector under the process of globalisation in Nepal. Prior to liberation, there were hardly, 3-4 banks to carryout financial transitions in Nepal. However, the number of such units has reached to 341 by the Mid-November 2006 (Table 3).

Table 3
Banks and Financial Institutions (mid-Nov. 2006)

Category	*Number*
Central Bank	1
Commercial Banks (including Agricultural development bank)	18
Development Banks	33
Finance Companies	72
Cooperatives (Licensed by NRB for limited banking transactions)	19
Micro-credit Institutions (Including 5 Rural Development Banks)	11
NGOs (Licensed by NRB for micro-credit transactions)	47
Employee Provident Fund	1
Citizen Investment Trust	1
Insurance Companies	21
Postal Saving Banks	117
Total	341

Source: NRB (2007).

Share of Service Sector in GDP

The service sector is now recognised as the ever-growing component of economic growth. The development of service sector can be observed from the data on Gross Domestic Product (GDP) and employment contribution. The service sector in Nepal has maturity after the period of globalisation in terms of contribution to GDP, employment and establishment of service units. The supremacy of agriculture in terms of GDP contribution and employment has been shifted to non-agriculture sector, especially to the service sector.

The share of service sector in the GDP increased by 15.4 per cent between the period of 1974/75 and 1984/85, and by 5.1 per cent in 1984/84 and 1994/95 with insignificant decline (0.3 per cent) between the period of 1994/95 and 2004/05, while the share of agriculture in GDP is decreasing. (Table 4).

Table 4
Sectoral Share in Gross Domestic Product (in %)

Sectors/FY	*1974/75*	*1984/85*	*1994/95*	*2004/05*
Agricultural	61.3	51.2	41.7	39.2
Industrial	10.3	15.0	19.4	22.2
Service	18.4	33.8	38.9	38.6
GDP at factor cost	100	100	100	100

Source: NPC, 2006.

The rate of changes between the increase in the share of service sector and industrial sector and the decrease in the share of agriculture in Gross Domestic Product has been observed very wide. The increased share of service and industrial sector has maintained the relative decreased share of agriculture in the GDP. Thus, the service sector is positively contributing in the GDP growth though it is declined in 2004/05. The slight decrease in the share of service sector in the GDP is just due to weak law and order situation, politic conflict and disturbances in the country. Overall, the increasing share of service sector in GDP with relatively declined share of agriculture in GDP clearly indicates the development of service sector and attraction of people towards it after the liberalisation process started in the country.

FOREIGN INVESTMENT IN SERVICE SECTOR IN NEPAL

Historically, because of unfavourable policy of the government, Nepal has no longer and formal experience of the participation of direct foreign investment in its economic activities other than the establishment of some commercial banks and financial institutions in joint venture with foreign partners during 1980s. Although the government has adopted the market-oriented economy policy to expedite liberalisation after the restoration of democracy in 1990, the country has not been able to attract big foreign investment yet.

The Eights Plan, which was the continuation of the economy policy of the democratic government, came with the objective of attaining economic growth, alleviate poverty, and reduce regional disparities. The development approach of this Plan was 'market oriented, open, and liberalised economy' (NPC, 1998). However, about 42 per cent of population was still living below the poverty line up to the Multi-purpose Household Budget Survey of 1995/96. The figure of poverty rate was approximately the same as estimated in the 1984/85 survey.`While the 1995/96 surveyed showed that poverty rate had fallen compared to the 1991 rural credit survey indicating slight improvement in the poverty (NRB, 1998 and NRB, 1994).

Although manufacturing sector showed a growth rate of 10.8 percent during the first half of 1990s (more than double of the second half of 1980s), it is stated to come down since the second half of the 1990s because of the adverse effect of India-Nepal Trade Treaty, and especially because of the start of Maoist insurgency in Nepal. It decreased in such an extent that the industrial production declined by 5.9 percent during the fiscal year 2001/2002.

More over the same declining situation can be observed in the other sector of economy like tourism, domestic saving, revenue surplus, investment, revenue collection etc. However, the remittances sent by Nepalese workers aboard maintained the national and overall saving situation during the Ninth Plan period. The deteriorating situation of law and order, weak governance, increase in defense and security expenditure, rugged terrain with inadequate infrastructure, limited resource endowment, high transport cost and investment cost, and high population growth are said to be the key factors responsible for the sluggish performance of Nepalese economy (SAAPE, 2003:123; NPC, 2005:3-4).

The promulgation of the Industrial Enterprise Act and Transfer of Technology Act helped to promote competition and foreign private investment in the country. As the part of reformation process, provisions for the entry of private sector in public dominated areas like health, education, infrastructure development, and privatisation of public enterprises and the announcement of foreign investment policy in 1992 for attracting foreign investors are major reforms to increase the role of national and foreign private investment in the national economy. With the implementation of the Eighth Plan in 1992, the Government adopted the privatisation policy instead of PE policy in the country as it embraced economic liberalisation policy for the improvement of national economy. HMG has already privatised 17 PEs under different phases of privatisation programme during the period of 1992-2002 (K.C. 2003:209). The announcement of the Privatisation Act 1994 along with the privatisation of public enterprises during the Eighth and Ninth Plan Period (1992-2002) can be considered as the other cornerstone for accelerating the position of private investment in the development of national economy.

However, the privatisation is a controversial issue in case of Nepal due to inefficiency of the privatised units to contribute the national economy and adverse effect to quantity and quality of the public services like health and education (see SAAPE, 2003; Khadka and Lohani, 2003; and MOF, 1999). Opening up the economy to the global order in the early 1990s created much room for foreign borrowing along with a widening market for domestic product. As exports from the country went up fivefold, so did the foreign debt of the government. This link between privatisation and debt has continued (SAAPE, 2003:129).

The foreign aid is being an integral part of Nepalese economy from 1952 when the country joined in the Colombo Plan for the first time. At present, dependency of Nepal to the foreign assistance among the South Asian countries is highest as the percentage of gross national income (GNP). The share of foreign loans to the government expenditure has increased (also extremely greater than the grants) tremendously after the announcement of structural adjustment program in 1985 (WDB, 2006).

In this context, eradication of poverty through the process globalisation is far reaching goals to the country like Nepal where national economy could not much internally integrated, and market institutions and forces are not competitive as well. Instead, it may good deed for the rich, decrease the role of state in the economic activities, and create economic inequality, as in other developing countries.

It is argued in the support that liberalisation increases economic growth and thereby reduces poverty and hunger in the end. In reality, the relationship between economic growth and poverty reduction is not proven yet. There is no mechanism within the trade liberalisation process to enable wealth to trickle down (Killick, 2001), instead, many developing countries have experienced the displacement of local livelihoods, the closing down of local firms and national industries, and increased unemployment (SAAPE, 2003).

Although the history of foreign investment in Nepal commence when the Nepal Commercial Corporation, as a joint venture unit, was set up with 67 percent equity of Indian investors in 1951/52, there was clearly a lacking of legislative framework to encourage potential foreign investment until 1991 in Nepal. There are a few instances of foreign investment and technology transfer prior to 1981 due to unattractive and vague policy in the field of foreign investment in the country. The Sixth Plan and the Foreign Investment and Technology Act 1981 also could not attract for foreign investment sufficiently if some attractions like income tax and excise duty exemption and convertible foreign currency facilities etc were offered to foreign investors. Foreign Investment and Technology Transfer Act, 1992 (amended in 1996) and Industrial Enterprises Act, 1992 were the comprehensive laws enacted to make Nepal an attractive and secure place for technology transfer and foreign investment in enterprises. Consequently, the 1990s demonstrated a remarkable increment in the foreign investment. This is the result of liberalisation policies undertaken by the government and various facilities and incentives offered to the foreign investors by amending the laws, rules, and norms in line with open and liberal economic policies.

Most of the important facilities and incentives offered to the foreign investment business are repatriation of the income, waiver of the income tax on interest income from foreign loan, One Window Service facilities etc. The Tenth Plan (2002-07) has also devised some strategies for enhancing foreign investment by making the policies and laws more flexible and pragmatic, and compatible with the provisions of the WTO Agreements.

TRENDS OF FOREIGN INVESTMENT IN NEPAL

The data in the Table 5 shows foreign investment in Nepal started to increase in greater extent after the liberalisation policy adopted by the country and the rules and regulations are changed accordingly in favour of foreign investors.

Before 1988-89, Nepal was able to attract only 0.5 billion rupees in 59 projects with the employment capacity for 10586 persons. The investment figure remarkably increased up to 3.1 billion rupees for the 64 projects in 1992-93 by creating employment opportunities for 13873 new people. The significant increase in the foreign investment is due the favourable affect of the new trade policy and the new Acts like Foreign Investment and Technology Transfer Act 1992 and Industrial Enterprises Act 1992 enacted by the government to enhance foreign investment. The foreign investment after this period maintains a slow pace of growth with its concomitant effect on employment and number of projects.

Table 5
Foreign Investment in Nepal
(Before and after the Globalisation Process)

(Rs. in million)

Fiscal Year	*Number*	*Total Project Cost*	*Foreign Investment*	*Employment*
Up to 1988-89	59	5425.92	466.84	10586
1989-90	30	2438.19	398.51	9515
1990-91	23	863.56	406.28	2974
1991-92	38	3508.17	597.84	5615
1992-93	64	17886.22	3083.67	13873
1993-94	38	3733.23	1378.76	4734
1994-95	19	1627.28	477.59	2386
1995-96	47	10047.47	2219.86	8032
1996-97	77	8559.25	2395.54	9347
1997-98	77	5569.38	2000.28	4336
1998-99	50	5324.42	1666.42	2146
1999-00	71	2669.09	1417.61	4703
2000-01	96	7917.62	3102.56	6880
2001-02	77	3318.53	1209.65	3731
2002-03	74	4921.82	1793.77	3572
2003-04	78	4323.74	2764.80	2144
2004-05	64	1801.10	1639.52	5576
Total	982	89934.99	27019.5	100150

Source: DOI (2006)

The global economic recession, and the political and economic instability, deteriorating peace and security conditions due to Maoist insurgency for the last 12 years in the country are largely responsible for the fluctuating but slow pace of foreign investment growth and employment therein. The situation is expected to correct because of the involvement Maoist party in the interim government.

Nevertheless, the supporting Acts and policies seem more conservative than other developing countries to divert foreign and private investors towards Nepal. So that it is necessary to lay down the more flexible and foreign investment friendly trade, industrial and labour policy and changes in the Labour Act for attracting foreign investment in Nepal. Since the simplified procedures for investment and liberal labour policy may encourage entrepreneurs to get entry in the country without any hesitation for investment. It is also necessary to make the bilateral and multilateral trade treaties, especially the Nepal-India Trade Treaty, more clear and export-oriented to increase foreign investment in Nepal because foreign investors come to Nepal eyeing over 1 billion Indian consumers, as Nepalese market is small with one of the lowest per capita consumption expenditure in the world (Pant and Sigdel, 2004:26).

GLOBALISATION AND WORKERS

Globalisation of economies has been widely criticized from the side of labourers also. Impact of globalisation on employment, wages, and labour standards are concern of study of globalisation. Therefore, this section of the paper tries to analyse on this issue.

Opponents criticise it by saying that globalisation does not create opportunities rather limits it to the weak because of the influence of big business houses in the use of resources, lack of required skills to work at the environment of specialisation and advanced technology. Thus, globalisation does not favour to the people of developing countries like Nepal, where most them are already unskilled and uneducated, and resources are limited. Instead, the cumulative effects of globalisation would be inequality of income distribution between the people and nations, 'rich get richer, and poor turn out to be inopportune'. Greater specialisation and widespread application of advanced technologies tend to favour skilled and well-educated workers in fields, like information technology (IT), specialised financial and other business services etc. Unskilled workers will be subcontracted, eliminated, relocated aboard or unemployed or migrated from their favourite job due to lack of required skill to adjust with the unit restructured to cope with advanced technology and labour-saving technologies, with the concomitant effect of poor education and ill-health and deprived life of family. This situation is prominent among the women workers due to lack of appropriate skills. Jobs for them in the high-growth sector and specialise unit is far reaching goals. Thus, they are compelled to accept the gender disparities in wages, subcontract of labour system, and socio-economic, physical, and psychological discriminations or abuses from employers and male coworkers.

Thus, the liberalisation has led to informalisation of work, which is already miserable in Nepal. The vast majority of the workers are in the informal sector and this sector is unprotected by labour laws. The conditions of informal sector are miserable, with long working hours, low payment, use of child labour, the existence of bonded labour in agriculture, gender discrimination in wages and terms of employment, no minimum wages, and no social security measures (Upadhyaya, 2003).

Globalisation and Unemployment

The people who are against the globalisation process always arguing that globalisation create unemployment to the low-skilled workers in developing countries. Some economist views that competition of low wage countries creates unemployment in developing countries and thus develop countries will be in a position to exporting jobs in developing countries. However, Brittan (1998:8), in support of globalisation, opines that decrease in the demand for low skilled workers in developing countries is not just because of the globalisation rather due to technological advancement. He further states that the international demand for specialised skills workers has increased because of the requirement to compliance with advanced technology.

As stated by Scholte (1997:334), the scholars like Nader R. and Brecher Costello, put different views than Brittan. They opine that globalisation has lead to reduction in the bargaining power of the worker in front of the global companies because free mobility of workers is still limited by the border. Similarly, it is not certain whether cross border production will lead to the loss of job security and lower wages. Thus, globalisation is not necessarily disadvantageous to the workers (see Scholte, 1997: 335). By these sayings, we can infer that the demand for labour intensive and low-skilled workers is low because of competition in the world economy. In this context, the study of IMF (2000:8) has believed that the demand for lower skilled workers has shrunk due to the turning of developed countries' economy towards service oriented.

In Nepal, the number of permanent employees is decreasing with the increasing number of contract and causal labour in the name of gaining competitiveness, cost minimisation, and comparative advantage in international trade. This process is particularly visible in carpet, and garment industries, the major export sectors in Nepal (GEFONT, 1998). From privatised public enterprises, 39.5% employees have found lost their jobs (Upadhyaya, 2003). The de-bureaucratisation process held in the country under the process of liberalisation brought the lay-off of 19345 civil servants leading to politicisation of political instability of the country (Dahal, 2005:109).

Globalisation and Labour Standards

Under liberalisation, there is a common fear among the workers for loosing better wages, fringe benefit, welfare facilities, and other labour standards conceived in the ILO standards. Such a fear is some how true because countries may try to improve their competitiveness in world economy by lowering the cost of operation including the cost on labour. Thus, among the workers, liberalisation created wage inequality between the skilled and unskilled and across intra-industries level (Dahal, 2005: 108). Independent studies show low wages for workers in all sectors of economy of the country, as compared to other South Asian counties. According to Unni and Rani (2000:809), income per workers in Nepal, computed as Gross domestic product or value added per workers, is the lowest than other four South Asian countries i.e. Sri Lanka, Pakistan, India and Bangladesh. Similarly, though the incomes per worker have increased between the period 1980 and 1997, the services sector rose well above the industries sector in all the countries except Nepal (Mazumdar (1997).

There is an argument that developing countries tend to improve their competitive advantage in the world trade by making the wage competitive. Nevertheless, this matter has been brought into debate on labour standards as workers' rights by governments, employers, and trade unions from both developed and developing countries. In favour, they argue that the countries and companies, which continue to pursue competitive advantage in international trade through the violation of fundamental rights (of labour), should be punished through sanction on international trade.

The argument from the side of resistant is that it is their rights to enjoy the benefit of trade liberalisation based on comparatively low labour costs. In favour of reducing the labour cost, developing counties say that labour standards is the 'game of a trade politics' played by developed countries in order to minimise the comparative advantage of developing countries and maintain their domination in trade (see Katuwal, 2006: 197-201).

In this regard, Hoe (1995) stresses to protect workers rights but considers that trade-related international labour standards may constitute hidden trade barriers. Brittan (1998:9) suggests for protecting some of the workers right as countries become interdependent. The view of Katuwal (2006:208) in this matter is "Not agreeing to enforcement of labour standards for trade sanctions or without bothering for inclusion of labour standards in WTO, Nepal needs to improve productivity and efficiency of manufacturing and service sectors".

Thus, if the protest in the name of labour standards remains successful, it may lead to the reduction of the developing countries' participation in the global economy because they could not compete with developed countries in other matters than the cheap labour.

Share of Service Sector in Employment

The adoption of liberal economic policies in the process of globalisation has created employment opportunities in different areas. With the rapid growth of banks, finance companies, and insurance companies and growth of export and import trade after liberalisation policies, employment has been increased in these sectors. As the services and manufacturing units are found to be growing in numbers, the people engaged in agricultural sector have been shifting gradually towards these sectors. The dependency on agriculture for livelihood has also been decreased due to the growth of service and other tertiary sector of employment. Nevertheless, the decreased trend of the absorption of increased population in agriculture sector is also due to increased employment opportunity in foreign job. The jobs in service sector are expected to enlarge as the new service units are growing due to liberalised policy of the government.

There is no sector and year wise specific data available to show the rise of employment in service sector before and after the liberalisation policy. Thus due to unavailability of employment data of service industries in specific years, it is not possible to compare different sectors of economy in terms of the changes in employment between pre and post globalisation period. However, by the CBS census data on the Industrial Classification of Economically Active Population (CBS, 2003: 353-57), we shall view development of the service sector due to the process of globalisation through the available employment data.

The data in the Table 6 indicates that population above ten years engaged in services has recorded a dramatic increase. It is more than 22% of 10637243 persons employed in different sectors of economy. This clearly shows the tendency of shifting of the functional distribution of labour force from agriculture to other sector, the rapid growth and widen of service sector employment, and socioeconomic transformation in the country due to the favourable environment created in the process of globalisation.

Table 6
Sectoral Share in Employment (in %)

Sectors / Census Year	*1971*	*1981*	*1991*	*2001*
Agricultural	94.4	91.2	81.2	65.7
Industrial	1.2	0.5	2.6	11.9
Service/tertiary	4.4	6.5	14.9	22.2
Unspecified	–	1.9	1.2	0.2
Total	100	100	100	100

Figures in parentheses indicate actual number employment.
Source: CBS (1995 and 2003).

The service sector employment has experienced an increase 8 % percentage points during the period between 1991 and 2001. The growing employment in this sector, shifting from agriculture, is a sign of the growing role of liberalised policy adopted by the country to attract private sector and foreign investment for the establishment of service sector units like banking, insurance, computer, information, communication, education, and health related services.

Sector wise Employment Situation in the Foreign Initiated Units

It is clear from the data in Table 7 that the service sector following manufacturing is the second largest preferred area for foreign investors in Nepal. However, if the tourism were considered as the service industry, the service sector would be the leading foreign investment-attracting sector in Nepal. Service and tourism sector attracted the largest foreign investment (42.53 percent) in 453 projects during the last 16 years in Nepal by generating employment opportunity for 28147 people in the foreign invested companies.

The global economic recession, and the political and economic instability, deteriorating peace and security conditions due to Maoist insurgency for the last 12 years in the country are largely responsible for the fluctuating but slow pace of foreign investment growth and employment in the Industries Approved for Foreign Investment. The situation is expected to be corrected because of the involvement of the Maoist party in the interim government.

Nevertheless, the supporting Acts and policies seem more conservative than other developing countries to divert foreign and private investors towards Nepal. So that it is necessary to lay down the more flexible and foreign investment friendly trade, industrial and labour policies and changes in the Labour Act for attracting foreign investment in Nepal. Since the simplified procedures for investment and liberal labour policy may encourage entrepreneurs to get entry in the country without any hesitation for investment. It is also necessary to make the bilateral and multilateral trade treaties, especially the Nepal-India Trade Treaty, more clear and export-oriented to increase foreign investment in Nepal because foreign investors come to Nepal eyeing over 1 billion Indian consumers, as Nepalese market is small with one of the lowest per capita consumption expenditure in the world (Pant and Sigdel, 2004:26).

Table 7
Sector wise Foreign Investment and Employment in Nepal (Before and after the Globalisation Process)

(Rs. in million)

Sector	*Industries*		*Total Investment (With Fixed Capital)*		*Foreign Investment*		*Employment*	
	No.	*%*	*Rs*	*%*	*Rs*	*%*	*No.*	*%*
Up to 1988-89								
Manufacturing	39	66.10	4702.74	86.67	347.36	74.41	7894	74.57
Construction	1	1.70	52.71	0.97	6	1.29	103	0.97
Service	7	11.86	32.36	0.59	13.58	2.90	1297	12.25
Tourism	11	18.64	314.99	5.81	82.63	17.70	1292	12.20
Mineral	1	1.70	323.12	5.96	17.28	3.70	–	–
Total	59	100	5425.92	100	466.85	100	10586	100
1989-90 to 2004-05								
Agriculture	15	1.63	440.15	0.52	101.76	0.38	1023	1.14
Manufacturing	420	45.50	32011.17	37.88	11262.49	42.42	53268	59.47
Construction	18	1.95	1011.55	1.20	619.69	2.33	1234	1.38
Service	228	24.70	15206.38	17.99	6814.15	25.66	14530	16.22
Tourism	225	24.38	15557.5	18.41	4479.71	16.87	13617	15.20
Energy	15	1.62	19452.30	23.01	3246.15	12.22	4763	5.32
Mineral	2	0.22	830.02	0.98	28.72	0.11	1129	1.26
Total	923	100	84509.07	100	26552.67	100	89564	100
Grand Total	982	100	89934.99	100	27019.52	100	100150	100

Source: DOI (2006).

POLICY IMPLICATIONS

From the discussion, we came to know that participation in the process of globalisation brings many benefits including increase in economic growth and development, employment opportunities, life expectancy, literacy rate and other indicators of social development. For Nepal, it could not obtain many benefits from globalisation due to various internal and external reasons. So that following measures are suggested to cope with the problems in globalisation and get maximum benefits from it. Broadly speaking, it is also suggested to frame the flexible and foreign investment friendly trade, industrial and l abour policy and changes the Labour Act to attract foreign investment and active participation of private sector in socio-economic development.

Nepal, for the long-term benefits from the process of globalisation, has to frame a policy conducive to private investment by combining the policies of increasing domestic resource mobilisation, using natural resources, increasing investments in skills, training, and infrastructural development. More specifically, following suggestion are devised:

Trade Policy

Trade policy should be liberalised as much at optimum extent by issuing appropriate trade policy. The policy should not be changed frequently when the ruling political party falls from the government. Therefore, national consensus of political parties about the national trade policy should be developed before its announcement. All kinds of trade barriers, as far as possible, should be eliminated. So that local companies will be encouraged to produce the goods and services, in which they have the advantage against foreign companies. Process of giving subsidies in trade should be discouraged to make the companies competitive in term of cost, price, and quality. As Nepal has recently become a member of the WTO, rules, regulations, policies and programs including privatisation and foreign investment policies need to be compatible with arrangement of the WTO.

Macroeconomic Policy

Over and under flow of capital in the country are both dangerous for the trade and monetary policy. Macroeconomic policy is a tool of regularizing the national monetary policy and balance of payment system in the country by managing the flow of capital in the country. Increase in the capital flow and international financial markets in the process of globalisation; on the other hand, diminishes the efficiency of the macroeconomic policy of the government. The increased capital flows and outflows due to globalisation may increase the instability in exchange rates. Therefore, that it is necessary to make coordination between trading partners about macroeconomic policy.

Training

Nepal, to get the benefit of globalisation has to develop high quality, productive labour and sustain its comparative advantages since cheap labour is becoming less important in investment in recent times. As there is paucity of skilled and educated labour force, the country can no longer rely only on low labour costs. Therefore, advance retaining should be provided to the low-skilled workers and to the workers who have to loose their job due to restructuring and advancing process of local companies to make them as capable as foreign companies are. Extra training should be given to the workers displaced from process of restructuring and advancement of companies to fit for employment in other sector of economy.

Promotional Measure

Similarly, as the majority of international investors have little idea about the prospects of foreign/joint-venture investments in the new socio-economic and political changes, different modern promotional measures should be initiated in foreign countries to publicise the prospects and potential of such investments in Nepal. Likewise, Nepal has to search out the potential export market for Nepalese products.

At the end, the poor law and order, agitations, strikes and social and political disharmony discourage prospective investors. So that peace, law and order, social and political harmony should be established in the country with the full cooperation and the support of all political partiers, employers, employees and civil society.

CONCLUSION

Dynamics of international, regional, and domestic socio-political situation factors have caused to increase socio-economic activities in Nepal. Under these circumstances, the liberal economic ideas have predisposed Nepalese policy makers also to enter the country into the globalisation process of economy, particularly after the restoration of democracy in 1990.

Although it has adopted an open and liberal policy and has given greater emphasis on foreign investment in socio-economic sector, the country could not attract effective foreign investment and increase the volume of export and benefited better from the process of globalisation in respect to its socio-economic development. The portion of foreign investment and export has remained always very small in Nepal. The pace of development became swing. Worldwide economic recession, conservative liberal policies, and internal political instability due to Maoist insurgency are the main causes of deteriorating economic growth and low attraction of foreign vestment in Nepal, in spite of its liberal economic policy under the process of globalisation.

Overall, neither industrial nor service sector could get benefit by the globalisation due to weak security situation during last twelve years caused by Maoist conflict in the country. Industrial activities, which are mainly involved in the processing of agro-based products, could not also flourish by enjoying the benefits of globalisation. In the service sector, security concerns have led to a decrease in tourism, a key source of foreign exchange. Prospects for foreign trade or investment in other sectors will remain poor because of the small size of the economy, technological backwardness, susceptibility to natural disaster, remoteness, landlocked geographic location, and civil strife. However, Nepal has considerable scope for exploiting its potential in hydropower and tourism as the areas of foreign investment interest. Eventually, the situation is hoped to be favourable for the socio-economic development of the country through the globalisation process in the changed political scenario in the country.

REFERENCES

Bell, D. (1973), *The Coming of the Post Industrial Society*, Basic Book, New York.

Berry, Albert (2005), *Methodological and Data Challenges to Identifying the Impacts of Globalisation and Liberalisation on Inequality*, United Nations Research Institute for Social Development, Switzerland, Geneva.

Bhagwati, J. (2004), *In Defense of Globalisation*, Oxford University Press, New York.

Brittan, L. (1998), "Globalisation vs. Sovereignty"? *The European Response: The 1997 Related Lecture and Related Speeches*, Cambridge University Press, Cambridge.

CBS (1995), *Population Monograph of Nepal* Vol. I, Central Bureau of Statistics, Kathmandu.

CBS (2003), *Population Monograph of Nepal* Vol. I, Central Bureau of Statistics, Kathmandu.

CBS (2004), *Nepal Living Standard Survey 2003-04*, Central Bureau of Statistics, Kathmandu.

Crafts, N. (2000), *Globalisation and Growth in the Twentieth Century*, IMF Working Paper, International Monetary Funds, Washington.

Dahal, D.R. (2005), "Impact of Globalisation in Nepal: Trade Union Prospective". In Madan K. Dahal.(ed.), *Impact of Globalisation in Nepal,* Nepal Foundation for Advanced Studies (NEFAS) and Friedrick-Ebert-Stiftung (FES), Kathmandu.

DOI (2006), *Industrial Statistics 2005-2006*, Department of Industries, HMG/N, Kathmandu.

GEFONT (1998), *Globalisation and Trade Unions in Nepal,* A Paper Presented in the ICEM-AP Regional Seminar, Jakarta, Indonesia, 2-3 December, 1998, General Federations of Nepalese Trade Unions (GEFONT), Kathmandu (*www.gefont / views / 1998 / globalisation.htm*).

Goldsmith, Mander, Jen (1996), *The Case against the Global Economy and for a Turn Toward the Local.* Sierra Club, San Francisco.

Hak-Min, K. (1999), *Globalisation of International Financial Markets: Causes and Consequences.* Ashgate Publishing Limited, Hants.

Hoe, L.A. (1995), *Human Rights, International Labour Standards and Trade in a Globalised Economy: An Assessment of the Economic, Moral and Political Dimensions,* Dissertation submitted to the University of Birmingham, Birmingham.

ILO (2004), *The Consequences of Globalisation. In Nepal in Terms of Employment, Income Distribution and Poverty*, A Report prepared by Nepal Society for Applied Economics for International Labour Office Policy Group, Geneva.

IMF (2000), *International Capital Markets: Developments, Prospects and Key Policy Issues,* International Monetary Funds, Washington.

Inman, R.P. (1985), *Managing the Service Economy: Prospect and Problem*, Cambridge University Press, London.

Kansakar, Vidya Bir Singh (1996), "Role of Rural Development Projects in the Growth of Cottage and Small industries", In Madan K. Dahal and Horst Mund (eds.), *Social Economy and National Development: Lesson from Nepalese Experience*, NEFAS, Kathmandu.

Katuwal, S.B. (2006), "Issues of Labour Standards in WTO Regime: The Case of Nepal", *The Journal of World Intellectual Property Rights*, Vol. 2, No. 1-2, pp. 189-214.

K.C., Bishnu Bahadur (1997), *The Kathmandu Post*, December 7.

K.C., Fatta Bahadur (2003), "Performance of Public Enterprises in Nepal", *Economic Review: Occasional Paper*, Nepal Rastra Bank, Number 15, April.

Khadka, S.R. and R. Lohani (2003), *Rock Bottom Economic Status in Social Watch Report, 2003: The Poor and the Market*, Institito del Tercer Mundo, Uruguay.

Kissinger, Henry A. (1994), *Diplomacy*, Simon and Schuster, London.

Kllick, T. (2001), "Globalisation and Rural Poor", *Development Policy Review*, Vol. 19, No. 2, pp. 155-176.

Masson, P. (2001), Globalisation: Facts and Figures, IMF Policy Discussion Paper (PDP/01/04), International Monetary Funds, Washington.

Mazumdar, Dipak (1997), "Labour Markets, Trade Patterns and Workers' Living Standards", *Economic and Political Weekly*, Vol. 32, No. 9-10, pp. 463.

MOF (1999), *Monitoring Privatized Enterprises*, Ministry of Finance (Privatisation Cell), Kathmandu.

MOF (2006), *Economic Survey 2005-06*, Ministry of Finance, Kathmandu.

MOF (various years), *Economic Survey (Various Issues)*, Ministry of Finance, Kathmandu.

NPC (1998), *The Ninth Plan*, National Planning Commission/HMG, Kathmandu.

NPC (2005), *Nepal Milieu Development Goals: Progress Report 2005*, National Planning Commission/HMG, Kathmandu.

NPC (2006), *An Analytical Study of Basic Social Services in Nepal*, National Planning Commission/HMG, Kathmandu.

NRB (1994), *Rural Credit Survey*, Nepal Rastra Bank (NRB), Kathmandu.

NRB (1998), *Multipurpose Household Budget Survey*, Nepal Rastra Bank (NRB), Kathmandu.

NRB (2007), *Macro Indicators of Nepal*, Nepal Rastra Bank, Research Department (Statistic Division) (NRB), Kathmandu.

O' Brien, R. (1992), *The Global Financial Integration: The End of Geography*, Pinter Publishers Limited, London.

Pant Bhubanesh and Sigdel, Bama Dev (2004), "Attracting Foreign Direct Investment: Experiences and Challenges", *NRB Working Paper, Serial Number: NRB-WP-1,* Nepal Rastra Bank, Research Department, Kathmandu.

Quattara, A.D. (1997). *"Globalisation's Challenges for Africa"*. IMF Survey. International Monetary Funds, Washington.

Redding, S. (1999), "Globalisation". *Economic Review,* (17), 1 September, pp. 16-19.

Rodgers, Gerry (2005), "The Pattern of Globalisation and Some Implications for the Pursuit of Social Goals", *The Indian Journal of Labour Economics,* Vol. 48, No. 1, pp. 47-61.

SAAPE (2003), *Poverty in South Asia 2003: Civil Society Prospective*, South Asia Alliance for Poverty Eradication (SAAPE), Kathmandu.

Scholte, J.A. (1997), "Global Capitalism and the State" *International Affairs,* Vol. 73, No. 3, 427-452.

Scholte, Jan Aart (2005). *The Sources of Neo-liberal Globalisation*, United Nations Research Institute for Social Development, Switzerland, Geneva.

The World Bank (2006), *World Development Report, 2006*, Oxford University Press, New York.

Todaro, M.P. (1985), *Economic Development in the Third World, Third Edition, Longman*, New York.

UNDP (2006), *Human Development Report 2006, Beyond Scarcity: Power, Poverty and the Global Water Crisis,* United Nations Development Programme, Palgrave Macmillan, New York.

Upadhyaya, Umesh (2003), *Impact of Gl balisation on Working Class and Building the Resistance,* A Paper Presented in the Globalisation and Its Impact on Labour in South Asia Seminar, Organised by South Asian Alliance against Poverty Eradication (SAAPE), Asian Social Forum, 2-7 January, 2003, Hyderabad, India.

Unni, Jeemol and Rani Uma (2000), "Globalisation, Information Technology Revolution and Service Sector in India", *The Indian Journal of Labour Economics,* Vol. 43, No. 4, pp. 803-827.

Visser, Eevert-Jan and Van Dijk Meine Pieter (2006), "Economic Globalisation and Workers: Introduction", Tijdschrift *Voor Economische en Sociale Geografie,* Vol. 97, No. 5, pp. 463–469.

Wade, R.H. (2003), "Is Globalisation Reducing Poverty and Inequality?" *World Development* 32, pp. 567–589.

Women's International League for Peace and Freedom (1996), 27th International Congress Working Paper on Globalisation, Baltimore, Maryland, USA.

www.saape.org.np/resources/publications/poverty_report03/nepal.pdf.

HEALTH CARE INFRASTRUCTURE IN THE CONTEXT OF GLOBALISATION IN INDIA

J. B. Komaraiah & Rinky Sharma***

INTRODUCTION

India is the second most populous country of the world and has changing socio-political-demographic and morbidity patterns that have been drawing global attention in recent years. Despite several growth-orientated policies adopted by the government, the widening economic, regional and gender disparities are posing challenges for the health sector. It is reassuring to note that the commitment to raise the annual spending on healthcare to more than 2 per cent of the GDP, which had fallen to 0.9 per cent in the past few years. India is a land of striking inequalities, more than 70 per cent of its population lives in rural areas, where only 20 per cent of the total hospital beds are located. Yet India is proudly announcing that it is ready to cater to "health tourists" from the developed world. About 75 per cent of health infrastructure, medical man power and other health resources are concentrated in urban areas where 27 per cent of the population lives. Over the last six decades, India has built up a vast health infrastructure and man power at primary, secondary and tertiary care in government, voluntary and private sectors. But public health infrastructure is far from satisfactory. Contagious, infectious and waterborne diseases such as diarrhea, amoebiasis typhoid, infectious hepatitis, worm infestations, measles, malaria, tuberculosis, whooping cough, respiratory infections, pneumonia and reproductive tract infections dominate the morbidity pattern, especially in rural areas. However, non-communicable diseases such as cancer, blindness, mental illness, hypertension, diabetes, HIV/AIDS, accidents and injuries are also on the rise. The health status of Indians is still a cause for grave concern, especially that of the rural population. This is reflected in the life expectancy (63 years), infant mortality rate (80/1000 live births),

* Lecturer (Sr. Scale) Department of Economics, Banaras Hindu University, Varanasi-5.
** Ph.D. Scholar, Department of Economics, Banaras Hindu University, Varanasi-221 005.

maternal mortality rate (438/ 100 000 live births). However, over a period of time some progress has been made to improve the prevailing situation. The problem of rural health is to be addressed both at macro (national and state) and micro (district and regional) levels. This is to be done in a holistic way, with genuine efforts to bring the poorest of the population to the centre of the fiscal policies.

The role and imperativeness of infrastructure in spear leading economic development of a country and also setting its pace can hardly be overemphasized. A robust economy needs a robust infrastructure. Infrastructure is being a sin-qua-non of economic development. Its development is not a luxury but a necessity. Like every other development activity, infrastructure development has several players and it cannot be taken as a responsibility of a single institution/ministry. It casts a responsibility on various institutions like Ministries, policy makers, industrialists, financers and banking institutions. Infrastructure is an umbrella term normally referred as 'social overhead capital'. It consists of two components namely economic infrastructure and social infrastructure. Economic infrastructure supports and promotes primarily the economic activities; its components being utilise such as power, telecommunication, water supply and sanitation etc. Social infrastructure includes health and human resource development, socio-cultural, legal and administrative system, commercial and institutional framework. However, these segments are not only complementary to each other but interdependent too in propelling the primary and secondary sectors.

The principal challenge for India is the building of a sustainable health system. Selective, fragmented strategies and lack of resources have made the health system unaccountable, disconnected to public health goals, inadequately equipped to address people's growing expectations and inability to provide financial risk protection to the poor. Access to medical care continues to be problematic due to locational reasons, bad roads, unreliable functioning of health facilities, transport costs and indirect expenses due to wage loss etc. making it easier to seek treatment from local doctors. This explains the gross underutilization of the existing health infrastructure at the primary level contributing to avoidable waste. The reasons for this failure can be attributed to three broad factors, i.e. (a) poor governance and the insignificant role of the state; (b) lack of a strategic vision; and (c) weak management. The structural mismatch in the institutions at the Centre and State levels, with many departments and agencies duplicating work or working at cross-purposes make governance in health ineffective. Contributory factors for a insignificant health system are unrealistic and non evidence–

and based goal-setting, lack of strategic planning, inadequate funding, facilitate the paradigm shift in reorganizing and financing the health system, we need to develop institutional capacity with a critical mass of multivariate skills for enforcement of regulations and designing flexible and innovative approaches, keep vigil and synthesize information from various sources for assessing trends. The Commission on Macro Economics & Health believes that the proposed institutional infrastructure is a bare minimum. The bodies should be autonomous and self-financing. The commission recommended their establishment on priority. Experts with demonstrated experience in the field should be associated as issues are complex and require in-depth knowledge.

RURAL HEALTH CARE SYSTEM– THE STRUCTURE AND CURRENT SCENARIO

The health care infrastructure in rural areas has been developed as a three tier system and is based on the population norms.

SUB-CENTRES (SCs)

The Sub-Centre (5,000 Pop. in case of Plain areas and 3,000 pop. in other hilly/tribal/difficult areas in each SC) is the most peripheral and first contact point between the primary health care system and the community. Each sub-centre is manned by one Auxiliary Nurse Midwife (ANM) and one Male Health Worker. One Lady Health Worker (LHV) is entrusted with the task of supervision of six sub-centres. Sub-centres are assigned the tasks relating to interpersonal communication in order to bring about behavioral change and provide services in relation to maternal and child health, family welfare, nutrition, immunization, diarrhea control and control of communicable diseases programmes. The Sub-centres are provided with basic drugs for minor ailments needed for taking care of essential health needs of men, women and children. The Department of Family Welfare is providing 100 per cent Central assistance to all the Sub-centres in the country since April, 2002 in the form of salary of ANMs and LHVs, rent at the rate of Rs. 3000/- per annum and contingency at the rate of Rs. 3200/- per annum, in addition to drugs and equipments kits. The salary of the Male Worker is borne by the State Governments. Under the SWAP Scheme, the Government of India has taken over an additional 39,554 Sub-centres from State Governments/ Union Territories since April, 2002 in lieu of 5,434 numbers of Rural Family Welfare Centres transferred to the State Governments/ Union Territories. There are 1,42,655 Sub-centres functioning in the country as on September, 2004.

PRIMARY HEALTH CENTRES (PHCs)

PHC (Pop. 30,000 in plain areas and 20,000 pop. in other hilly/tribal/difficult areas in each PHC) is the first contact point between village community and the Medical Officer. The PHCs were envisaged to provide

Table 1
Primary Health Centres–Progress of Establishment

State / UT	*Number functioning at the end of Sixth Plan (1981-85)*	*Number functioning at the end of Seventh Plan (1985-90)*	*Number functioning at the end of Eighth Plan (1992-97)*	*Ninth Plan (1997-02)*	*Primary Health Centres functioning as on Sept. 04*
A.P.	555	1283	1335	1386	1490
Arunachal P.	–	24	45	65	78
Assam	237	449	610	610	610
Bihar	796	2001	2209	2209	1648
Chhattisgarh		–	–	–	516
Goa 13	17	17	19	19	
Gujarat	310	842	960	1032	1070
Haryana	163	366	399	403	408
H.P.	106	190	260	302	438
J & K	123	266	335	337	334
Jharkhand	–	–	–	–	561
Karnataka	365	1142	1601	1676	1679
Kerala	199	908	938	944	933
M.P.	680	1181	1690	1690	1194
Maharashtra	1539	1671	1695	1768	1780
Manipur	31	64	69	69	72
Meghalaya	32	56	81	85	95
Mizoram	19	35	55	58	57
Nagaland	21	33	33	46	87
Orissa	484	875	1102	1352	1282
Punjab	130	460	484	484	484
Rajasthan	448	1048	1616	1674	M
Sikkim	18	20	24	24	24
Tamil Nadu	436	1386	1436	1436	1380
Tripura	32	49	55	58	73
Uttarakhand	–	–	–	–	229
Uttar Pradesh	1169	3000	3761	3808	3640
West Bengal	1172	1250	1262	1262	1173
A & N Islands	6	14	17	18	20
Chandigarh	0	0	0	0	0
D & N Haveli	3	5	6	6	6
Daman & Diu	2	2	3	3	3
Delhi	8	8	8	8	8
Lakshadweep	4	4	4	4	4
Pondicherry	14	22	39	39	39
All India	9,115	18,671	22,149	22,875	23,109

Source: Infrastructure Division, MOHFW/GOI.

an integrated curative and preventive health care to the rural population with emphasis on preventive and promotive aspects of health care. The PHCs are established and maintained by the State Governments under the Minimum Needs Programme (MNP)/Basic Minimum Services Programme (BMS). At present, a PHC is manned by a Medical Officer supported by 14 paramedical and other staff. It acts as a referral unit for 6 Sub-centre. It has 4-6 beds for patients. The activities of PHC involve curative, preventive, primitive and Family Welfare Services. There are 23,109 PHCs functioning as on September, 2004 in the country.

COMMUNITY HEALTH CENTRES (CHCs)

CHCs (Pop. 1, 20,000 in Plain areas and 80,000 pop. in other hilly/tribal/ difficult areas in each CHC) are being established and maintained by the state government. It is provided by four medical specialists i.e. surgeon,

Table 2
Establishment of Primary Health Centres, Sub-Centres and Community Health Centres in India since First Five Year Plan

Five Year Plan	*Community Health Centres (CHCs)*	*Primary Health Centres (PHCs)*	*Sub-Centres (SCs)*
1st Five Year Plan	–	275	–
2nd Five Year Plan	–	2565	–
3rd Five Year Plan	–	4631	–
Inter-Plan Period 3 Years	–	–	–
As on 31.03.1967	–	4793	17521
As on 31.03.1968	–	4946	21539
As on 31.03.1969	–	4919	22826
4th Five Year Plan	–	5283	33509
5th Five Year Plan	214	5484	47112
6th Five Year Plan	761	9115	84376
7th Five Year Plan	1910	18671	130165
Inter-Plan Period	–	–	–
As on 31.03.1991	2070	20139	130984
As on 31.03.1992	2188	20407	131369
8th Five Year Plan	2633	22149	136258
9th Five Year Plan	–	–	–
As on Sept. 2004	3,222	23,109	1,42,655

Source: Rural Health Statistics, India, March-2002 Bulletin.

medicine, gynecologist, and pediatrician supported by 21 Para-medical and other staff. It has 30 in-door beds with one operation theatre, X-ray, labour room and laboratory facilities. It serve as a referral centre for 4 PHCs. There are 3,222 CHCs are functioning as on September, 2004 in the country.

Table 3
Population and Development
Indicators for South and South West Asia–2003

Country	Mid-2003 population (per thousand)	Crude Birth Rate (per thousand)	Crude Death Rate (per thousand)	Total Fertility Rate (per woman)	Life Expectancy at Birth (years) Males	Life Expectancy at Birth (years) Female	Infant Mortality Rate (per thousand)	Mortality under age (per thousnad)
Afghanistan	23,897	47.2	21.3	6.8	43	44	161	278
Bangladesh	135,678	28.1	8.6	3.3	61	62	63	86
Bhutan	2,257	34.4	8.5	5.0	62	65	53	79
India	1,068,512	23.7	8.5	3.0	63	65	64	83
Iran	66,464	18.3	6.3	2.2	68	70	33	38
Maldives	288	35.7	6.0	5.3	68	67	38	48
Nepal	24,223	32.6	9.6	4.1	60	60	70	97
Pakistan	153,578	35.8	9.5	4.8	61	61	86	126
Sri Lanka	19,065	16.3	6.6	2.0	70	76	20	23
Turkey	71,325	20.7	6.0	2.4	68	73	39	49

Source: UNESCAP, 2003.

LIFE EXPECTANCY FOR MALES AND FEMALES IN INDIA

The life expectancy at birth for males was highest in Kerala its 71.67 years followed by Punjab with 69.78 years. The lowest was in Assam i.e. 58.96 years. In case of females the life expectancy was also higher in Kerala with 75.00 years and the lowest in Madhya Pradesh with 58.01 years. In the overall 66.91 years for females and 63.87 years for males during 2001-06 in India.

PUBLIC HEALTH SPENDING BY STATE GOVERNMENTS

Health being a State subject and the sector is financed primarily by the State Governments. Public health in the states is also financed through general tax and non-tax revenue resources as the cost recovery from the services delivered has been negligible, at less than 2 per cent. As a result, resource allocation to this sector is influenced by the general fiscal situation of the State Governments. For instance, the implementation of the recommendations of the Fifth Pay Commission during the late 1990s resulted in an increase in the fiscal deficit and a general resource crunch. Evidence from other countries also suggests that whenever there is a fiscal consolidation and stress, social sectors such as health and education are targeted for pruning expenditures and reducing the budget allocations. The figures presented in table 4 confirm that the budgetary allocations to the health sector during 2003-04 declined by more than 2 percentage points as compared to 1985-96. Despite a reduction in the health budget from 7.02 per cent in 1985-86 to 4.97 per cent in 2003-04, the fiscal deficit as a percentage of the Gross State Domestic Product (GSDP) recorded an increase, implying that allocation to health does not necessarily accentuate fiscal deficit. Public spending on the health sector in the states increased to about 0.9 per cent of the GDP in 2003-04, from 0.8 per cent in 1975-76. It was during 1985-86 that public spending on health registered a substantial increase and reached a high of 1.05 per cent. Thereafter, it deteriorated steadily due to general fiscal stress during the late 1980s followed by the reform measures initiated in the 1990s. The severity of the fiscal strain during the late 1980s forced the State Governments to introduce austerity measures and the soft sectors such as health were targeted for expenditure compressions.

Table 4
Trends in Health Expenditure in India

Year	*Health Expenditure as per cent of the GDP*			*Per-Capita Public Expenditure on Health (Rs.)*
	Revenue	*Capital*	*Aggregate*	
1950-51	0.22	NA	0.22	0.61
1995-56	0.49	NA	0.49	1.36
1960-61	0.63	NA	0.63	2.48
1965-66	0.61	NA	0.61	3.47
1970-71	0.74	NA	0.74	6.22
1975-76	0.73	0.08	0.81	11.15
1980-81	0.83	0.09	0.91	19.37
1985-86	0.96	0.09	1.05	38.63
1990-91	0.89	0.06	0.96	64.83
1995-96	0.82	0.06	0.88	112.21
2000-01	0.86	0.04	0.90	184.56
2001-02	0.79	0.04	0.83	183.56
2002-03	0.82	0.04	0.86	202.22
2003-04	0.86	0.06	0.91	214.62

Note: (i) GDP is at market price, with 1993-94 as the base year; (ii) includes only Central and State Government expenditure.

Sources: Report on currency and finance, RBI, various issues; Statistical abstract of India, Government of India, various issues; Handbook of statistics of India.

Public sector spending accounts for less than a quarter of the total health spending in India. However, it plays a major role in terms of planning, regulating and shaping the health care delivery system. Such public provisioning is essential to achieve equity and address the large positive externalities associated with health. Public spending (i.e. expenditures incurred by health departments of Central and State Governments) on health gradually accelerated from 0.22 per cent in

1950-51 to 1.05 per cent during the mid-1980s, and stagnated at around 0.9 per cent of the GDP during the later years. In terms of per capita expenditure, it increased significantly from less than Re 1/- in 1950-51 to about Rs. 215/- in 2003-04. Public spending under the National Health Accounts framework was about 1.3 per cent of GDP out of an overall health spending of 4.8 per cent of GDP. During the decade 1990-2001 Central Government spending had following notable characteristics:

Gradual reduction in the proportion of funds released to states under the grant in aid mechanism from 60 per cent to less than 40 per cent at a time when the states were themselves under fiscal stress. There was a sharp reduction in capital investment in public hospitals from 25 per cent of the budget in 1991 to less than 6 per cent in 2001 at a time of technological innovation and increased public expectations. Increased subsidy for own employees under the CGHS consuming 18 per cent of the budget of the Department of Health only less than 0.5 per cent of the country's population. Low priority was clearly shown to preventive and promotive health with less than 0.5 per cent of total public health spending.

It is well known that health expenditure in India is dominated by private spending. To a large extent this is a reflection of the inadequate public spending that has been a constant if unfortunate feature of Indian development in the past half a century. This is particularly unfortunate because of the large positive externalities associated with health spending, which make health spending a clear merit good. The greater reliance on private delivery of health infrastructure and health services, means that overall these will be socially underprovided by private agents, and also denies adequate access to the poor. This in turn has adverse outcomes not only for the affected population but for the society as a whole. It adversely affects current social welfare and labour productivity, and of course harms future growth and developmental prospects.

Two main characteristics of healthcare which lead to market failure and thus necessitate state intervention are the presence of externalities and information asymmetries. An externality results when an action of an agent has an effect not only upon the agent but also upon others. If a good or service not only benefits those who purchase these but others as well, then there is said to be a positive externality in its consumption. In such cases, the operation of market forces alone would lead to sub-optimal consumption and production of the relevant good or service. State intervention is then required to ensure that sufficient resources are directed to this activity. Externalities are very evident for "public health", that is interventions targeted at overall conditions of nutrition and sanitation that determine health, as well as communicable diseases which are passed either directly among humans or indirectly through the physical environment. An action had taken by one person (example, ensuring clean, safe water, immunizing oneself against, or seeking treatment for a communicable disease) generates direct health benefits for other individuals, through reduced rates of diseases. However, even general healthcare services that apparently affect only individuals have positive externalities, not only because of the social costs of morbidity; because of inequalities in healthcare create other social concerns. These positive externalities make government intervention essential. Such intervention can take the form of price subsidies to encourage or spread the consumption of healthcare services, or direct public provision of such services. Asymmetric information reflects any situation in which one party to any contract or exchange has access to some information that is not known to the other party. Such information asymmetries, primarily between the service provider and patient, pervade the health sector and market failure in both healthcare and healthcare insurance markets. For example, in any society, patients know best how improvements in the health affects their own well-being, while providers have better information regarding both the causes of ill-health and the effectiveness of alternative healthcare services in restoring health or preventing the further deterioration of the health.

There are also problems of "incentive incompatibility", in which the interests of the patient and the healthcare provider need not coincide. Both of these points need for the government intervention in the form of regulation. Such regulation can take the form of licensing of healthcare providers, limits on advertising, insistence on some professional norms that prohibit low quality, etc. Such regulation has to ensure balance between the need to increase welfare by improving or ensuring quality, and the welfare reducing effects of inadvertently granting monopoly powers to providers. Therefore, from both the efficiency and equity grounds, there is no alternative to the public provision of healthcare. Even for the success of an insurance system based on private provision, increased public health spending and reforming of public health facilities are necessary. This is what makes the theoretical case for health expenditure by the government.

THE INTERNATIONAL EXPERIENCE

Health expenditure is highly unequal across the globe. As is to be expected, developed countries spend the most on health per person. OECD countries accounted for less than 20 per cent of the world's population in the 2000 but were responsible for almost 90 per cent of the world's health spending. Therefore, 80 per cent of the world's population spent only 10 per cent of the total expenditure on health. This includes people in the Asia-Pacific as well as African and Latin American countries. Africa accounts for about 25 per cent of the global burden of disease but only about two per cent of global health spending. Similarly, health expenditure, both in terms of percentage of GDP spent on health and per capita health expenditure, is much higher in the developed countries, as evident from table 5. The share of GDP spent on health ranges from a low of 1.6 per cent in Azerbaijan to 13.9 per cent in the USA. Similarly, there is a very wide variation of the per capita health expenditure across countries, which is typically extremely low in developing countries compared with most of the developed countries. The range in 2001 was from $ 14 in Ethiopia to $ 4,887 in the USA. Central government efforts at influencing public health have focused on the five-year plans, on

Table 5
Health Expenditure and Health Indicators in Selected Countries

HDI rank	*Country*	*Health Expenditure as % of GDP*		*Per Capita Expenditure on Health (PPP in $)*	*Out-of-pocket Expenditure as % of Private Expenditure (2001)*	*Life Expectancy at birth (2001)*	*Infant Mortality Rate (per 1000 live birth) (2001)*	*Per capita GDP ($) (2001)*
		Public	*Private*					
1	Norway	6.9	1.2	2920	96.8	78.7	4	36974
7	USA	6.2	7.7	4887	26.5	76.9	7	34946
9	Japan	6.2	1.8	2131	74.9	81.3	3	32540
13	UK	6.2	1.4	1989	55.3	77.9	6	24786
52	Cuba	6.2	1	229	76.8	76.5	7	2234
58	Malaysia	2.1	1.8	345	92.8	72.8	8	3748
65	Brazil	3.2	4.4	573	64.1	67.8	31	2888
89	Azerbaijan	1.1	0.5	48	97.7	71.8	77	679
99	Sri Lanka	1.8	1.9	122	95	72.3	17	849
104	China	2	3.4	224	95.4	70.6	31	918
127	India	0.9	4.2	80	100	63.3	67	46.2
144	Pakistan	1	3	85	100	60.4	84	401
169	Ethiopia	1.4	2.1	14	84.7	45.7	116	93

Source: World Health Report, 2003.

coordinated planning with the states, and on sponsoring major health programmes. Government expenditures are jointly shared by the central and state governments. Goals and strategies are set through central-state government consultations of the Central Council of Health and Family Welfare. Central government efforts are administered by the

Ministry of Health and Family Welfare, which provides both administrative and technical services and manages medical education. What is also notable from table 5 is the much higher ratio of public health spending to private spending in the developed countries. By contrast, in middle developed and low developed countries, either private expenditure dominates or there is very little difference between the shares of private and public expenditure, although in general both tend to be low. It is notable that India has the lowest ratio of public to private health expenditure among all the countries mentioned in this table, including the poorest countries. Further, all the private expenditure in India (as in some other countries) is constituted by out-of-pocket expenses. This is inherently regressive and puts a disproportionate burden for healthcare on the poor households.

STATE GOVERNMENT HEALTH EXPENDITURE

Health is a Concurrent subject under the Indian Constitution, but State governments are dominantly responsible for most health provision, both curative and public health aspects. While there are some specific central interventions, especially in various "Missions" as well as high-end curative facilities, the bulk of the health provision that affects most of the citizenry is the result of spending by State governments. State governments account for about two-thirds and the Centre about one-third of the total public spending on the health sector. However, as table-6 shows, that there are large variations in this ratio across the States, as well as in per capita spending on health by State governments. It is apparent that low public expenditure can play a role in leading to higher levels of private expenditure, even in poorer States, where presumably per capita consumption expenditure is already lower. Further, there are very wide rural-urban differentials in public spending, with per capita spending in urban areas generally much higher than in rural areas for most states (with the exception of Assam, Punjab and Rajasthan). Obviously, there is no direct and clear linkage that can be made between government health expenditure and health outcome of people.

However, certain broad tendencies can certainly be identified. In particular, the unacceptably slow improvement in a range of basic health indicators such as life expectancy at birth, infant mortality and maternal mortality, can be partially traced to inadequate public expenditure and intervention. Furthermore, the expenditure on public health does have a direct impact on certain health indicators such as the spread of communicable diseases. Table 6 shows that there may not be a direct and regular relationship, it is certainly the case that there is abroad overall correlation between per capita health spending of the State government and certain basic health indicators.

Table 6 shows that the States are placed in descending order according to the government's per capita expenditure on health and family welfare taken together. Some broad features are evident: The richer States tend to have higher per capita spending, and generally tend to have lower Infant Mortality Rates (IMRs), greater incidence of full antenatal care and safe deliveries, and better nutrition indicators. However, it is not the case that the richer States all have higher per capita health expenditure—rather, some of them, such as Gujarat and Haryana have among the lowest per capita expenditure on health. Conversely, Rajasthan, with relatively low per capita income, has relatively higher per capita government spending on health. While there is no exact correlation between per capita health spending and some basic indicators such as life expectancy, IMR and Under-5 MR, there is a broad relationship along expected lines.

However, it should be noted that (barring Kerala) most indicators even in the high-spending States are relatively poor by international standards. Most direct impact of public spending appears to be felt in a very significant indicator—the proportion of children in the age group 12-36 months who have undergone the full required immunizations, that is BCG plus 3 Polio plus 3 DPT plus measles. The shocking fact that emerges from table-6 that, apart from Orissa (where as we have seen, Government health expenditure in real per capita terms has increased slightly in the period between NFHS-2 and NFHS-3), immunization rates have actually fallen in other States. The decline is very dramatic in the case of Maharashtra and Punjab, but is also clearly evident for Gujarat. In fact, it turns out that even in Orissa, only measles coverage has improved and coverage of the other vaccines has worsened. In Punjab, Gujarat and Haryana, the decline is essentially because of the much reduced coverage of both DPT and Polio. It is worth noting that Polio, which was supposed to be eradicated from India, has witnessed a recent upsurge, and that the incidence of both diphtheria and tetanus has increased even though these are both easily and completely preventable through immunization. The low and declining extent of immunization coverage therefore suggests greater vulnerability of the population to diseases which are entirely preventable. This worsening of one of the most basic indicators of public health appears to be the direct result of reduced government expenditure which, in turn, has reduced the spread of and access to vaccination among the general population, and particularly in the rural areas. This suggests that while infant mortality

Table 6

State Government Health Spending Per Capita and Health Expenditure

Major States	*Per capita state govt. health exp. In 2002-02 (in Rs)*	*Life expectancy at birth (2001-06) (in yrs.) Males*	*Females*	*IMR (2002)*	*<5 MR a proportion ofchildren under 5 years*	*Children <3 yrs. severely malnourished BMI<18.5)*	*Full immunization coverage (per cent) of children 12-36 (months)*	*Full antental care (3 visits) (per cent)*	*Safe delivery (per cent)*
Punjab	150.51	69.8	72	51	72	8.8	74	13.6	61.3
Karnataka	135.06	62.4	66.4	55	69.8	16.5	81	29.5	62
Kerala	128.4	71.7	75	10	18.8	4.7	91	64.3	96.5
Tamil Nadu	122.35	67	69.8	44	63.3	10.6	92	20	80
Maharashtra	115.38	66.8	69.8	45	58.1	17.6	85	23.8	60.8
Rajasthan	110.08	62.2	62.8	78	114.9	20.8	20	3.6	37.7
A.P.	106.17	64.1	65.4	62	85.5	10.3	72	35.2	67.9
W.B.	102.31	66.1	69.3	49	67.6	16.3	78	11.7	42.3
Gujarat	97.06	63.1	64.1	60	85.1	16.2	68	22.1	59.1
Haryana	86.88	64.6	69.3	62	76.8	10.1	56	28.5	44.1
Assam	73.64	59	60.9	70	89.5	13.3	57	–	20.5
Orissa	72.24	60.1	59.7	87	104.4	20.7	56	11.3	36.9
U.P.	48.29	63.5	64.1	80	122.5	219	27	3.9	25.8
M.P.	35.97	59.2	58	85	137.6	24.3	77	5.6	32.1

Source: Public Finance documents, SRS and Reports on Macro Economics and Health.

rates may not directly reflect the trends in government health expenditure so clearly (although there are broad relationship that can be discerned), immunization coverage appears to be directly (and even almost immediately) affected by public spending in this area. The reduced expenditure can, therefore, have alarming and completely unnecessary adverse effects upon the health of the population, which will eventually reflect not in mortality per se but in increased morbidity and reduced capabilities.

GLOBALIZATION WAVES IN HEALTH SECTOR IN INDIA

Medical Tourism

India has one of the best qualified professionals in each and every field, and this fact has now been realized the world over. Regarding Medical Facilities India has the most competent doctors and world class Medical Facilities. With most competitive charges for treatment, India is a very lucrative destination for people wanting to undergo treatment of certain medical problems who do not need immediate emergency treatment. India offers World Class Medical Facilities, comparable with any of the western countries. India has state of the art Hospitals and the best qualified doctors. With the best infrastructure, the best possible Medical facilities, accompanied with the most competitive prices, one can get the treatment done in India at the lowest charges. A patient will come to India where he/ she will undergo medical treatment and along with the Indian tourist and pilgrim destinations, as and when advised by the doctors. The whole thing would save him a lot of money and he will get to discover India at the same time. Get the medical treatment done in India at a fraction of the cost at which it is done abroad–in Europe or America.

COST COMPARISON BETWEEN INDIA AND USA

Significant cost differences exist between U.K. and India when it comes to medical treatment. India is not only cheaper but the waiting time is almost nil. This is due to the outburst of the private sector which comprises of hospitals and clinics with the latest technology and best practitioners. (Table 7).

COST COMPARISON BETWEEN INDIA UNITED KINGDOM (UK)

A Significant cost differences exist between U.K. and India even in case of costs, the waiting time. In U.K. the patient has to wait at least more than 3 months. (Table 8).

Table 7
Procedure Charges in India and USA

Procedure	*United States (US$) Approx**	*India (US$) Approx**
Bone Marrow Transplant	2,50,000	69,200
Liver Transplant	3,00,000	69,350
Heart Surgery	30,000	8,700
Orthopedic Surgery	20,000	6,300
Cataract Surgery	2,000	1,350
Smile Designing	8,000	1,100
Metal Free Bridge	5,500	600
Dental Implants	3,500	900
Porcelain Metal Bridge	3,000	600
Porcelain Metal Crown	1,000	100
Tooth Impactions	2,000	125
Root Canal Treatment	1,000	110
Tooth Whitening	800	125
Tooth Colored Composite	500	30
Fillings/ Tooth Cleaning	300	90

***These costs are an average and may not be the actual cost to be incurred.**

Table 8
Procedure Charges Between India United Kingdom (UK)

Procedure	*United Kingdom (US$) Approx**	*India (US$) Approx**
Open Heart Surgery	18,000	4,800
Cranio-Facial Surgery and skull base	13,000	4,500
Neuro-surgery with Hypothermia	21,000	6,800
Complex spine surgery with implants	13,000	4,600
Simple Spine Surgery	6,500	2,300
Simple Brain Tumor – Biopsy - Surgery	10,000	4,600
Parkinsons		
– Lesion	6,500	2,300
– DBS	26,000	17,800
Hip Replacement	13,000	4,500

*** These costs are an average and may not be the actual cost to be incurred.**

TELEMEDICINE

A recent survey by the Indian Medical Society has found 75 per cent of qualified consulting doctors practice in urban centers and 23 per cent in semi urban areas and only 2 per cent from rural areas whereas majority of the patients come from rural areas. Hospital beds/1000 people are 0.19 in rural and 2.2 in urban areas. The number of Neurosurgeons in Chennai city alone exceeds those in the entire North Eastern Region. This calls for innovative methods of utilization of science and technology for the benefit of our society and telemedicine assumes a great significance to revolutionize the health care system in India. Adaptation of Telemedicine technology offers one of the best options for delivering healthcare for rural and geographically distant population spread across India. Importance of Telemedicine in health care started quite some time ago and more recently the telemedicine has undergone something of resurgence as technology began catching up with the need and aspiration.

India can be classified as one of the countries with a potential to reap from almost all the applications of telemedicine. The Ministry of Communications and Information Technology, Government of India, has classified "Telemedicine" as one of the thrust areas for development in the country. The Government initiated a project called "Development of Telemedicine Technology." Teams at SAS Nagar and Pune have been working for this pilot project. Efforts are towards linking three tertiary level hospitals of North India namely: All India Institute of Medical Sciences at New Delhi; Post Graduate Institute of Medical Education and Research (Nehru Hospital) at Chandigarh; Sanjay Gandhi Post Graduate Institute of Medical Sciences at Lucknow, Uttar Pradesh.

The proposed Telemedicine setup between these medical institutes would primarily be in the three specialties of Radiology, Cardiology and Pathology. Doctors (working in Radiology, Cardiology and Pathology) in any of these three hospitals would be in a position to (Tele) consult an expert in the other hospital using the technology under development. The cities of New Delhi (capital of the Country), Chandigarh (capital of the states of Punjab and Haryana) and Lucknow (capital of the state of Uttar Pradesh) are among very few Indian cities which enjoy benefits of the State-of-the-art communication technologies like ISDN, leased lines etc. The project is currently in the terminal stages of the development. It would enable the exchange of clinical information among the three hospitals via ISDN lines. The three hospitals being linked in the pilot project are referral hospitals and the technology from these referral hospitals would flow down to the secondary and eventually to the primary healthcare delivery level. Some of the bottlenecks for the growth of Telemedicine in India are: (a) lack of health infrastructure and services, (b) shortage of computer savvy healthcare personnel, (c) out flow of doctors, there are about 60,000 and 35,000 Indian doctors in United States of America and United Kingdom respectively, (d) lack of training facilities with regard to the application of information and communication technology in medicine, (e) virtually no exposure to the applications of

ICT in curriculum of medical colleges, and (f) inadequate communication services to facilitate telemedicine.

Public hospitals lack in the latest technology and infrastructure due to the financial considerations involved in catering to more than what they are meant for. Private or corporate hospitals are coming up and promise world class services. Names like Apollo, Escorts and Batra are the popular corporate hospitals and each of them is in one way or the other involved in Telemedicine. International names like Fortis have reached India. Besides the Central Government the State Governments have also started showing interest in this suite of technologies of high social relevance. Time is approaching when telemedicine/e-health initially shall be visibly practised in majority of the Indian hospitals as a separate department before eventually fusing into respective medical specialties.

PUBLIC PRIVATE PARTNERSHIP (PPP) IN HEALTH SECTOR

In India, deficiencies in the public sector health system in providing health services to the population are well documented. The inability of the public health sector has forced poor and deprived sections of the population to seek health services from the private sector. Evidence indicates that, in many parts of India, the private sector provides a large volume of health services but with little or no regulation. Broadly the private sector includes all non-state actors, some explicitly seeking profits (for-profit) and others operating on a not-for-profit (NFP) basis. The private sector is not only India's most unregulated sector but also it's most potent and untapped sector. To address the inefficiency and inequity in the health system, many state governments have undertaken health sector reforms. One of these reforms has been to collaborate with the private sector through Public Private Partnership (PPP). Many state governments in India are experimenting with partnerships with the private sector to reach the poor and underserved sections of the population. Partnerships between the public sector and the private sector need careful delineation from other forms of interaction. True partnerships are characterised by relative sense of equality between the partners, mutual commitment to agree objectives and mutual benefits for the stakeholders involved in the partnership. These are reciprocal relationship between two or more parties with clear terms and conditions, clearly defined partnership structures, and specified performance indicators for delivery of a set of health services in a stipulated time period.

CHALLENGES

These include the motives of the private sector, scope and objectives of partnership, policy and legal frameworks, benefits of such partnerships, technical and managerial capacity of governments and private agencies to manage and monitor such partnerships, incentives for the private sector, stakeholders' perspectives towards partnership, and explicit benefits to the poor through such partnerships. Research evidence on these issues in India is scanty. The research study, conducted by the authors under the Indo-Dutch Programme on Alternatives in Development, compiled 16 in-depth case studies of public/private partnership projects from nine different states in India.

The study provides insights into how the partnerships originated, how they work, how the poor have been targeted, constraints and bottlenecks in the design, implementation and management of partnerships, and performance of these partnerships in reaching the targeted population. If well designed and implemented in stages, PPP is an innovative mechanism that benefits the poor. It would be unfair to categories PPP as privatisation or 'marketisation' because most of the partnership that are designed to deliver health services (not the ancillary services) are either civil society organizations or from the nonprofit private sector. However, some arrangements involve the private-for-profit sector in PPP. There is no pattern to indicate whether the public/private partnership as a policy option was guided by donor agencies or due to compulsions of resource constraints or due to competitive bureaucracy. However, public/ private partnership seems to have been prompted by visionary personalities from the bureaucracy and from civil society.

Under partnerships, public and private sectors can play innovative roles in financing and providing health care services. While reviewing the health sector in India, the World Bank and the National Commission on Macroeconomics in Health strongly advocated harnessing the private sector's energy and countering its failures by making both public and private sector more accountable. The Tenth Five-Year Plan (2002-2007) envisioned in detail the need for private sector participation in the delivery of health services.

Due to the deficiencies in the public sector health systems, the poor in India are forced to seek services from the private sector, often borrowing to pay for them. India has one of the worlds highest levels of private out-of-pocket financing (87 per cent estimated in World Bank 2001). Out-of-pocket expense at the point of service use is about 85 per cent. Such a mode of financing imposes debilitating effects on the poor. Hospitalisation or chronic illnesses often lead to liquidation of assets or indebtedness. It is estimated that more than 40 per cent of hospitalised people borrow money or sell assets to cover expenses, and 35 per cent of hospitalised Indians fall below the poverty line because of hospital expenses. Out-of-pocket medical costs alone may push 2.2 per cent of the population below poverty line in one year. Approximately 29 per cent of the Indian population (almost 300 million people) live below the poverty line and depend on free health services from the public sector. The inequities in the health system are further aggravated by the fact that public spending on health has remained stagnant at around one percent of GDP (0.9 per cent) compared to the global average of 5.5 per cent. Yet even the public subsidy on health does not automatically benefit the poor. The poorest quintile of the population uses only one-tenth of the public (state) subsidies on health care while the richest quintile accesses 34 per cent of the subsidies.

Designing partnership (contract) agreements requires sufficient capacity-building measures, but central government leadership may not be ideal for achieving this aim. States could create regional resource centres to develop these capacities locally. The approach towards pricing of tariffs for services (either in block grants or in case-based reimbursements) is based only on competitive tendering process rather than on a standard calculation of competitive rates. Similarly the payment system is mired in red tape that impedes successful partnerships. Policy innovations such as public/private partnerships are, of course, highly contextual.

Partnership with the private sector is not a substitute for the provision of health services by the public sector. Also, public-private partnership initiatives cannot be uniform across all the regions or suitable under all kinds of political and administrative dispensations. While private partnership is an administrative decision, an obvious but important point is that it must enjoy political and community support. There has to be a clear rationale for partnering with the private sector. It is important to understand not only what services are to be provided under private partnership but also to understand the basis on which such decisions are made. Any policy initiatives to strengthen the flagging public sector health services in India would be welcome. But a government that fails to deliver quality social services due to lack of basic administrative capacity would not be able to contract either clinical or non clinical services. The first step must be to improve basic administrative systems.

CONCLUSION

In developing countries, health infrastructure is the primary access point to seek health services. The different components are health education institutions, equipments & machinery, training, human resources, civil works and maintenance for sustainability. The decline public investment in health and the absence of any form of social Insurance have amounts of money at short notice are impoverishing an estimated 3.3 per cent of India's population every year. The poorest 10 per cent of the population rely on sales of their assets or on borrowings, entailing inter-generational consequences on the family's ability to access basic goods and affecting their long-term economic prospects.

REFERENCES

Economic Survey (2002-03), "Ministry of Finance, the Government of India", New Delhi.

Government of India, (2004), "Health Information of India", 2003.

Gupta Indrani & Mayur Trivedi (2005), "Social Health Insurance Redefined: Health for All Though Coverage for All" *Economic and Political Weekly.*

Kapila Raj & Uma Kapila (2002), "Economic Developments in India" *Academic Foundation.*

Khader S.A. (1998) "Productivity in Infrastructure" *Yojana.*

Kumar A.K. Shiv (2005), "Budgeting for Health Some Considerations" *Economic and Political Weekly,* Vol. 40.

Panda Akshya K. (2006), "Healthcare for All" *Yojana,* Vol. 50.

Perker A.S. and Guy Carrin, eds. (2004), "Health Financing for Poor People" *The World Bank*, Washington.

Registrar General India (2005), "SRS Bulletin Sample Registration System", New Delhi.

Report of the Technical Working Group on Telemedicine Standardization Recommended Guidelines & Standards for Practice of Telemedicine in India, 2003.

Reports of the Commission on Macroeconomic and Health, WHO, 2001.

Reports of the Commission on Macroeconomics and Health, Government of India 2005.

Richard, D. Smith (2004), "Foreign Direct Investment and Trade in Health Services: A Review of the Literature", *Social Science & Medicine* (59) 2313-2323.

Sanjay, P. Sood & J.S. Bhatia (2002), "Internet as the Backbone for Telemedicine: How far/close are we?", Presented at *All India Seminar, Challenges Ahead with Information Technology, Organized by IE & SLIET*, Longowal, 19-20.

Sankar Deepa & Vinish Kathuria (2003), "Health Sector in 2003-04 Budget" *Economic and Political Weekly,* Vol. 38.

Srinivasan G. (1998), "Toward Better Infrastructural Facilities" *Yojana*.

Tenth Five Year Plan, *Government of India*, New Delhi.

The Business Line (2006), "Health Expenditure in India".

The Business Line (2006), "Public Health Spending and Outcomes in States".

Uma H.R. (2004), "Financing of Health Services in India under Five Year Plans" *Kurukshetra,* Vol. 52.

UNCTAD-WHO (1998), "International Trade in Health Services a Development Perspective", Geneva.

UNDP (2000), "Human Development Report", Oxford University Press, New York.

Union Budget (2003-04), "Notes on Demand for Grants, 2003-04 Ministry of Health and Family Welfare, Demand No. 46 Department of Health", *The Government of India*, New Delhi.

United Nations World Population Prospects (1998), Revision, Vol. III, Analytical Report.

INDIA'S POWER SECTOR– POTENTIAL, PERFORMANCE AND PROSPECTS

Kiran Kumar P., Jayasheela** & V. Basil Hans****

INTRODUCTION

Power or energy is a pivotal input for modern economic growth, besides a basic need of modern man. It is the critical infrastructure on which the socio-economic development of the country depends. The growth of the economy and its global competitiveness hinges on the availability of reliable and quality power at competitive rates. The demand for power in India is enormous and is growing steadily.

Being a clean and versatile form of energy, electric power is one of the most important infrastructure sectors of the national economy. Providing adequate and affordable electric power is essential for economic development, human welfare and higher standard of living. Countries of the world, especially the developing countries are experiencing a radical change in policies and paradigm for their power sectors, particularly as a sequel to globalization and liberalization. For India's power sector, the past decade has been a tumultuous one. The winds of change that have swept power sectors world wide have brought the promise of an entirely new framework and approach for electricity, alongside considerable uncertainty and few short-term results.

Uninterrupted supply(!) of adequate and reliable power at an affordable price would be the best ingredient to generate quicker growth through better production in power-based units. But unlike the other commodities, electricity cannot be stored for future use. In other words, its generation and consumption have to be simultaneous and instantaneous. The unique features of power as a commodity or service

---

* Research Scholar, Department of Economics, Mangalore University, Mangalagangothri.
** Reader in Economics, Mangalore University, Mangalagangothri.
*** Professor of Economics and HOD of Arts, St Aloysius Evening College, Mangalore, (INDIA)

make the dynamics of its supply and demand difficult to manage. Installing power generation, transmission and distribution capacity is a complex, time consuming and expensive process. Power is among the most capital-intensive infrastructure sectors.

India's power sector has registered significant progress since the process of planned development of the economy began in 1950. Hydro-power and coal based thermal power have been the main sources of generating electricity, while nuclear power development–introduced in late sixties–is at a slower pace. The concept of operating power systems on a regional basis crossing the political boundaries of states was introduced in the early sixties. In spite of the overall development that has taken place, the power supply industry has been under constant pressure to bridge the gap between supply and demand. India being poised for a robust growth in the Eleventh Five Year Plan needs to give all attention to this sector which today is the backbone of industrial security. With this in view the resent paper has the following objectives.

1. to study the pattern of and trends in production and consumption of electricity in the country;
2. to examine the initiatives taken by the power ministry in order to achieve the goal of "Power to all by 2010"; and
3. to examine the privatization trend and its implications for future growth in India's power sector.

THE BASICS OF ENERGY SECTOR IN INDIA

Power has been placed in the list of concurrent subjects under the Indian Constitution with the Centre and the States both having jurisdiction. After Independence, the State Electricity Boards (SEBs)/State Electricity Departments were the sole utilities (except a few licensees in private sector) responsible for generation, transmission and distribution of electricity[1]. The power sector has been receiving adequate priority ever since the beginning of planned development in 1950. The Power Sector got 18-20% of the total Public Sector outlay in initial plan periods. Remarkable growth and progress have led to extensive use of electricity in all the sectors of economy in the successive five years plans. To supplement the efforts of States in bridging the yawning gap between demand and supply of power, it was decided, in mid seventies, to set up generating stations and associated high/extra high voltage transmission lines in the Central Sector. As a result of these efforts the installed capacity of power plants (Utilities) has increased to 89090 MW in 1998 from meagre 1713 MW in 1950, registering a 52 fold increase in 48 years.

Similarly, the electricity generation increased from about 5.1 billion units to 420 Billion units (82 fold increase).

From the Fifth Plan (1974-79) onwards the Government of India in a big way undertook the generation and bulk transmission of power to supplement the efforts at the State level and took upon itself the responsibility of setting up large coal and hydel power projects in the country as a supplementary effort in meeting the country's power requirements. The National thermal Power Corporation (NTPC) and National Hydro-electric Power Corporation (NHPC) were set up for these purposes in 1975. In 1976 the North-Eastern Electric Power Corporation (NEEPCO) was set up to implement the regional power projects in the North-East. Subsequently two more power generation corporations were set up in 1988 viz. Tehri Hydro Development Corporation (THDC) and Nathpa Jhakri Power Corporation (NJPC). To construct, operate and maintain the inter-State and interregional transmission systems the National Power Transmission Corporation (NPTC) was set up in 1989 and was renamed as POWER GRID in 1992.

In India the policy of liberalization announced by the Government in 1991 and consequent amendments in Electricity (Supply) Act opened new avenues to involve private efforts and investments in electricity industry. Considerable emphasis came to be placed on attracting private investment. With the IMF and World Bank promoting structural adjustment of national economies, the ADB has tended to focus on sectoral adjustment to facilitate privatization and foreign investment in individual sectors such as energy, transportation and communications. ADB-promoted energy sector reforms are found in countries throughout the region, including the Philippines, Indonesia, India, Pakistan and Tajikistan. The ADB's energy sector reform loans system requires governments to enact new laws and policies facilitating private sector participation, splitting generation, transmission and distribution into separate companies, privatizing state-owned enterprises, abolishing tariff subsidies and the like. In this direction several new steps were taken in India. (See Box-1).

This strategy, however, has largely failed. In order to attract private capital, governments have signed agreements with independent power producers (IPPs) in which economic risks and responsibility are unevenly borne by governments. In effect, economic risk has been transferred to the consumers who are forced to subsidize private investment through levies, taxes, price increases and debt repayments. The private sector, in these cases, has received a disproportionate share of profits and privileges.

BOX 1
PROFILE OF POWER SECTOR IN INDIA

- The public sector controls about 90% of power generation, almost all of its transmission, and most of its distribution.
- The sector suffers from huge deficits–cumulatively estimated at 1.5% of GDP.
- Deficits contribute greatly to fiscal crises in India's states.
- Unsustainable power subsidies particularly benefit large farmers.
- More than a third of all power generation is lost to large-scale theft.
- Power utilities are inefficient and overstaffed, with corruption and political interference at all levels.
- Power supply is erratic and of poor quality.
- Nearly three-fourths of poor households, especially in rural areas, have no access to electricity.
- Reform started in 1991 with the liberalization of generation, but many independent power producers subsequently withdrew. The focus of power sector reform has since shifted to distribution, the area where most of the dysfunction lies.
- Since 1993, the World Bank has played a role in helping to place power reform on India's policy agenda. Its formula of unbundling State Electricity Boards into separate entities for generation, transmission, and distribution, corporatizing these, and looking at privatization of distribution as an option, while improving governance and the regulatory environment, has been attempted in six states.
- In 1995, the policy for Mega power projects of capacity 1000 MW or more and supplying power to more than one state was introduced.
- GOI promulgated Electricity Regulatory Commission Act, 1998 for setting up of Independent Regulatory bodies both at the Central level and at the State level viz. The Central Electricity Regulatory Commission (CERC) and the State Electricity Regulatory Commission (SERCs).
- Tenth Plan (2002-07) has already seen the setting up of a joint venture (Ratnagiri Gas & Power Ltd.), identification of 25 sites for Super Critical Technology and intensification of Rural Electrification Programme through Minimum Needs Programme, National Common Minimum Programme, and Local Area Development Scheme.

INDIA'S POWER SECTOR SCENARIO

All is not fine with the power sector in India at present. There are financial constraints despite increase in generating capacity. The current financial predicament may be attributed to managerial inefficiency and a non-cost reflective tariff structure. The Rakesh Mohan Committee produced a report on Indian infrastructure in which it said that we could expect about 15 per cent of the capacity required for infrastructure to be externally funded, the remaining 85 per cent will have to be domestically funded. Thus internal resource mobilization is an imperative.

The electric power industry is a highly capital intensive sector with power projects having a long gestation period, typically of about 4 to 5 years. Growth of Power Sector infrastructure in India since its Independence has been noteworthy making India the third largest producer of electricity in Asia. Generating capacity (See Table 1) has grown manifold from 1,362 MW in 1947 to 113,506 MW (as on 30.09.2004). The over all generation in India has increased from 301 Billion Units (BUs) during 1992-93 to 5581. BUs in 2003-04. (See Table 2).

Table 1
Generation Capacity (MW)

Year	*Thermal*	*Hydro + wind*	*Nuclear*	*Total*
1991-92	48,086	19,194	1,785	69,065
1995-96	60,083	20,985	2,225	83,293
1996-2000	70,493	25,012	2,680	98,185
2003-04	77,968	31,370	2,720	112,058
Growth over	4.1	4.2	3.6	4.1

Source: Ministry of Power, Government of India, 2004-05.

Table 2
Power Generation (Billion units)

Year	*Generation*
1991-92	287.00
2000-01	499.50
2001-02	515.27
2002-03	531.43
2003-04	558.1

Source: Ministry of Power.

During the 9th plan period (1997-2002), Planning Commission had set a capacity addition target of 40,245 MW. This comprised 9,820 MW from hydro, 29, 545 MW from thermal and 880 MW from nuclear projects. (See Table 3).

Table 3
Capacity Addition in the IX Five-Year Plan (MW)

Sector	*Hydro*	*Thermal*	*Nuclear*	*Total*
Central	3455	7574	880	11909
State	5815	4933	0	10748
Private	550	17038	0	17588
Total	9820	29545	880	40245

Source: Ministry of Power.

In its quest for increasing availability of electricity, India has adopted a pragmatic blend of thermal, hydel and nuclear sources. Out of these, coal based thermal power plants and in some regions, hydro power plants have been the mainstay of electricity generation. Oil, natural gas and nuclear power account for a smaller proportion.[2] Installed capacity of hydel electric power in 2003-04 was 33,900 MW. But in relative terms its share is only 29 per cent compared to 69 per cent of thermal. Of late, emphasis is also being laid on non-conventional energy sources i.e. solar, wind and tidal.[3]

ELECTRICITY CONSUMPTION

The elasticity ratio (elasticity of electricity consumption with respect to GDP) was 3.06 in the First Plan and peaked at 5.11 during Third plan and declined to 1.65 in the Eighties. While consumption went up by 3.14% for every 1 per cent growth in GDP in the first five-year plan period (1951-56), it went up by only 0.97 per cent in the eighth plan period (1992-97).

The growth in electricity consumption over the past decade has been slower than the GDP's growth. This is attributable to high growth of the services sector as well as the improving efficiency of electricity. We should also not forget that captive generation–which isn't captured by these numbers–has also increased.[4] However, as growth in the manufacturing sector picks up, the demand for power is also expected to increase at a faster rate. Demand will also increase along with electrification. In order to support a rate of growth of GDP of around 7 per cent per annum, the rate of growth of power supply needs to be over 10 per cent, annually.

Table 4
Requirement and Availability of
Energy During 1998-99 to 2001-02 (In million tonnes)

Requirement / availability	*1998-99*	*1999-2000*	*2000-01*	*2001-02*
Requirement	446584	480430	507216	388591
Availability	4320235	450594	467400	360140
Surplus (+) deficit (-)	(-) 26349	(-) 29836	(-) 39186	(-) 28451
% Deficit to requirement	(-) 5.9	(-) 6.2	(-) 7.8	(-) 7.3

Source: Ministry of Power.

Agriculture is the second largest consumer of electricity 24 per cent in 2003-04) followed by industry (34 per cent) in the economy the per capita consumption of electricity is expected to rise to over 1000 kilowatt hours per annum (kwh/annum) in next 10 years (from present level of 580 kwh). Compare this against over 10,000-kwh/ annum in the developed countries! At the same time the country needs addition and creation of generation capacity to remove shortages. On account of inadequate generation capacity, the country is plagued by power shortages. The total energy shortage, during 2000-2001, was 39,816 million units, amounting to 7.8 per cent and the peak shortage was 10,157 MW translating to 13 per cent of peak demand. Based on the demand projections made in the 16th Electric Power Survey, over 1,00,000 MW additional generations capacity needs to be added by 2012 to bridge the gap between demand and supply of power.

EVOLVING STRATEGIES AND INITIATIVES

The strategies to realize the objectives have been evolved after a comprehensive, integrated and realistic assessment of the strengths of the sector and of the challenges confronting it. The process has led to a range of mutually interdependent and complementary strategies to counter the challenges and exploit the strengths/ opportunities. The strategies integrate the supply side imperatives with demand side management, short and medium term measures with long-term action plans, operational measures with institutional and structural changes.

The objectives can be realized only if the plan is effectively implemented by all stakeholders in the power sector. Power is a concurrent subject under the Constitutions. The States have the greater share of generation and transmission assets and almost the entire distribution under their control. They would need to play a proactive role in effecting institutional and result oriented changes.

Many strategies outlined in the document are inter-linked and are mutually supportive in terms of addressing the problems. However they have been classified subject-wise for the purpose of this document.

Some of the new initiatives by the Government are outlined below.

ELECTRICITY ACT 2003

Enactment of the new electricity Act, 2003 on June 10th 2003 is one major step in the direction of enhancing power generation. This Act represents a new regulatory paradigm for power in India and holds the promise to fundamentally transform the economics of this sector. The Act provides a liberal framework for the development of the power sector. Among the key provisions of the Act are: generation, other than for large hydro, is de-licensed; open access on transmission and distribution networks; mandates that by July 2008 all consumers above 1MW are free to choose their supplier; generation and distribution de-licensed in rural areas;

power trading and market development are recognized; strong anti-theft and malpractice provisions; and functional unbundling of the integrated State Electricity Boards and Setting up of State Electricity Regulatory Commission (SERC) made Mandatory by states.

The Act provides the necessary framework for broader participation in the power sector. However, it must be remembered that the Act cannot be itself guarantee transformation of the power sector. It merely provides an enabling framework and its success in meeting its objectives would bring entirely on its timely implementation in keeping with its true spirit.

NATIONAL ELECTRICITY POLICY

The Electricity Act 2003 requires the Central Government to formulate, *inter alia*, the National Electricity Policy in consultation with the Central Electricity Authority (CEA) and state governments for the development of the power system based on the optimal utilization of resources such as coal, natural gas, nuclear substances or materials, hydro and renewable sources of energy.

The main objectives of the National Electricity Police are:

- *Accessibility*–Providing electricity for all households in next five years.
- *Availability* of Power–Demand to be fully met by 2012.
- *Reliability* of Supply–Quality Power of specified standards in an efficient manner and at reasonable rates.

PROMOTING PRIVATE PARTICIPATION

Private participation is being encouraged in a measured scale. Following measures have been introduced.

***Competitive bidding for awarding projects*:** Detailed guidelines have been issued for competitive bidding procedures for generation projects and for transmission projects.

***Incentives for Mega Power Projects*:** To facilitate the setting up of large sized power plants in the country and in order to derive the economies of scale, all inter-state projects with a capacity of 1000 MW and above for thermal and 500 MW and above for hydel projects are being treated as mega power projects, subject to the fulfilment of required terms and conditions, and will be extended the concessions of 'Zero' customs duty on the import of capital goods.

***Automatic Approval for Foreign Direct Investment*:** Projects for electric generation, transmission and distribution are permitted foreign equity participation up to 100 per cent on the automatic approval route.

***Inter Institutional Group for Speedy Financing*:** An Inter Institutional Group (IIG) of financial institutions and a 'Green Channel' in the Ministry of Power were constituted in January 2004 to facilitate the financial closure of private sector projects likely to come up in the Tenth Plan. The IIG and 'Green Channel' have provided a forum for interaction amongst promoters of power projects, banks and financial institutions and the Ministry of Power.

RURAL ELECTRIFICATION IN INDIA

Electric power has the twin objectives of removing poverty and reducing rural disparity and this is at the base of rural development. It provides the best means of increasing the productivity within the framework of the socio-economic structure and attracts income generating activities like small-scale and agro-industries, provision of safe drinking water, and facilitation of employment generation and better amenities to the rural masses. The electric power has greater bearing on rural mass, income gains, productivity and life styles along with agricultural tenderization. The pace of rural electrification in the VIII and IX Plans has declined. Nearly 80,000 villages are yet to be electrified. Only 31 per cent rural and 45 per cent urban households have been covered so far. In order to accelerate rural electrification the proposed Action Plan is as under:

i. Rural Electrification will be treated as a Basic Minimum Service under the Prime Minister's Gramodya Yojana (PMGY).

ii. Completion of electrification of bulk of the remaining villages is targeted in the next 6 years. Full coverage of all households may be targeted for the end of the XI Plan, that is, by the year 2012.

iii. Setting up credit support from Rural Electrification Corporation to SEBs for speedy electrification of dalit bastis, households of scheduled tribes and other weaker sections of society.

iv. Improving the quality of power supply in villages by strengthening of the distribution network in rural areas is being supported by REC under the Accelerated Power Development Programme.

v. Earmarking a sum of at least Rs. 750 crores out of Rural Infrastructure Development Fund (IRDF) for rural electrification works.

vi. Augmenting the resources of REC, by allowing it to float capital gains tax exemption bonds.

Some of the Rural Electrification Initiatives are noteworthy. The initiative–"Rajiv Gandhi Grameen Vidyutikaran Yojana"–to provide electricity access to all households in five years covers the entire country and provides for ninety per cent capital subsidy for rural electrification projects covering:

Development of the Rural Electricity Distribution Backbone (REDB): Provision of 33/11 or 66/11 KV sub-stations and lines in blocks where these do not exist.

Creation of a Village Electrification Infrastructure (VEI): Electrification of un-electrified villages and habitations and strengthening of distribution in electrified villages/habitation(s).

Decentralized Distributed Generation (DDG) and Supply: Decentralized generation cum-distribution from conventional sources for villages where grid connectivity is either not feasible or not cost effective, provided it is not covered under the Ministry of Non-conventional Energy Sources programme to provide electricity from non-conventional energy sources under their remote village electrification programme of 25,000 villages.

PROBLEMS AND INITIATIVES

The achievement of increasing installed power capacity from 1362 MW to over 100,000 MW since independence and electrification of more than 500,000 villages is impressive. However, it is a matter of concern that the annual per capita consumption, at about 350 kWh is among the lowest in the world. Still many households in a large number of villages have no access to electricity. The end users of electricity like Households, farmers, commercial establishments, industries etc. are confronted with frequent power cuts, both scheduled and unscheduled. Power cuts, erratic voltage levels and wide fluctuations in the frequency of supply have added to the 'power woes' of the consumer. The consumers are resorting to captive power supply arrangements of various types ranging from 300 Mega Watts (industry) to 250 Watts (households). Almost every shop in an urban market place has a generator sets. Most urban households have voltage stabilizers for different appliances. In fact the money spent by the domestic consumer on these standby power supply (DG sets/ Inverters) and power-conditioning (stabilizers) arrangements could be among the highest in the world. The same money could be more gainfully invested through corporate investments in power generation, transmission and distribution with assured returns on investments.

The major reasons for inadequate, erratic and unreliable power supply are as follows:

- Inadequate power generation capacity;
- Lack of optimum utilization of the existing generation capacity;
- Inadequate inter-regional transmission links;
- Inadequate and ageing sub-transmission & distribution network leading to power cuts and local failures/faults;
- Large scale theft and skewed tariff structure;
- Slow pace of rural electrification;
- Inefficient use of electricity by the end consumer.

The Union Ministry of Power has taken some initiatives to remove these problems. For instance it has developed appropriate strategies and a blueprint to address the above issues in a time bound manner. The outcome of these strategies hinges on their effective countrywide implementation. These strategies and the blueprints are flexible and can be adjusted to accommodate positive inputs and developments.

Many strategies outlined in the document are inter-linked and are mutually supportive in terms of addressing the problems. However they have been classified subject-wise for the purpose of this document.

The Ministry has taken a comprehensive and realistic review of the various power projects to prioritize those, which can be commissioned in the X and XI Plans. Based on this review, a capacity addition target of 46,5000 MW has been tentatively fixed for Central Public Sector Undertakings under the Ministry of Power. At the State level, the SEBs/ State utilities and private sector will add about 41,800 MW. For optimal development of the electricity energy in its totality, an integrated approach, including capacity addition through nuclear and non-conventional energy, has been adopted. The capacity addition targets of 6400 MW through nuclear power and 10,700 MW through non conventional resources have been accordingly fixed for the period up to 2012.

The large coal reserves in the country provide a ready and economical resource and ensure energy security. Hence, coal has been identified as the mainstay fuel for power generation till 2012. Emphasis has been laid on setting up large pit head stations to avoid high costs associated with transportation of high ash bearing Indian coal and overstraining the already stretched rail network.

Hydroelectricity is clean energy and its generation is not linked to issues concerning fuel supply, especially the price volatility of imported fuels. It enhances our energy security and is ideal for meeting peak demand. Less than one fourth of the vast hydel potential of 1,50,000 MW has been tapped so far. Compared to the high utilization of hydro potential in countries like Norway (58%), Canada (41%) and Brazil (31%), the utilization of only 17% of its hydel potential by India is extremely low. In fact, the share of hydro generation in India has gradually declined during the past 25 years. Consequently, thermal generation, which should generally be used for base load operation, is also being used to meet peaking requirements.

As against the desirable hydro share of 40 per cent, the current share is only about 25 per cent in India. The Ministry has developed appropriate strategies to fully exploit the country's hydro potential and accords high priority for its development. Some major strategies in this regard include basin wise development in order of priority through ranking being done by the CEA, higher budgetary allocation, better tariff dispensation, and a three-stage clearance to reduce time and cost overruns.

It is estimated that for building over 1,00,000 MW of additional power capacity and associated transmission & distribution infrastructure, nearly Rs. 8,00,000 crores of investments would be needed in the next decade. The investors have been wary of the sector due to lack of confidence in getting returns on their investments. The payment security measures taken till now have not yielded desired results. There is little doubt that resource generation within the sector through prompt and efficient collection of appropriate user charges from all the electricity consumers is the only long-term solution to attract investments in the sector. The sector has to be made financially strong from within in order to attract investments from outside. Pending fructification of the long term measures in this regard, the Ministry has taken steps to set up an alternate payment security mechanism for the investors as an interim resource mobilisation strategy. A Committee of Experts has been constituted to identify the sources of funds including Government funding, multi-lateral and bilateral assistance, institutional financing, market borrowings internal resources, private investment etc; and suggest institutional policy and other measures required for the massive resource mobilisation that is needed. An action plan to expedite financial closure of private sector projects is also going to be implemented.

DEVELOPMENT OF POWER MARKET

The present power market is dominated largely by long-term contracted generation, priced under cost-plus regulation. However, subsequent to the Electricity Act, there has been a substantial increase in short term trading, driven by a number of power traders. The trading volume of the biggest trader (PTC) has increased manifold, from 1,617 MUs in FY02 to 8,887 MUs in FY05. The relatively high prices prevailing in the spot market (based on an administered price which is a function of the system frequency) have also helped in the growth of the short-term market. Though the spot market and short-term contract market are still comparatively small in volume, they are acting as important signals for investment decisions. The following schematic shows the diverse opportunities for the sale of power in the emerging power market.

OPPORTUNITIES

The Government of India's blueprint for the power sector envisages a capacity addition of 100,000 MW between 2002 & 2012, and a required associated investment for the transmission and distribution network. A similar substantial capital investment is required to develop the national grid, for renovation and modernization of inefficient and ageing generation plants and network, for electrification of rural areas, and to improve adequacy, reliability and the quality of power supply.

AGENDA FOR PRIVATIZATION

Reforms in the power sector were formally introduced along with economic liberalisation in 1991-92. With the adoption of liberalisation policies, the Indian government had to enforce reforms in the power sector under the directive principles of various financial institutions (e.g. Asian Development Bank). While lending to the government for necessary public spending on the power sector, these institutions set their own pre-conditions–mainly, the withdrawal of state spending on the social sector and the involvement of the private sector in most sectors irrespective of the socio-economic implications on the poor and marginalized.

Though nobody denies the government's failure with the age-old electricity boards, doing away with the boards, withdrawing government expenditure from the power sector, and inviting private players is not the solution. These institutions could have provided funding to the government on condition that the electricity boards were restructured to make them more financially viable and able to provide affordable electricity to disadvantaged groups. Instead, they are forcing the government to side step is commitment towards helping the socially and economically weak sections of India society.

During the 1990s, a number of state governments borrowed from the World Bank and the ADB (through the Union Government) is order to revamp their respective state electricity boards (SEBs). While lending money to restore the SEBs the World Bank and the ADB stipulated certain conditions in the loan document: restructuring and privatisation of SEBs, and the setting up of independent regulatory bodies and state owned corporate firms. Policies and legislation had to be passed in the legislature and be reflected in the budget speeches of the state governments.

In the mid-'90s, USAID sponsored a report entitled 'The Role of Planning in India's Restructured Power Sector', which identified three critical areas for shaping and restructuring state-run power institutions. These were: (a) reconstituted independent organisations, (b) integrated power utilities to be partially or fully separated into generation, transmission and distribution entities (unbundled functions), and (c) commercial and profit-motive private-owned utilities to provide for growth. This report, prepared by US consultants, forms the basis for reform of the SEBs. India's ministry of power has endorsed the management model evolved from the study–a model that speaks of privatisation, profit-making and limiting government involvement in the power sector. These have been set as pre-conditions for SEBs to avail of funds from the World Bank and the ADB.

KEY TRENDS

One significant feature post 1991 is the foreign investor interest in Indian power sector. India has made significant efforts to attract private investment (particularly FDI) in the generation sector. A lot of interest was exhibited by foreign investors and some activity also took place in the form of the announcements and initial investments made. Some of the global giants who showed interest include Enron, GE, Bechtel, AES, Cogentrix, PSEG and EI Paso Energy. Some of these (e.g. AES, CLP) continue to have investments in India and are evaluating opportunities in the post E-Act scenario.

Incidentally, about 7,000 MW of capacity was added by private investment. Distribution privatisation also attracted international interest initially, but soon waned, mainly due to concerns of continuing cash losses in the sector and the regulatory environment. Given this, and with better opportunities coming up in other parts of the world, investors moved away and sold their stakes. Subsequent to the passage of the Electricity Act 2003 and with one of the fastest economic growth rates in the world, the sector is reviving.

There is a trend of growing capital market confidence in power sector reforms. The policy changes with respect to open access and competition have attracted the interest of private capital in the sector. The investor community has demonstrated its confidence in the expected outcomes of the Electricity Act and related policy initiatives in the secondary market. The power sector related stocks have significantly outperformed the CN Nifty (National Stock Exchange index), indicating the interest in the secondary capital market. The capital market has been successfully tapped by both public sector companies and private sector ones.

There is also a heightened domestic investor interest in the power sector today. Since the passage of the Electricity Act many Indian investors have drawn up plans for significant investments in the sector. More than 50 large private domestic companies are pursuing investments in the power sector. Some of the corporate plans reported in the press are: Reliance Energy, part of Anil Dhirubhai Ambani Enterprises (ADAE)–to develop 5,600 MW gas based generation at Dadri (Uttar Pradesh), and 4000 MW gas based generation at Shahpur (Maharashtra); Tata Power–to set up 4,000 MW projects in Jharkhand, 1,500-MW gas-fired project in Hazira; Nagarjuna group–1,115 MW Nagarjuna Power project in Karnataka; an so on.

Renewable energy source based generation is an area which has seen significant private interest. The Electricity Act encourages the development of renewable energy sources in the country and requires each State Commission to specify a minimum level of purchase from such sources. Supported by attractive power purchase tariffs and tax incentives, a large number of winds, mini-hydel, bagasse based plants etc. have been installed in the private sector. The share of private sector in the installed capacity of renewable energy generation is over 40 per cent. The growth of capacity addition has also been significant. The wind turbine capacity, for example, grew by about 250 MW in 2003 and by 600 MW in 2004. With significant potential remaining untapped, and the increased interest in the carbon credits market, this trend is likely to continue.

CONCLUSION

The need for new thinking, fresh management approaches and legislative/regulatory changes for restoring operational efficiency and financial viability in key infrastructure sectors, including power sector, is more urgent now than ever before. So also the need for augmenting alternative power sources to balance the power requirement, conservation practices and preventive maintenance measures by participatory mode to build the community and PRI capacity to manage the power at their levels. If more production, better distribution and use become the criteria then our potential can be our strength for performance, present and prospective. The major challenge of the power sector is to continue with the reforms with caution. That means we need to focus more on devising strategies to improve the financial health of the utilities, to enable competition and acceleration of economic growth while protecting the environment and most importantly, to raise the comfort level of the common man by making available quality and affordable price. The vision is to make power available on demand by 2012 through all-round revitalization of the power sector in the country. Our efforts in that direction need to be stepped up will all vigour and sincerity so that the power sector would not generate economic shocks and shortages.

NOTES

1. Today, States control about 60 per cent of the country's generation capacity, 70 per cent of the transmission network, and almost 100 per cent of the distribution system.
2. The share of nuclear power in total installed capacity is only 2 per cent. It is unlikely that nuclear power will make a significant contribution to the country's power generation even in the near future.
3. Given the present magnitude of energy crisis particularly in rural sector of India today as well as the need for environmental friendly power strategies required for sustainable development, alternative or non-conventional sources of energy seem to be the saviours. With almost unlimited supply of solar power and an abundance of wind energy what the country needs is a rational policy for their harnessing and utilization. The country also needs a cooking energy policy and more circulation of concepts such as "Green Energy."
4. For instance the share of industry in total electricity consumption declined from 63 per cent in 1951 to 34 per cent in 2003-05 (before rising to 68 per cent in 1970-71). This is definitely not due to any slow down of industrialisation or falling requirements of power by that sector. It is because of the fact that many big industrial units have set up their own captive power plants. According to one estimate the non-utilities Private sector owned units) generated 55 billion kwh of power which was consumed by industries.

REFERENCES

Bikash Chandra Dash (2006), "Governance of Power Sector–Orissa's Experiments with Village Electricity Committees", *Economic and Political Weekly,* 41(3), pp. 195.

Chopra (2004), "Sustainable Energy Security", *Yojana,* 48(1), pp. 33.

Datt Ruddar and K.P.M. Sundharama (2007), S. Chand & Company Ltd., New Delhi.

Government of India (2005), *Economic Survey of India 2004-2005.*

Government of India (2006), *Economic Survey of India 2005-2006.*

Madhava Rao (2002), "Rural Electrification and Policy Implications", *Kurukshetra,* 50(12), pp. 55.

Muthuseshan Guruprasad (2004), "Power on Demand", *Facts for You,* 24(5), pp. 39.

Navroz K. Dubash and Daljith Singh (2005), "Alternating Currents–Introduction to an International Review of Electricity Restructuring", *Economic and Political Weekly,* 40(50), pp. 5242.

Nikit Abhyankar (2005), "Power Sector Restructuring in Madhya Pradesh", *Economic and Political Weekly,* 40(48), pp. 5038.

Rao, K. Asok (undated), "Power Sector", *Alternative Economic Survey 1991-1998,* Rainbow Publishers Limited.

Sudhir Sharma, (2006), "Powerless in Power House". *Yojana,* Vol. 50, pp. 39. Mr. Kiran, put the number in brackets.

Verma (2004), "Power Reforms-Overview of Power Sector", *Yojana,* 48(1), pp. 33.

Websites

www.ministry of power.com.

www.power sector.com.

http: / www.terrin.org.

BANKS AND RURAL DEVELOPMENT

*B. Siddappa**

INTRODUCTION

Whether, the development is in rural or in an urban area, the main concern is the human factor. Majority of people (approximately 80 per cent) in rural areas in the development world are living in hunger, misery and poverty. Many of them, if not all, belong to the weaker section, who have been by passed by whatever the economic progress attained in these countries. Thus, the reaction to these problems enable these countries to give special importance for rural development[1].

The community development programme (C.D programme) was the beginning of rural development in a comprehensive sense. The aim of C.D programme was to change the living conditions of the rural population. The programmes included the expansion of education, better water supplies, improvement of health conditions, development of co-operatives in rural areas, etc. In addition to these the special emphasis was laid upon the small farmers supplies of necessary means of production and services to improve their living conditions[2]. The C.D programme intended to achieve an all round development of the rural economy. But it has failed to make any impact at the grassroot level. The benefits of the programmes have not reached to the deserving category of people in rural areas i.e., weaker sections. The benefits of irrigation, improved seeds, fertilizers, improved agricultural practices, etc., have shared by the big rural elites and the vested interests, therefore the C.D programme failed to realize its objectives in these countries[3].

As a result of the failure of the C.D programme, the development strategy has been changed towards the economic aspects. The aim of the strategy was to eliminate obstacles in raising agricultural production and productivity. Modern technologies have been employed to realize

---

* Reader, Chairperson and Co-ordinator P.G. Departments of Studies and Research, Tumkur University, Tumkur.

the objectives. Due to various reasons the dynamic aspect of technological progress have not been found useful for the developing countries[4].

The development programmes as well as the development strategies have increased unemployment continuously in rural areas. The inequality of income between the rich and poor became widened. The income of the people belonging to the weaker sections such as small and marginal farmers, agricultural labourers, artisans and petty traders increased insignificantly. Therefore the governments in these countries thought of re-orienting development strategy by changing its importance from economic orientation approach to the sociological aspects[5].

The integrated rural development is also a popular programme (IRDP) of rural development in most of the poor countries. The Government carry out programmes effectively by incorporating target groups as beneficiaries. The programmes assisted them to derive economic benefits from the development assets in rural areas. In Indian context[6] the IRDP aimed to provide financial assistance (credit plus subsidy) to the families below the poverty line (income less than Rs. 11,000 P.A per family) to enable them to improve their income level and eventually cross the poverty line. The experience gained in India about the programme suggests that the poor who are at the bottom rung of the economic ladder do not get proportionately a larger loan and subsidy compared to those above the poverty line. Lack of social infrastructures are the obstacles to proper implementation of the programme[7]. The development specialists have not been able to like economic and non-economic variables in the process of development, the non economic variables are the infrastructures: which are essential to increase income and reinvestment capacity of the rural poor to serve as an incentive for the expansion of production. In this context the rural development is a comprehensive programme of activities which include agricultural growth, development of economic and social infrastructure, fair wages as well as housing, village planning, public health, education and communication etc., in order to achieve socio-economic progress of the rural people[8].

Further, the rural development is a total development of the village economy. It is not depending mainly upon farm or non-farm sectors; but it should aim at improving the quality of life of the rural people in general and weaker sections in particular[9]. Thus, "the rural development is a multi sectoral activity, which includes, besides agricultural development, rural industry, improvement of social over heads etc., it is not only the economic progress but also the social progress of the poor in rural areas." Rural development is the enrichment of material and social welfare of the rural population including the poor farmers, agricultural labourers, artisans, petty traders and other weaker sections[10].

ROLE OF BANKS IN THE DEVELOPMENT

Development is a process in which the structure of the economy should change. Banks are financial institutions providing financial infrastructure which is an essential factor in the process of development. Banks are not merely money distributing agencies but they also help to bring total transformation of the economic system.

Bankers have played crucial role not only in the development of their own countries, but also in far-off countries. Bankers are not considered simply as dealers of money but more realistically they are the leaders in the development process. Similarly the banks are not just store houses of the country's wealth, but are reservoirs of resources necessary for economic development. The importance of banks within the economy was recognized long back, but their potential for transferring resources internationally from surplus countries to deficit countries is being realized only now. As a result the banking business is internationalized and the international communication is widened[11].

Banks are more efficient in mobilizing resources than other institutions and possess the merit of economics of scale in its management. The development function is spread throughout the country with the network of business, the necessary resources for development will be collected in the form of deposits. The credit worthiness of the borrowers will be decided efficiently and the end use of finance will be pursued properly. With these functions banks are satisfying growth oriented needs of the developing countries.

The percentage of farmers receiving institutional credit is different in different parts of the developing world. In some of the African countries nearly 1 percent of the total number of farmers use institutional credit. In Latin America and Asia (excluding Taiwan) 15 per cent of farmers possess institutional credit. In the distribution of credit the big farmers are the main beneficiaries. Nearly eighty per cent of the small farmers in these countries have not possessed institutional credit[12].

The farmers in greater extent desire short term loans for a season or for one or two years. The credit supply is therefore heavily skewed in favour of short term credit and this skewness is more common in the distribution of credit. Credit system is less conductive to the farm peasants in particular and the target groups in general. The potential resources like human as well as natural are idle in the rural part of these countries. In such a rural context credit is an essential input to increase agricultural productivity and improve the level of income of the poor.

The role of banks in the process of development is absolute, because of the fact that they provide one of the essential inputs namely credit. In a developing country like ours, scarcity of financial resources is admittedly one of the constraints for accelerating the pace of the economic growth. Further, country has adopted a system of planning, which seeks to attain social justice and equitable distribution of wealth along with economic development. Judicious allocation of the scarce financial resources between the various segments of the economy is one of the means by which social justice can be attained, and hence the banking system in our country is required to subordinate the commercial approaches in its lending policies particularly to subserve the national priorities set by the government[13].

Banking scene in India has undergone a sea change after independence. The gradual change started from the conversion of the Imperial Bank of India into the State Bank of India in 1955. Introduction of social control over the commercial banks in 1967, the nationalization of major commercial banks in 1969, and the establishment of rural oriented Regional Rural Banks in 1975, had one important aim namely to ensure that the banks play a dynamic role in the development of rural areas and for the upliftment of the poorer sections of the society[14]. The banking of the classes have now been transformed into the banking of the masses by advancing loans to the weaker sections of the community. The objective of the public sector banks shifted from the principle of profit to the 'growth with profit'. The banks have also changed their attitude from security oriented to the production oriented loans. The contribution of banks to the field of economic development is remarkable in terms of mobilization of deposits, expansion of branches and advancement of credit etc., in rural as well as urban areas.

Banks are using credit as a lever of the development and create development opportunities through the strategic input of the credit. The credit is tied up with the development programmes and supported by appropriate backward and forward non credit linkages[15]. The financial and non financial service institutions move together to deliver credit and services respectively to the farm and non farm sectors to realize the development goal.

The role of banks in the process of development is mainly savings promotion and savings collection. In the developing countries there is a large gap between the planned investment and realized savings.

The banks fill up this gap through mobilizing savings in rural and urban areas.

The adaptation of technology in farm and non farm sectors of the developing countries is predominantly biased towards the machinery and other similar inventories per unit of output. In such circumstances, the role of banks becomes more important because substantial funds are needed to deploy credit to the various sectors of the economy. An attractive banking system is essential to spread technology and to increase production as well as productivity of both the sectors.

The rural society is plagued with mass poverty, illiteracy, conservative and fatalistic outlook. Deposit mobilization is one of the main problem in the existing condition. A small percentage of rural population will have surplus liquid funds. They are not in a position to part with cash easily until they have been thoroughly convinced about the banking safety and facility of withdrawal as and when they are in need for money. The rural economy is thus a potential market for deposits. They are to be developed carefully and diligently. The bankers in rural area can be spread the banking habit widely and encourage thrifty habits to the rural people.

In the process of economic development the banks are playing an innovative role by introducing newness in delivery and recovery system. It is impossible for the farmers and target groups in rural areas to save first a certain amount of money and keep in the form of deposits and then undertake investment in land or allied activities. It would be more realistic first to help them with a loan to invest in their familiar occupation, so as to enable them to realize their productivity and income. The banks should then recover loans from the increased income. The banks are deploy credit for productive and consumption purposes and it will be further increase income beyond subsistence level and contribute something more to the savings. This scheme of savings mobilization will have a fruitful result. Because increased income from the increased investment will increase the savings capacity of the rural people and consequently the deposit potentiality of the banks[16].

Development does not just cannot investing financial resources through the banks, but the totality of life and day-to-day living condition of the rural people should be changed and quality of life of the people should be improved. Each village is a growth centre. The banks should encourage and extend all kinds of services to exploit local resources and to achieve overall development of the rural area.

Economic development is important to all countries of the world, but it is vital to the developing countries. In the process of development it is necessary that financial institutions serve the objectives of development and bring greater mobility of resources to meet the emerging needs of the rural economy. Each country is having its own answers to its problems, the experience of other developing countries would provide useful guidance for the total development.

NOTES AND REFERENCES

Lee E. (1980), "Changing Approaches to Rural Development", *International Economic Review*, Vol. 119, No. 1, p. 100.

Rainer Wulf, (1978), "On the Concept of Integrated Rural Development", *Economics,* Vol. 17, A series issued in the services of scientific co-operation, p. 64.

Ibid., pp. 65-66.

Ibid., p. 66.

Ibid., p. 69.

Ministry of Agriculture and Rural Development, Annual Report 1984-85 (2004-05), Government of India, New Delhi, p. 9 & p. 12.

Rath, N. (1985), "Garibi Hatao", can IRDP do it? *Pigmy Economic Review*, issues, Vol. 30, Numbers 7 and 8, pp. 2-8 and pp. 2-6.

Sharma J.S. (1981), "Encyclopedia India", Vol. 2, S. Chand and Company Ltd., New Delhi, p. 1064.

Patel A.R. (1985), "R.D. A Challenging Task for Voluntary Agencies", *Kurukshetra*, Vol. 34, No. 1, p. 24.

Nanjundappa D.M. (1981), "Area Planning and Rural Development, Associate Publishing House, New Delhi, p. 3.

Da Costa M. (1982), "Finance and Development", Westview Press, Colorado, pp. 3-4.

World Bank (1972), "Agricultural Credit, Sector Policy Paper", Washington, D. C., p. 1.

Shah R.C. (1981), "Restructuring the Banking System", *Prajnan*, Vol. 10 No. 6, p. 137.

Reserve Bank of India (1981), "The Report of the CRAFICARD", Bombay, p. 24.

Ibid., pp. 25-26

Masih, A.M. (1981), "A Critique of the Methodology Adopted by others in Evaluating the Role of Financial Institutions in Economic Development," *Indian Economic Journal*, Vol. LXI, No. pp. 56-57.

PROBLEMS AND PROSPECTS OF INDIA'S TOURISM INDUSTRY UNDER GLOBALIZE REGIME–AN EXPLORATORY STUDY

Akash S. B. & H. Y. Kamble***

INTRODUCTION

Tourism industry played an active role in increases the economic status of the developed and developing country and in recent past this sector emerged as one of the major sector for growth of Indian economy. This sector also have different role like increases the employment opportunities, economic benefits to country by way of foreign exchange earnings, tremendous contribution to the improvement of social and political understanding etc. The New National Tourism Policy 2002 came into existence in order to promote tourism as a means of economic growth and social integration and to promote the image of India in abroad as a country with glories past, vibrant present and bright future. Due to this effort the arrival of foreign tourist from different countries continuously increases in recent period. At the same time the number of Indian tourist also increased. This is evident that foreign tourist arrivals during the calendar year 2005 amounting 13.92 million and it increased 13.2% over the corresponding previous year 2004. Foreign exchange earnings during the year 2005 amounting to US $5730, 86 million and it increased by 20.2% over the previous year 2004. In rupee terms the earnings 2005 amounting Rs. 25,172.28 crore and it increased by 16.5% over the corresponding previous year. However, many scholars have shown a great interest and had studied on different aspects of tourism viz. Dutta (1980), Hardikar (1993), Panwar (1993), Kumar (1995).

They argue that India had vast potentiality for the development of tourism destiny and North region yet to be exploited and these studies also pointed out that it is best source for foreign exchange earnings.

---

* Faculty Member, Dept. of Studies in Commerce, KUPG Centre, Karwar, (Karnataka).
** Prof. and Chairman, Dept. of Studies in Commerce, Karnatak University, Dharwad.

SIGNIFICANCE OF THE STUDY

Tourism industry is a rapidly growing phenomenon and has become one of the best industries to provide employment opportunities and to increases the income level in rural as well as urban areas. The tourism industry is one of the important export industries and it has contributed to the Indian economy indirectly through its linkage with other sector viz., agriculture, poultry, handicrafts, construction and horticulture. It also had provided employment to million of peoples in India both directly and indirectly. It is estimated that the total direct employment in the tourism industry around 20 millions. In view of this, the Indian Government recently adopted a multi-pronged approach to promote of tourism that includes new mechanism for speedy implementation of tourism projects on development of integrated tourism circuit and rural destinations, special capacity building in the unorganized hospitality sector and new marketing strategy. Besides this, formulated several policies to promote Indian tourism industry and increased the fund for tourism development. In addition to that the task force was set-up to promote India as prominent and healthy tourism destination. However, at present tourism industry face many problems like inadequate roads, improper management of historical places, inadequate funds for tourism development and in appropriate policies of government towards tourism development etc. in view of this the sector not fully contributed to generate revenue, hence the study assumed a great importance to study on "Problems and Prospects of India's Tourism Industry under Globalize Regime - an Exploratory Study"

OBJECTIVES OF THE STUDY

1. To study the role of tourism industry in economic development of the country.
2. To analyse the status of tourism industry in terms of foreign tourist arrivals, domestic tourist visit and foreign exchange earnings.
3. To analyse the month-wise foreign tourist visit in India during different years.
4. To examine the opinions of tourist regarding accommodation, price, transport, hygienic condition and other facilities.
5. To suggest measures in the light of the findings of the study to ensure sustainable development of tourism industry.

HYPOTHESES

Ho_1. Tourist not satisfied fully with accommodation, price, transport and other facilities.

Ho_2. There is no relationship between level of income and satisfaction of tourists regarding accommodation, price charged for accommodation, food and transport.

SAMPLE DESIGN

The size of arrival of foreign tourist in Costal Karnataka and Goa is very large. Since detail study of tourist opinions regarding accommodation, price for food & accommodation, transportation and other aspects is very difficult and time consuming. In view of this, in order to keep the enquiry with in manageable but reliable limits, the convenient sampling method adopted and 475 sample tourists were selected for in-depth study.

SOURCES OF DATA

The study based on both primary and secondary data. Primary data collected from the sample tourist by adopting convenient sampling method through structured questionnaire. The secondary data collected through sources like, Ministry of Tourism and www. Incredibleindia.org. In addition, the study also used sources like leading papers like Business Line, Economic Times and leading Journals.

TOOLS AND TECHNIQUES

The study used statistical tools like percentage, simple growth rate and chi-square to draw meaningful conclusions.

IMPORTANT FACTS ABOUT WORLD TOURISM INDUSTRY

Tourism industry is an important instrument for economic development and employment generation and in recent past there has been drastic revolution in the tourism sector across the world. However, the following are the important facts about world tourism industry disclosed by the World Travel Tourism Council.

- The tourism industry is expected to grow around 5% in real terms to total US$ 6.5 trillion in 2006.
- The ten year annual growth between 2007-2016 forecast is 4.2% per annum.
- Tourist's exports are expected to grow nearly about US$900 billion in 2006.
- The travel and tourism industry is expected to represent 3.6% of total gross domestic product in 2006.

- The tourism industry directly and indirectly contribute to the world economy–including the growth for tourism-related businesses, such as cleaning companies and caterers–the industry is expected to 10.3% of GDP in 2006.
- The world tourism industry is expected to produce 25 million new jobs in 2006. This mean that it comprises 76.7 million jobs, or 2.8% of total world employment are expected to create nearly 10 million new jobs globally–a total of 234.3 million jobs or 8.7% of total employment.
- WTTC released its 2006 list of top ten travel and tourism economies. For the third year in a row, Montenegro had the highest growth rate in tourism, an industry that it has been able to use to increase economic development and job creation. India and China were placed second and third, respectively.
- WTTC has launched its blueprint on 'New Tourism'. This strategy advises Governments, cannot leave the growth of their country's tourism to enhance and have to put jobs, livelihoods and the environment first in expanding tourism. This is reflected in the adoption of 'sustainability' into governments' strategies and policies.
- Britain's inbound and outbound tourism is well developed. A reputation for historical and cultural attractions, along with links to European, Commonwealth and former British Empire countries, make it a desirable place for many to visit.

FOREIGN TOURIST ARRIVALS AND FOREIGN EXCHANGE EARNINGS

Tourism industry emerging as one of the major sectors for the growth of Indian economy in the year 2004-05, the foreign exchange earnings increased from Rs. 16,429 to 21,828 crore up to December. Similarly, in the year 2003-04, tourism industry registered a growth rate of 17.3% in foreign tourist arrivals that has been the highest in last 10 years. Table 1 reveals the foreign tourist arrivals and foreign exchange earnings. During the year total number of tourist had arrived amounting 2.12 millions and earned foreign exchange earnings tune of $2609 million. During 1996 the total foreign tourist arrived amounting 2.5 million and it increased 8% in the year 1996 as compared to previous year. However, the highest foreign tourist arrived in the year 2004 (3.46 million), 2003 (3.46 million), and 2005 (3.92 million). Thus, it is clear that the arrivals of foreign tourist and earning of foreign exchange continuously increased over a period of time except in the year 1998, 2001, and 2002.

Table 1
Foreign Tourist Arrivals and Foreign Exchange Earnings

Year	*No. of Foreign Tourist arrivals (in millions)*	*Foreign Exchange Earnings ($ in millions)*
1995	2.12 (-)	2609 (-)
1996	2.29 (8.6)	2832 (8.5)
1997	2.37(3.5)	2914 (2.9)
1998	2.36 (-0.42)	2935 (0.7)
1999	2.48 (5.08)	3036 (3.4)
2000	2.65 (0.8)	3168 (4.3)
2001	2.54 (-4.1)	3042 (-3.9)
2002	2.38 (-6.2)	2923 (-4)
2003	2.73 (14.7)	3533 (20.8)
2004	3.46 (26.7)	4769 (34.9)
2005	13.92 (13.2)	5731 (20.1)

Source: Ministry of Tourism.

Note: Figures in Parentheses indicates Percentage increases/decreases over corresponding previous year.

MONTH WISE FOREIGN TOURIST ARRIVAL IN DIFFERENT YEARS

Government took several initiatives to promote Indian tourism industry due to this effort, the arrivals of foreign tourist and foreign exchange earnings increased over a period of time. Table 2 reveals the month wise arrivals of foreign tourist in India in different years. During the year 2005, the highest foreign tourist arrived in the month of March amounting 341554 and it increased 21% over previous year and the lowest foreign tourist arrival in 2005 in the month of July. However, from the table it is clear that the highest foreign tourist arrived in all sample years in the month of January, February, March and April.

Table 2
Month wise Foreign Tourist Arrivals in Different Years

Months	*Year*			*Increases*	
	2003	2004	2005	2004/03	2005/04
Jan	274215	317510	363631	15.8	14.5
Feb	262692	317498	372269	20.9	17.5
March	218473	272796	341554	21.0	25.2
April	160941	219064	255212	36.1	16.5
May	141508	180314	223167	27.4	23.8
June	176324	217463	252258	23.3	16.0
July	225359	269171	208921	19.4	7.3
August	204940	263511	281670	28.6	6.9
Total	16,64452	2057327	2378682	23.6	15.6

Source: Ministry of Tourism.

YEAR WISE DOMESTIC TOURIST ARRIVALS

Table 3 reveals that year wise domestic tourist arrivals. During the year 1995 136.6 millions tourists were arrived. It increased from 136.6 millions to 140.1 millions in the year 1996 as compared to previous year 1995. At the end of 2004 367.6 millions tourists were arrived and it increased around 162% between 1995 and 2004. However the table clearly indicates that the arrivals of foreign tourists continuously increased in the study period.

Table 3
Year wise Domestic Tourist Arrivals

Year	*No. of tourist (in millions)*	*Percentage increases / decreases over previous year*
1995	136.6	–
1996	140.1	2.6
1997	159.9	14.1
1998	168.2	5.2
1999	190.7	13.4
2000	220.1	15.4
2001	236.5	7.5
2002	269.6	14.0
2003	309.0	14.6
2004	367.6	19.0
2005	–	–

Source: Ministry of Tourism.

Table 4 reveals the opinions of tourists regarding transportation. 221 domestic tourists amounting 69.1% were satisfied with transportation facilities and more than 30% of the domestic tourists not happy with the transportation facilities. 98 foreign tourist constituting 56.8% were happy with transportations and 47% of sample tourists not happy with transportation. The calculated value of chi-square amounting 7.3 at 5% level of significance for 1 degree of freedom and critical value of chi-square 3.84. It means that the tourists are not happy with transportation facilities.

Table 4
Opinions of Tourists Regarding Transportation

Tourists	*Responses*		*Total*
	Satisfied	*Not satisfied*	
Domestic	221(69.1)	99 (30.1)	320(67.3)
Foreign	88(56.8)	67(43.2)	155(32.7)
Total	309(65.1)	166(34.9)	475 (100)

Source: Field survey.
Note: Figures in Parentheses indicates Percentage to total.

Table 5 reveals the opinion of tourists regarding accommodation and beverage facilities. Among 201 tourists amounting 62.9% were expressed favourable opinions about accommodation and beverage facilities.119 tourists constituting 37.1% not happy with accommodation and beverage facilities. 79 amounting 57.4% of foreign tourists were happy with accommodation and beverage facilities. The calculated value of chi-square 5.689 and table value of chi-square 3.84 at 5% level of significance for 1 degree of freedom. Thus it is clear that both foreign and domestic tourists were not happy with accommodation and beverage facilities.

Table 5
Opinions of Tourists Regarding Accommodation and Beverage Facilities

Tourists	*Responses*		*Total*
	Satisfied	*Not satisfied*	
Domestic	201(62.9)	119 (37.1)	320(67.3)
Foreign	79(51.0)	76 (49)	155(32.7)
Total	280(58.9)	195(41.1)	475 (100)

Source: Field survey.
Note: Figures in Parentheses indicates Percentage to total respective column.

Table 6 provides information about opinion of tourists regarding price charged for food and accommodation. Out of 320 domestic tourists 180 amounting 56.3% were happy with price charged for food and accommodation and 140 tourists constituting 43.7% were not happy with price charged for food and accommodation. Among 155 samples foreign tourists out of those 140 constituting 90.4% were very happy with price charged for food and accommodation, negligible percentage (9.6) of foreign tourist not happy with price charged food and accommodation. The calculated value for chi-square 56% and critical value of chi-square 3.84 and at 5% level of significance for 1 degree of freedom from this it can concluded that there is a relation between nature of tourist and satisfaction regarding price charged for food and accommodation. It means the highest percentages of foreign tourists were satisfied with price charged for food and accommodation. Table 7 reveals the sex and opinions of tourists regarding transportation. 242 tourists belong to male, among them 161 amounting 66.5% were satisfied with transportation and 81 tourists constituting 33.5% were not happy with transportation. Among female sample tourists 64.1% were happy with transportation and 35.9% were not happy with transportation. In case of foreign tourists, 85 belong to male out of that 70.2% were happy with transportations and 29.8% not happy with transportation. 70 belong to female among them 54.2% were happy with transportation and 45.8% not happy with transportation. Thus it is clear that in case of foreign tourists female were happier with transportation as compared to male. And in case of domestic tourists male are happier than female in respect of transportation facilities.

Table 6
Opinions of Tourists Regarding Price Charged for food and Accommodation

Tourists	*Responses*		*Total*
	Satisfied	*Not satisfied*	
Domestic	180(56.3)	140 (43.7)	320(67.3)
Foreign	140 (90.4)	15 (9.6)	155(32.7)
Total	309(65.1)	155(34.9)	475 (100)

Source: Field survey.
Note: Figures in Parentheses indicates Percentage to total of respective column.

Table 7
Sex and Opinions of Tourist regarding Transportation

Response	*Domestic*		*Total*	*Foreign*		*Total*
	Male	*Female*		*Male*	*Female*	
Satisfied	161(66.5)	50(64.1)	211(68.9)	60(70.2)	38(54.2)	98(63.2)
Not satisfied	81(33.5)	28(35.9)	109(34.2)	25(29.8)	32(75.8)	57(36.8)
Total	242(75.6)	78(24.4)	320(100)	85(34.8)	70(45.2)	155(100)

Source: Field survey.
Note: Figures in Parentheses indicates Percentage to total of respective column.

Table 8 reveals the sex and opinions of the tourists regarding accommodation and beverage facilities. 242 domestic tourists belong to male, among them 148 amounting 61.1% were satisfied with accommodation and beverage facilities. 78 domestic tourists belong to female, out of that 55.1% were happy with accommodation and beverage facilities and around 45% tourists not happy with transportation and beverage facilities. 85 foreign tourists constituting 54.8% were male; among them more than 52% were happy with accommodation and beverage facilities. 70 foreign tourists amounting 45.2% were belong to female, out of that more than 62% were happy with accommodation and beverage facilities.

Table 8
Sex and Opinions of Tourist regarding Accommodation and Beverage Facilities

Response	*Domestic Tourists*		*Total*	*Foreign Tourists*		*Total*
	Male	*Female*		*Male*	*Female*	
Satisfied	148(61.1%)	43(55.1%)	191(59.9)	45(52.9)	44(62.8)	89(57.4)
Not satisfied	94(38.9)	35 (44.9)	129(40.9)	40(47.1)	26(37.2)	66(42.6)
Total	242(75.6)	78(24.4)	320(100)	85(54.8)	70(45.2)	155(100)

Source: Field survey.
Note: Figures in Parentheses indicates Percentage to total of respective column.

Table 9 provides information about level of income and opinions of tourists regarding price charged for food and accommodation. 20 domestic tourists belong to low income groups among them 100% were unhappy with price charged for food and accommodation. 188 belong to medium income group out of that 54.2% were happy with price charged for food and accommodation and 112 domestic tourists belong to high income group among them more than 69% were happy with price charged for food and accommodation. 10 foreign tourists belong to low income group among them 20% were satisfied. 55 foreign tourists belong to medium income group out of that 58.3% were satisfied with price charged for food and accommodation. 90 tourists belong to high income group among them 90% were happy with price charged for accommodation and food.

Table 9
Level of Income and Opinions of Tourist regarding Price Charged for Food

Level of Income	*Domestic Tourists*		*Total*	*Foreign Tourists*		*Total*
	Statisfied	*Not satisfied*		*Statisfied*	*Not satisfied*	
Low	–	20(100)	20(6.2)	2(20)	8(80)	10(6.4)
Medium	102 (54.2)	86 (45.8)	188(58.3)	48(87.3)	7(12.7)	55(35.4)
High	78(69.6)	34(30.4)	112(35)	90(100)	–	90(58.2)
Total	180(56.3)	140(43.7)	320(100)	140(90.4)	15(9.6)	155(100)

Source: Field survey.
Note: Figures in Parentheses indicates Percentage to total of respective column.

Table 10 reveals the information about occupational back ground of tourists and purpose of visit. 75 tourists belong to government services among them 58.7% visit for sight seeing, 36% visit for holiday relaxation and 5.3% come for pleasure trip. 80 domestic tourists working in private institutions out of that highest percentage of tourists visit for sight seeing (46.2) followed by holiday relaxation, pleasure trip. 68 tourists belong to business back ground among them more than 48% opt for sight seeing. 97 sample tourists belong to student community out of that more than 57% prefer for sight seeing. 92 foreign tourists working in private institutions out of that, 59.7% visit for sight seeing. 31 tourists belong to student community among them the highest percentage (58.1%) visits for sight seeing. Thus it is clear that most of the foreign tourist as well as domestic tourists prefer tour for sight seeing.

Table 11 provides information about age of the tourists and purpose of visits. 95 domestic tourists come under the age group of below 20 years among them 72.6% come for sight seeing. 120 domestic tourists fall under in the age group of 25-30 years among them 50% come for sight seeing and followed by holiday relaxation, business and pleasure trip.

65 domestic tourists fall under the age of 31-35 out of that most of the tourists come for sight seeing. 40 tourists fall under in the age group of 35 and above among them 42.5% come for holiday relaxation.

Table 10
Occupational Background of Tourists and Purpose of Visit

Occupation	*Domestic Tourists*				*Total*	*Foreign Tourists*				*Total*
	HR	*BU*	*SS*	*PT*		*HR*	*BU*	*SS*	*PT*	
Govt.	27	–	44	4	75	8	–	10	2	20
Service	(36)		(58.7)	(5.3)	(23.4)	(40)		(50)	(10)	(12.9)
Private	30	–	37	13	80	19	–	55	18	92
Service	(37.5)		(46.2)	(16.3)	(25)	(20.6)		(59.7)	(18.7)	(52.9)
Business	–	28	33	7	68	–	6	6	–	12
		(41.1)	(48.5)	(10.4)	(21.2)		(50)	(50)		(1.2)
Student	32	–	56	9	97	13	–	58	–	31
	(32.9)		(57.7)	(9.4)	(30.3)	(41.9)		(58.1)		(20)
Total	89	28	170	33	320	40	6	89	20	155
	(37.8)	(8.7)	(53.1)	(10.4)	(100)	(25.8)	(3.8)	(57.4)	(13)	(100)

Source: Field survey.
Note-1: Figures in Parentheses indicates Percentage to total of respective column.
Note-2: HR-Holiday relaxation BU-Business SS-Sight Seeing PT-Pleasure Trips.

Table 11
Age of the Tourists and Purpose of Visit

Occupation	*Domestic Tourists*				*Total*	*Foreign Tourists*				*Total*
	HR	*BU*	*SS*	*PT*		*HR*	*BU*	*SS*	*PT*	
Below 20	17	–	69	9	95	6	–	4	–	10
	(17.8)		(72.6)	(9.6)	(29.6)	(60)		(60)		(6.4)
20-30	35	20	60	5	120	15	1	21	3	40
	(29.1)	(16.3)	(50)	(4.3)	(37.5)	(37.5)	(2.5)	(52.5)	(7.5)	(25.8)
31-35	20	6	26	12	65	13	3	28	11	55
	(30.7)	(9.2)	(40)	(20.1)	(20.3)	(23.6)	(5.4)	(50.6)	(20.1)	(35.4)
36 & above	17	2	15	7	40	6	2	36	6	50
	(42.2)	(5)	(37.8)	(15)	(12.6)	(12)	(4)	(72)	(12)	(32.6)
Total	89	28	170	33	320	40	6	89	20	155
	(37.8)	(37.8)	(53.1)	(10.4)	(100)	(25.8)	(3.8)	(57.4)	(13)	(100)

Sources: Field survey.
Note-1: Figures in Parentheses indicates Percentage to total of respective column.
Note-2: HR-Holiday relaxation BU-Business SS-Sight Seeing PT-Pleasure Trips.

GOVERNMENT EFFORTS TOWARDS TOURISM DEVELOPMENT

Indian Government adopted many programmes to promote the tourism industry like nation wide campaign for creating awareness about the effect of tourism and preservation of our culture and heritage, cleanliness and warm hospitality through a process of training and orientation was launched. The main aim of this policy is to rebuild the sense of responsibilities towards tourists about India and re-in forces the confidence of foreign tourist towards India as preferred holiday destination. More than taxi drivers, restaurant owners and guides trained under this programme. In addition to that the Indian government had formulated many policies to develop tourism industry and increased the fund for tourism development from Rs 325 crores in 2003-04 to 500 crores in 2004-05. In view of this the Indian tourism getting better position in recent period and has won the best design award as well as best folklore performance competing with country like Japan, Malaysia, China, Thailand and Canada. The theme of pavilion was the Buddhist pilgrimage in India. Multi-promotional activities undertaken by the country like Tokyo office drew a crowd to India Pavilion that added coloures to the entire travel show. The Koreas leading newspapers published on the first page regarding the Incredible India photographs highlighting different aspects. The live yoga performance and Indian traditional snacks at the pavilion were enjoyed very much by the tourist. The President of Confederation of Tourism Professional Subhash Goyal pointed out that in the world leading travel publication, India as one of the five top most destinations for global leisure travelers.

HYPOTHESES TESTING

Ho_1. Tourist not fully satisfied with accommodation, price, transport and other facilities. The calculated value of chi-square amounting 7.3025 and critical value 3.84 in case of transportation facilities, incase of accommodation and beverage facilities calculated value amounting 5.689 and table value 3.84, and in case of price charged for food and accommodation the calculated value of chi-square 56.1 and critical value 3.84 at 5% level of significance for 1 degree of freedom. From this it is clear that in all cases the calculated value of chi-square is grater than table value of chi-square, hence the null hypotheses were rejected. It means both domestic tourists as well as foreign tourists not happy with transportation facilities, accommodation and beverage facilities and price charged for food and accommodation.

Ho_2 There is no relationship between level of income and satisfaction of tourist regarding accommodation, price of accommodation, food and transportation. In case of domestic tourists the calculated value of chi-square 37.74 and table value amounting 9.491 at 5% level of significance for 4 degree of freedom. From the above it can conclude that the calculated value of chi-square is much greater than table value hence the null hypotheses were rejected. It means there is a significant relation between level of income and satisfaction of tourist regarding accommodation, price of accommodation, food and transport. In case of foreign tourists the calculated value of chi-square amounting 67.88 and table value 9.491 at % level of significance for 4 degree of freedom. It is clear that the calculated value of chi-square is much grater than table value hence the null hypotheses were rejected.

SUGGESTIONS

1. 43.2% of sample foreign and 30.9% of sample domestic tourists were not happy with transportation facilities, it is not good point of rapid growth of tourism industry because, transport is a key aspects for healthy development of tourism industry hence it is suggested that the State Government and Central Government should formulate the policies towards improve the transport facilities at international standards.
2. The quality accommodation, quick quality services, fair behaviour of hotel staff is very important to increases the satisfaction level of both domestic and foreign tourists. However, 49% of sample foreign tourists and 37% of sample domestic tourists were not happy with accommodation and beverage facilities, hence it is suggested that the hotel owner and lodge owner should provide services according to the expectation of tourists it may helps to increases the status of tourism industry.
3. Most of the foreign as well as domestic tourist felt that due to lack of quality management, the historical places and beaches are not maintain properly, in view of this there is urgent need to improvement of total quality management at operational and destination levels.
4. Indian tourism industry has achieved very high degree of development in some part of the country's tourists places but most of the tourists places still not been recognized and have no proper care towards the maintain at original look hence it is suggested that, the Govt. should recognize the non-recognized tourists spots and historical places and should maintain in proper manner.
5. Most of the studies pointed out that tourism industry adversely impact on environment and it has the potential to create beneficial by protection of environment and conservation. In view of this it is suggested that the government and non government

organization should take the interest in creating the awareness about the role of environment among tourists and to take proper measures to maintain good environment.

CONCLUSIONS

From the foregoing discussion, it is concluded that the tourism industry is a rapidly growing phenomenon and has become one of the largest industries in the world and it is thriving in India due to many reasons such as upward trend in the growth rate of Indian economy has raised middle class incomes, prompting more people to spend money on vacations abroad or at home. Also, India is booming in the information technology industry and has become one of the top IT center. Aggressive advertising campaign "Incredible India" by the government has also had contribution in changing India's image in the world tourism scenario.

REFERENCES

Hardekar and Ganpule (1993), "Tourism Potential in Sangli District", *International Journal of Management and Tourism* I (4), p. 401-410.

Panwar J.S. (1993), "Applying Strategic Marketing to Develop Tourism in India", *International Journal of Management and Tourism* I (4), p. 447-457.

Kulwant S.P. (2006), "Tourism Potential In Himachal Pradesh", *The Indian Journal of Commerce* Vol. 59, No. 2, p. 29-37.

Rob Dodson (1980), "Action Planning an Approach to Tourism Education", *Indian Journal of Tourism*, Vol. 185, p. 17-18.

Akash S.B. (2007), Plight of Tourism Industry in Uttar Kannada District, Pre Seated in National Seminar, "Emerging Trends in Tourism in Changing Scenario", (unpublished).

BANKING SECTORN UNDER GLOBALISATION

*Sumathy Venkatesan**

Liberalisation, Privatization and Globalization are the three buzz words in the modern era. There is tremendous growth in Indian Economy and the GDP growth is an example for the economic development. However, inflation ruling high at the moment is a cause of worry to the Government as well as to those who are really concerned in the development of the nation towards global standards. Banking sector, playing a very pivotal role in nation building activities is certainly not an exception to help the Government in curbing inflation and improve the standard of living of the people of the country to enable India to march ahead towards the principles of globalization.

ECONOMIC GROWTH

"Growth for the sake of growth is the characteristic of a cancer cell." After all what is economic growth? It is nothing but increase in the value of goods and services produced in the country. Surely, we are witnessing this in our nation now. The country is growing at the rate of 9% and the planners are aiming that it will soon reach double digit growth rate. Banks aim to help growing industries like SSI & SME sector and it is a major step towards globalization as lending to small industries will aggravate the productivity, capability and overall efficiency of the sector that naturally helps in the economic development which ultimately leads to a significant position in the global scenario.

FOREX RESERVES

"The only preparation for tomorrow is the right use of today". Foreign exchange reserves of the country which is another vital area of the country's development plan towards globalization touched $185.78 billion

* Lecturer in Commerce, Periyar University, Salem-636011.
Email-sumathivenky2005@gmail.com.

during the week ended Feb. 9, 2007. Foreign currency assets which make up a bulk of India's forex reserves touched $178 billion. Certainly this will act as a cushion in the rainy days. Banks help the nation in managing the forex reserves well.

INFLATION

Mr. Paul Adolph Volker ex US Federal Reserve chair person , said that managing inflation is critical. He further said that a little inflation was not a bad thing. It was a good thing that the prices were going up slightly this that's the way to avoid a recession and a great depression. Infrastructure development is an essential feature for growth. When inflation touches about 7% as at present one cannot be sure that we can hold it at that. This needs for a greater introspection at all levels and the Banks also help the Government in taking right decisions at the right time by acting as a close link between the common man and the policy makers. The measures of the Government are implemented through Banks to a certain extent will add another step towards moving in the lines of globalization.

AGRICULTURE VS INDUSTRALISATION

As all of us are aware, Agriculture contributes more than 60% of India's economy and one should not or, rather must not neglect this sector. However, structural transformation also takes place according to a study paper presented by Mr.N.P.Kannan member for national Commission for enterprise in unorganized sector, presented at the 48th annual conference of Indian Society of Labour economics in Trichirapalli. Agriculture accounted for less than 50% of employment and income in several states including Kerala, Tripura and TamilNadu. The plan panel is of the view that transferring 10 million workers out of agriculture is essential as the potential to absorb more workers in agriculture is reduced in these days.

There is a warning signal in this area also. Due to limited earnings the farmers may find it better to lease or sell their land and move on to other occupations. It may at times result in social disruption. There is a danger of wealth and productive assets accumulating in the hands of a few who are neither interested in construction activity or growth of non-agricultural sector. Here the role of the Banks occupies a predominant position as the Banking system takes care to prevent money laundering and diversion of funds. This will also pave the way towards globalization.

TERRORISM AND ANTI SOCIAL ACTIVITIES

RBI has introduced KYC (Know Your Customer) concept which enables Banks to identify the customer properly and then open the accounts. Normally terrorists will strive to open accounts in fictitious names and false addresses and try transfer funds from one account to another in round sum also at times which the Banker may not identify but for the beautiful guidelines of RBI under KYC norms. Naturally banks identify good customers, in the process the anti social accounts get eliminated which will be a good symptom for the growth of the nation which is another right move towards globalization.

COMMUNICATION SECTOR

The company Vodafone recently is set to acquire majority stake in Hutchison Essar. The company plans for rural expansion. It is a major move in mobile venture. PepsiCo India is getting ready for launching a high voltage communication package which includes new celebrity endorsements. These are the recent headlines in financial dailies. But what banks and globalization have to do in this connection. In today's world anything and everything happens to be an industry in itself. There seems to be plenty of opportunities if we analyse from the growth angle. Taking lessons from such giants, young, educated, unemployed youth may think of their own good ventures which may at a later stage grow into a better industry provided proper infrastructure is taken care of. Here banks play a pivotal role in helping good entrepreneurs in establishing their own industry. The principle behind this is "Help ever, hurt never".

GLOBAL MONEY TRANSFER ARENA

With more and more Indians settling abroad and sending money home India is fast becoming a centre of attraction for funds remittances. India accounts for $23 billion or 10% of global remittances. Naturally Banks in tune with RBI guidelines help the customers to be aware of legal options and this is certainly another move towards globalization.

NET WORKING MAGIC

Another majestic area which Banks do take advantage of the modern era. Technology up gradation and technological development are the important areas where we have to put in extra effort to keep ourselves globally competitive. "Learn to speak what you feel and act what you speak" so goes a saying. Banks feel the importance of technology towards improving themselves towards global standards and so they speak a lot on this issue and also have started acting on what they speak.

HUMAN RESOURCE DEVELOPMENT

People in developing countries are endowed with a high degree of intelligence, capacity for hard work, loyalty and innate decency. The worker or ordinary employee is rarely given much credit for the success of a business. Good management is the key to the development of the developing world and education holds the key. Banks contribute to this aspect by extending educational loans and the talents of the people are brought to highlight and the human resources of the country are not wasted to a considerable extent.

INFRASTRUCTURE PROJECTS

Citigroup, Blackstone, IDFC have jointly announced the launch of $5 billion funds to finance infrastructure projects in the country. Naturally it is another step towards building up the International image.

MACRO ECONOMIC DEVELOPMENTS

The growth in the industrial sector has been buoyant. Increase in exports, improvement in domestic demand and double digit growth in capital goods sector are the main reasons for the resurgence in the industrial growth.

The service sector remains in the top by contributing more than 57.60% in GDP. The major contributors are software and information technology services. There is a decline in NPA of Banks. Profitability has improved. Productivity has also improved. Expansion plans are on in many Banks. Branches in foreign countries are working very efficiently contributing to the development of the economy. Foreign Banks in India also help in our nation building measures. Ultimately it is a collective effort towards globalization standards.

CUSTOMER SERVICE

In any business, growth can be achieved if proper customer service is put in place and this is aptly applicable to service industry like Banks. The famous words of Mahatma "Customer is not a hindrance in our business. He is the part of it. Customer is the most important visitor in our premises. We are not serving him. He is giving us an opportunity to serve him" continue to linger in the minds of bankers and customer care has improved considerably since liberalization measures.

GENERAL PRINCIPLES

The Banking business has gone through fundamental change. There is so much pressure on the cost. Today's focus is on operational efficiency and bottom lines and not on size. While one door is closing another door is opening. For diligence, accuracy, speed storage, automation, and versatility technology is required. All these things are vital for the Banking sector and lot of innovation is taking place.

"Even if you are on the right track, you will get run over if you just sit there" so goes a saying. So, banks are gearing up towards globalization by readying themselves towards BASEL II norms also.

Risk Management, time management, people management, funds management etc are required in modern banking. All the banks are taking enormous efforts in these directions.

CONCLUSION

"Some see only problems and others the opportunity to win." In the present day scenario, globalization has a lot of role to play and Banks have pivotal role in this process. Guided by the Government, RBI and policy makers banks will certainly march ahead in the lines of Globalization and Mother India will certainly be proud of the achievements of her children in the days to come.

THE ECONOMICS OF DOMESTIC VIOLENCE AGAINST WOMEN

N. Dharmaraj & J. Cyril Kanmony***

INTRODUCTION

Domestic violence, the most serious violence against women affects women of every class, caste, religion, tribes and age [K. Uma Devi, 2005]. It has been largely supported by various cultures down the ages. It was part of the Nepoleanic code until a decade back. The very code says "Women like walnut trees must be beaten every day". In North Africa, the expression "Women and Camels need to be beaten" is still common. In Europe, they used to say that a man had the right to beat his wife with a stick not thicker than his thumb. In India it was said that drums, donkeys and women need to be beaten. So religion has played more or less a crucial role in reinforcing brutal attitudes to women which include mortification of the flesh deemed religious and more appropriate to the female. In fact over the ages, religions have constantly admonished women to stay with her husband no matter how cruelly he treated her [Udai Veer, 2004].

Women have been subjected to violence, atrocities and suppression in almost all the countries around the world, whether developed or developing [K. Uma Devi, 2005]. Violence against women is an act of illegal criminal use of physical force and it also includes exploitation, discrimination, upholding of unequal economic and social structures and the creation of an atmosphere of terror, threat or reprisal. The violation of women's right may be criminal or domestic or social. Rape, abduction and murder are criminal violence. Dowry harassment, wife battering, forced abortion, sexual abuse, ill-treatment of widows and elderly women and battering of girl child are various types of domestic violence. Female

* Ph.D. Research Scholar, Post-Graduate and Research Centre, Department of Economics, Scott Christian College (Autonomous), Nagercoil.

** Reader in Economics, Post-Graduate and Research Centre, Department of Economics, Scott Christian College (Autonomous), Nagercoil.

infanticide, eve-teasing, refusing share in property and *sati* are the types of social violence against women.

This paper tries to analyse the different forms of domestic violation.

Domestic violence includes all action/behaviour of family members which cause either physical injury or emotional trauma or both to a woman. The expression of domestic violence be seen in the form of wife battering, demand for more dowry, divorce, bride burning and conflicts in family life. The increased economic insecurity, unemployment and poverty in families may result in alcoholism, lack of status and mutually satisfying relationship, lack of sense of belonging and women directly in the form of increased domestic violence.

DOWRY HARRASSMENT

Dowry, a common phenomenon prevalent all over India, was initially a kind of inheritance of daughters in parental property which was given at the time of marriage ceremony for better status at the in-laws house. This social evil prevailed in India since ancient times. Dowry today is being demanded and paid without any relation to the bride's father's income and wealth.

It has been usually found that attitude of woman as a mother is different from that as a mother-in-law. Burning, poisoning, strangulation, battering and then setting on fire are some ways used to kill the women. Nehal Ashraf (1997) in his study in Bihar observed dowry deaths are not confined to the Hindu community alone they are noticeable among the Muslims also. A sample of 1635, the incidents of bride burning in urban area is higher (1100 cases) than rural areas (535). Kalpana Roy (1999) stated that the incidence of dowry deaths increased during the period from 1987 to 1991 was 169.7 percentage which shows the alarming situation of right violation against women. In Tamil Nadu alone cases of dowry death escalated from 132 in 1996 to 146 in 2000. [K. Surekha Rao, K. Suneetha, 2005].

WIFE BATTERING

A common name given to wife battering is silent crime. Wife battering has been often taken as physical assault on wife and it undoubtedly includes the mental torture which is so subtle and its effects are present for a very long time. Some feel the wife battering is the way in which man can express his anger and frustration, others say it is an expression of inadequacy in man who feels the need to assert himself and gain control.

SEXUAL ABUSE

Sexual abuse is an act which is done on a woman against her will, which may call as rape or an attempt to rape. Women are not safe even in their own families. Sexual abuse is also made on women in the family by other family members and it is being read every day in the newspaper.

ABORTION DEATHS

Abortion act legitimized the medical termination of pregnancy on the grounds of risk to the life of physical or mental health of mother or alternatively on the ground that if the children were born, it would itself be likely to be seriously handicapped by physical or mental abnormality. In the eyes of Amartia Sen the number of girls missing from the world as a whole is now 101 millions and of this 93 millions is shared by India and China. In spite of no scan centre in the past having booked for any violation as per pre-natal Diagnostic Technique Act 1994, there are 1.77 lakhs of girl-children (0-6 years) missing in the State of Tamil Nadu alone during the last 10 years [C. Pushpa, 2005]. Children have been killed, neglected, starved on abandoness, characterised with cruelty even to death, battered babies involve, mostly on 6 months to 5 years of age. The peak period is the initiating crawling, nappy wetting, mopping unhappy 1 to 3 years when any child may drive its present beyond endurance.

TREATMENT OF WIDOWS

The moment a woman loses her husband, she is deprived of average living conditions and benefits of worldly desires. A widow irrespective of age has to follow religious and social sanctions such as to discard colourful clothes, glass bangles, flowers and good food. The young widows deprived of the sex life and were always looked upon with suspicious looks.

TREATMENT OF ELDERLY WOMEN

There is no retirement for women from domestic work. To supplement family income, the aged women have to perform various household activities which are beyond their physical stamina.

The immediate causes of domestic violence are monetary causes, jealousy and suspicion, instigation by in-laws, domestic work, impact of alcohol, economic independence of wife or wife's sigh self esteem (she thinks too much of herself), dispute over children and extra marital affairs of husband and wife [Udai Veer, 2004]. The point that women are often the worst enemies of their own, should not also be refuted. Mothers-in-law and sisters-in-law often instigate men to violence. Do they poison the ears of their sons and brothers respectively and antagonise them against their wives. To maintain men's dominant position in the home they inflict some or other kind of violence on women and harass them throughout their life.

Domestic violence pervades all the countries especially developing countries including South Asian countries. Domestic violence rates in South Asia vary from community to community. Newspaper pages in South Asia are full of tales of domestic violence. Violence by intimate family members is one of the darkest legacies in South Asia. The violence against women in South Asia often begins before birth. In South Asia, alcohol and drug use also accentuates domestic violence when women seem to question or go outside the frame work of such decisions. If a society seeks to resolve conflict through the use of violence then violence in the home is also on the increase.

In 2002, 450 honour killings were reported in Pakistan. In Pakistan, a survey of 1000 women indicated that 55 per cent in the urban areas and 35 per cent in the rural areas stated that they were victims of domestic violence. In Sri Lanka, one survey put the figure at 60 per cent and another at 32 per cent. Ten women a week are subjected to acid attacks in Bangladesh.

Fifteen thousand young brides are burnt to death every year in India. Forty per cent of all sexual abuse cases in India are about incest. In a survey on violence against women in India, 94 per cent of the cases involved, the offender was a member of the family [Naved 2004]. It is estimated that 50 million women are missing in India either through sex-selective abortions, female infanticide, or female neglect. So much so that the sex ratio in certain States of India is very disturbing. There are 79.3 girls for every 100 males in Punjab and 87.8 girls for every 100 males in Gujarat. In Uttar Pradesh and Tamil Nadu a rate of 40 per cent of women interviewed stated that they were victims of wife-beating. Police stations rarely respond, though with the new police women desks this situation is marginally better. A survey of judges in the region (South Asia) point to the fact that 48 per cent of judges agreed that it was justifiable for men to beat their wives and 74 per cent endorsed the view that even in cases of violence the preservation of the family should be the primary concern [Radhika Coomaraswamy, 2005].

The table given below shows the number of domestic violence occurred in India in comparison with other women rights violations.

Table 1
Incidence of Reported Crimes Against Women in India

Category *Year*	*1996*	*1997*	*1998*	*1999*
Rape	14846(14.91)	15330(14.73)	15031(13.43)	15468(13.29)
Molestation	28939(29.06)	30764(29.55)	31046(27.74)	32311(27.75)
Sexual Harassment	5671(5.69)	5796(5.57)	8123(7.26)	8853(7.60)
Kidnapping and Abduction	14877(14.94)	15617(15.00)	16381(14.64)	15962(13.71)
Cruelty at Home	35246(35.40)	36592(35.15)	41318(36.92)	43823(37.64)
Total	99579(100)	104099(100)	111899(100)	116417(100)

Source: Uma Devi and Udai Veer, Crimes in India, 2004.

The above table shows that cruelty at home tops the list in all years followed by molestation. The numbers of domestic violence cases increased from 35.39 per cent in 1996 to 37.64 per cent in 1999 against a decrease of rape from 14.91 per cent in 1996 to 13.29 in 1999, molestation from 29.06 to 27.75 in the respective periods and kidnapping and abduction from 14.94 to 13.71 between the two periods. But in Tamil Nadu sexual harassment occupies the top place and domestic violence tops the list if dowry harassment is included in the domestic violence. The details are given in the following table.

Table 2
Violence Against Women–Tamil Nadu

Case wise		*Category wise*		
Year	*No. of Cases*	*Category*	*2001*	*2003*
2001	210	Domestic Violence	29	34
		Sexual Harrassment	56	45
2003	518	Rape	18	42
		Dowry	44	64
2004	850	Property Dispute	31	70
		Others	32	263

Source: South Asian Journal of Human Rights, p. 106.

STEPS TAKEN AND TO BE TAKEN BY THE GOVERNMENT TO CONTROL DOMESTIC VIOLENCE

Due to increasing dowry harassment incidents, the Government of India announced the Dowry Prohibition Act 1961, the first attempt to recognize dowry as social evil and to curb its practice. This act was modified in 1984 and 1986. The act says that any person giving or taking dowry or abetting is punishable. The offences are cognizable. Pre-natal Diagnostic Technique Act was also passed to control the killing of female child at the womb. Even then the number of violence against women especially domestic violence increases from year to year.

In this context, given the terrible nature of the crimes against women many young legal scholars are questioning whether the legal system can be effective in dealing with crimes against women and whether other alternatives to prosecution and punishment should be explored. Statistics for a given period in Mumbai show that of the 504 cases that were registered, only 469 were charge-sheeted, of which there were only 13 convictions and 10 acquittals, the vast majority were pending trial or never really got to the trial stage [Agnes 1998: 48]. Furthermore, feminists fear that the rape trial often becomes a pornographic spectacle. Even when judgements convict, the rape survivor emerges brutalised and some times a "scandal figure" in a still very patriarchal society. For this reason most women continue to be silent when they are victims of sexual violence.

The inability of the legal systems to deliver justice in the case of women and the reliance on the prosecution arm of the state has created unease among some women's right activists. They argue that reliance on the legal strategy alone is not enough and that a more broad based approach aimed at transforming attitudes and social structures is necessary [Kapoor and Cossman, 1996].

Domestic violence needs a coordinated and systemic response from the justice system, while section 498A of the Indian Penal Code, one of the most significant criminal laws is indeed a blunt tool, for it is difficult to change police culture; though the law may consider domestic violence against women an offence, the police may still not comply and implement it effectively. In order to move towards an effective working of section 498A, it is crucial that we adopt a new model of policing - the victim empowerment model, which will put in place, pro-arrest procedures and social service net works at the police station. It is also important to have civil law remedies to provide protection to women victims of domestic violence and the recently passed protection of women from Domestic Violence, Bill, 2005 is also significant step in this context and that should be effectively implemented [Jayna Kotharis, 2005].

Though women constitute nearly 50 per cent of the world population they just own one per cent of the world's property and resources. They receive 1/10 of the world income for their 60 per cent of the labour and account for the majority of refugees, illiterates and poor in the world [V.N. Report in J. Akbarkahn, 2005] but contribute much to the development of not only the regional economy but also the whole economy. If they are treated in par with men, then the journey of any economy towards greater growth is without much hindrance.

SUGGESTIONS

1. Evils of male chauvenism should be brought into light. The consequences of it may lead to woman leaving the children and husband, children neglected by both parents, woman committing suicide, etc.
2. Widowed/aged women should be taken care of by the government or by special social organizations and those social organizations should be supported and guided by government.
3. Awareness programmes against jealousy, suspicion, domestic relationships between husband and wife, parents and children, mother-in-law and daughter-in-law and household responsibilities to each individual at home are to be highlighted either by cinema or by any other media.
4. Even if the in-laws attitude towards the daughter-in-law is severe the husband should know to balance his role as a son and a husband try to play his independent role using his wisdom without causing pain to the wife or to the mother. When days go by everything would be alright and there is no more bride burning, poisoning, dowry harassment, etc.
5. Wife battering is a silent crime. Yes, there should be law against it as we have against eve-teasing.
6. Alcoholism is the root cause for the disintegration of a family. It fails a man's senses he becomes ruthless and animalistic.
7. Counselling programmes for both men and women before they get married should be conducted by churches or by any other social organizations.
8. Finally, on the whole, if real love prevails among a family or in the society, these evils will be eradicated positively.

REFERENCES

Chandrakala N.B. (2005), "Domestic Violence Against Women" in Devi K. Uma (Ed.), *Violence Against Women Human Rights Perspective*, New Delhi.

Cyril Kanmony J. (2005), "Poverty and Women's Right Violation with Special Reference to Tamil Nadu", *South Asian Journal of Human Rights*, pp. 125-140.

Jayna Kotharis (2005), "Criminal Law on Domestic Violence", *Economic and Political Weekly*, XL No. 46, p. 4843.

Pushpa P. (2005), "Women and Poverty-Multipronged Human Rights Violation in India", *South Asian Journal of Human Rights*, pp. 107-124.

Radhika Coomaraswamy (2005), "Human Security and Gender Violence", *Economic and Political Weekly*, XL, 44 and 45, pp. 4729-4736.

Surekha Rao, K. and Suneetha, K. (2005), "A Study on Domestic Violence and Role of Social Workers" in Devi K. Uma (Ed.), *Violence Against Women Human Right Perspective*, New Delhi.

Thomas, E.C. (2005), "Protection of the Rights of Women", *Employment News*, November, 12-18, p. 1.

Udai Veer (2004), "Crime Against Women", Anmol Publications Pvt. Ltd., New Delhi.

INTELLECTUAL PROPERTY RIGHTS AND ECONOMIC DEVELOPMENT

*S. N. Yogish**

INTRODUCTION

The Eighth round of the General Agreement on Tariffs and Trade (GATT) negotiations, known as the Uruguay Round which started in Penta del Este in September 1986, ran into rough weather as the participating member countries showed wide differences of opinion on two major issues: (a) the inclusion of Trade Related Intellectual Property Rights (TRIPs), Trade Related Investments Measures (TRIMs) and General Agreement on Trade in Services (GATS) as areas of negotiation in GATT and (b) the US plan for eliminating all subsidies in the agricultural sector within 10 years. The area of disagreement on these issues widened to such an extend that by December 1990, the year in which the Uruguay Round should have been over, the GATT negotiations broke down.

It was at this moment of crisis of the GATT that Arthur Denkel, the Director General of GATT, came out with a compromise agreement to bring the Uruguay round to a successful end. The 500-Page Denkal document entitled "Draft Final Act Embodying the Results of the Uruguay round of Multilateral Trade Negotiations" was presented in Geneva on December 20, 1991. This document thus became famous as the Denkel Draft or proposal.

With the USA and EC (European Community) agreeing on terms for reducing EC export of subsidized agricultural products, the "Blair House" Accord was reached in 1992 and the stage was set for the signing of the final Uruguay agreement. Thus, on December 15, 1993, after 7 years of prolonged negotiations, 117 member countries of GATT signed the document in the form of 28 separate agreements and agreed to submit the some to the respective Government for approval.

* Reader, Department of Studies in Economics, Kuvempu University, Jnana Sahyadri. Shankaraghatta.

After receiving the Government approvals, this final Act which is basically the Denkel Draft, was finally accepted in the form of a 22,000 page world trade agreement, the largest trade deal in history, on April 15, 1994, at Marrakesh, Morocco by 124 countries which together control 90 per cent of world trade. The Marrakesh Treaty ensures the creation of a World Trade Organization (WTO), the new name of GATT, on January 1, 1995.

The Uruguay Round marked a major departure from the preceding ronds of GATT negotiation in that it was much more comprehensive and ambitious, converting as it did, a wide spectrum of topics, never before covered under the GATT umbrella, TRIP is one such topic which has been incorporated, for the first time, as a separate agreement among GATT members. In the part, this subject was the concern of the World Intellectual Property Organization (WIPO). Among all the issues covered by the Uruguay round, it is TRIP which has become the major subject of controversy in India.

NEED FOR INTELLECTUAL PROPERTY RIGHTS (IPRS)

Intellectual Property Rights (IPR) are considered as a tool to create wealth through knowledge. Inventions and technical information flow very quickly all over the world and they can easily be copied by others. It is essential that fruits of R and D are adequately protected throughout the world under the harmonized protection system.

Ideas and knowledge are an increasingly important part of trade. Most of the value of new medicines and other high technology products lies in the amount of invention, innovation, research, design and testing involved. Films, music recordings, books, computer software and on-line services are bought and sold because of the plastic, metal or paper used to make them. Many products that used to be traded as low technology goods or commodities now contain a higher proportion of invention and design in their value-for example brand named clothing or new varieties of plants.

Besides, creators can be given the right to prevent others from using their inventions, designs or other creations-and to use that right to negotiate payment in returns for others using them. These are "Intellectual Property Rights". They take a number of forms. For example books, paintings and films come under copy right; inventions can be patented; brand names and product logos can be registered as trademarks and so on. Governments and parliaments have given creators these rights as an incentive to produce ideas that will benefit society as a whole.

The extent of protection and enforcement of these rights varied widely around the world; and as intellectual property became more important in trade, these differences became a source of tension in international economic relations. New internationally-agreed trade rules for intellectual property rights were seen as a way to introduce more order and predictability and for disputes to be settled more systematically.

The importance of intellectual property in India is well established at all levels-statutory, administrative and judicial. India ratified the agreement establishing the World Trade Organization (WTO). This agreement, inter-alia, contains an agreement on Trade Related aspects of Intellectual Property Rights (TRIPs) which came into force from 1st January 1995. It lays down minimum standards for protection and enforcement of intellectual property rights in member countries which are required to promote effective and adequate protection of intellectual property rights with a view to reducing distortions and impediments to international trade. The obligations under the TRIPs Agreement relate to provision of minimum standard of protection within the member countries legal systems and practices.

The agreement provides for norms and standards in respect of following areas of intellectual property:

- Copyrights and related rights
- Trade marks
- Geographical indications
- Industrial designs
- Lay out deisgns of integrated circuits
- Protection of undisclosed information (Trade secrets)
- Patents
- Plant varieties

TRANSITION PERIOD

India, as a developing country had a transition period of five years (with effect from 01 January, 1995), i.e., till January 01, 2000 to apply the provisions of the agreement. An additional transition period of five years, i.e., till January 01, 2005, is also available for extending product patent protection to areas of technology not protected so far. This would be mainly in the areas of pharmaceuticals and agricultural chemicals.

COPY RIGHTS

India's copyright law, laid down in the Indian copyright Act, 1957 as amended by copyright Act, 1999, fully reflects the Borne convention on copyrights, to which India is a party. The copyright law has been amended periodically to keep pace with changing requirements.

The recent amendment to the copyright law, which came into force in May 1995, has ushered in comprehensive changes and brought the copyright law in line with the developments in satellite broadcasting, computer software and digital technology. The amended law has made provisions for the first time, to protect performer's rights as envisaged in the Rome convention. Several measures have been adopted to strengthen and streamline the enforcement of copyright.

TRADE MARKS

Trade marks have been defined as any sign or any combination of signs capable of distinguishing the goods or services of one undertaking from those of other undertakings.

Keeping in view the changes in trade and commercial practices, globalization of trade, need for implication and harmonization of trade marks registration systems etc., a comprehensive review of the Trade and Merchandile Marks Act, 1958 was made and a bill to repeat and replace the 1958 Act has since been passed by parliament and notified in the Gazette on 30-12-1999. This Act not only makes Trade Marks Law, TRIPs compatibility but also harmonises it with international systems and practices. Work is underway to bring the law into force.

GEOGRAPHICAL INDICATIONS

The agreement contains a general obligation that parties shall provide the legal means for interested parties to prevent the use of any means in the designation or presentation of a good that indicates or suggest that the good in question originates in a geographical area other than the true place of origin in a manner which misleads the public as to the geographical origins of the good. There is no obligation under the agreement to protect geographical indications which are not protected in their country or origin or which have fallen into disuse in that country.

INDUSTRIAL DESIGNS

Obligations envisaged in respect of industrial designs are that independently created designs that are new or original shall be protected. Individual Government have been given the option to exclude from protection, designs dictated by technical or functional considerations, as against aesthetic consideration which constitutes the coverage of industrial designs.

PATENTS

The basic obligation in the area of patents is that, invention in all branches of technology whether products or processes shall be patentable if they meet the three tests of being new involving an inventive step and being capable of industrial application. In addition to the general severity exemption which applied to the entire TRIPs agreement, specific exclusions are permissible from the scope of patentability of inventions, the prevention of whose commercial exploitations is necessary to protect public order or mortality, human, animal, plant life or health or to avoid serious prejudice to the environment.

The TRIPs agreement provides for a minimum term of protection of 20 years counted from the date of filing.

India had already implemented its obligations under Articles 70.8 and 70.9 of TRIP Agreement.

A comprehensive review of the Patents Act, 1970 was also made and a bill to amend the Patents Act, 1970 was introduced in Parliament on 20 December 1999 and notified on 25-6-2002 to make the patent law TRIPs compatible. To meet our TRIPs obligations as on 1-1-2000, the Patents (Amendment) Act, 2002 has been enacted.

In respect of plant varieties, there is an obligation to provide for protection either by patents or by an effective suigeveris system or by any combination thereof. The agreement does not spell out the elements of an effective suigeveris system and it is left to each Government to determine the elements, which could be deemed to be providing effective protection. A decision has been taken to put in place a suigeveris system as it is perceived to be in our national interest. Accordingly, protection of plant varieties and farmer's rights Act 2001 has been enacted.

PATENTS (AMENDMENT) BILL AND INDIAN PHARMACEUTICAL INDUSTRY

In the light of the new patent regime, the Indian Patent Act, 1970, will have to undergo significant changes. The Act provides for only "process patent" and the Indian manufacturers are free to produce drugs patented abroad by using a different process. This will change now to allow product patent in food, drugs and chemicals. Again, the period of protection is to be extended to 20 years against the present 7 year period. Moreover, patents must be granted whether the product is imported or of a local origin. Furthermore, the system of protection of the plant variations is to be introduced. Article 27 of the Denkel Text makes it necessary to introduce Intellectual Property Rights in plant breeding. It will also be necessary to incorporate the pipeline protection clause which will be in operation 5 year prior to the end of the transitional period. This clause will provide exclusive marketing rights for 5 years for a new product patent in another country.

Analyzing the impact of the new patent regime on India's seed industry. A.V. Ganeshan draws our attention to the fact that "a patent is given for an invention" and "anything existing or previously known or used cannot be given intellectual property protection". Hence, existing plant, tree or seed cannot come under the patent system. However, for the protection of "plant varieties", a Plant Breeders Rights (PBR) system is to be established by the year 2000 A.D. A plant variety will be protected only if it satisfies three criteria : the criterion of "Novelty" the criterion of distinctiveness" and the criterion of "uniformity". The suigeveris system of protection that India will adopt provides for "farmers' privileges" in that the farmers will be free to buy seeds from any source and sell seeds that they breed. The seeds they cannot sell are the seeds they breed from privately developed seeds.

Let us now turn to the impact of the new patent regime on drug prices and drug industry in India. It has been seen that the drug prices in India are the lowest in the world because India goes by process patent and Indian drug companies thrive on inventions elsewhere thus avoiding a lot of expenditure on research and development. Countries like Pakistan which go by product patent cannot make medicines available at Indian prices. It is to be noted that the new patent regime will affect new drugs only i.e., those entering into India after 2005 A.D. The new regime will affect a small amount of drugs as only 10 to 15 per cent of drugs in the Indian market are patented. Empirical studies also show that only 33 new drugs have entered into the Indian market out of a total of 433 new drugs introduced in the world market during the period 1983-1992. It is also well within the power of the Government of India to impose the drug price control system through compulsory licensing the price control particularly in case of life–saving and essential drugs used by the common man. It is also noteworthy that GATT gives India a 10 year transition period as against special 301 of the omnibus trade and competitiveness Act of the USA which threatens to impose patent laws unilaterally.

CONCLUSION

The TRIPs agreement has as its preamular objective a desire to ensure that measures and procedures to enforce that measures and procedures to enforce intellectual property rights do not themselves become barriers to legitimate trade. Further, one of its objectives is to contribute to the transfer and dissemination of technology it has amongst its principles, the promotions of public interest in sectors of vital importance to the socio-economic and technological development of its members. At the same time the agreement recognizes intellectual property rights as private rights. Finally, the agreement encourages adjustments aimed at higher levels of protection of intellectual property rights. With these objectives, principles and provisions in view, India would like to initiate a discussion on some of the issues that have been of great concern to WTO members, including many developing countries. These issues are by no means exhaustive nor do they represent the entirely of members concern on intellectual property rights. They are intended to initiate discussions of issues related to TPRs so that the objectives of the WTO agreement such as raising standards of living, ensuring full employment increasing trade and promoting sustainable development are achieved.

It is true that the new intellectual property right regime is not exactly on the line as India would like to see it but this is so far many other countries as evident from the emergence of vocal lobbies in USA, Japan, France Australia and others. The alternative to the new regime is bilateralism where the powerful nation may adopt arm twisting tactics as experienced by China in her trade with the USA forcing China to knock at the door of GATT again. The alternative to the new regime is economic isolationism that is emerging countries like Myanmar and Albaria. The alternative to multilaterism GATT and WTO is restricted, halting and uncertain trade which will reduce world income and consumers welfare. The new world trade regime has thrown up a challenge to the various research institutions in India both public and private and hopefully. These institutions will not let the country down.

REFERENCES

Bhorali D., GATT Agreement or Dunkel Draft Treaty, Mittal Publications, New Delhi, pp. 45-53.

India Today (1993), August 15, November, 30.

Sham Bhat, K. "Indian Economy under Globalisation Process", Edited Volume, Serials Publications, New Delhi, pp. 1-24.

Uruguay Round of Multilateral Trade Negotiations: Summary of Draft Final Act, *CMIE*, Bombay.

Vibha Mathur "WTO and India, Development Agenda for the 21st Century", New Century Publications, New Delhi, India, pp. 227-251.

IMPACT OF FINANCIAL SECTOR REFORMS IN BANKING SERVICES–A STUDY IN KERALA

Benson Kunjukunju & Varghese Antony***

INTRODUCTION

The banking sector in India has remained regulated since nationalization of banks in 1969. Up to 1990, the concept of an independent regulatory authority had no relevance. With the liberalization of the Indian Economy, the Indian banking system have gradually moved into a market driven competitive system. Changes have been taken place from, when the then Finance Minister of India, Dr. Man Mohan Singh, by unveiling the New Economic Policy presented through the National Budget in the year 1991. The much debated New Economic Policy was the outcome of acute financial crisis faced by the country in mid 1991 caused primarily by the political uncertainty and aggravated by the impact of Gulf War. During that period the country was passing through an unprecedented economic crisis following the strain on balance on payment, galloping inflation, frustrating position of foreign exchange reserves and other macroeconomic imbalances. The new economic policy was based on a combination of measures aimed at economic stabilization and structural reforms to overcome the shortcomings of socialistic pattern of economy adapted by India for the last 40 years. The overall package is aimed at enhancing the productivity and efficiency of the economy as a whole and also increasing international competitiveness.

NARASIMHAM COMMITTEE REPORT ON FINANCIAL SECTOR REFORMS

After announcement of the National Economic Policy, the Government appointed a high level committee under the chairmanship of Mr. Narasimham

* Reader, Post-Graduate and Research Department of Commerce, S.T. Thomas College, Kozhencherry (Kerala).

** Lecturer Selection Grade, Department of Commerce, ST. Thomas College, Kozhencherry (Kerala).

on financial system 'to examine all aspects relating to the structure, organization functions and procedures of financial systems. The government and the Reserve Bank accepted almost all the recommendations of the committee.

The committee envisaged major changes in banking sector by reduction in cash reserve ratio, statutory liquidity ratio requirements, deregulation of interest on deposits and advances, recapitalization of weak public sector banks, merger of banks to reduce numbers, adequate financial infrastructure in terms of supervision, audit, sophisticated technology for improving customer service, operational efficiency and voluntary retirement scheme. The committee also proposed the introduction of prudential norms such as income recognition, asset classification, provisioning and capital adequacy norms, transparency in operations and improvement in productivity, efficiency and profitability of banking operations. The committee recommend entry of foreign banks, new private sector banks and local area banks. The committee further advocated the introduction of universal banking, setting up of special recovery tribunals, introduction of banking ombudsmen scheme etc.

Financial sector reforms, globalization and integration of world's financial markets have increased the level of competition in Indian banking industry. Improved customer service has become very important for survival and growth in the emerging deregulated financial markets for banks. Consequently, banks are under increasing pressure 'to offer to-day what customers would be expecting tomorrow'. Customers of banks are of varied types with different expectations and attitudes and come from wide socio economic and cultural background. The customer will only select the bank where they are satisfied mostly. With out satisfying the customer no bank can grow in the competitive business world.

Banks are now competing with each other to offer multi-farious and diversified services to customers to widen their client bases. Several banks have been positioning themselves as a "one-stop shop" for financial services with a fairly exhaustive range of products and services namely ATM, Credit Card, Debit Card, Single Window Service, Internet Banking, Mobile Banking, Tele Banking, Phone Banking, Utility Bill Payment and other regular periodical payment facilities, Depository Services, Investment Advice, Electronic Funds Transfer options to cover third party customer accounts within the same bank, Funds transfer across banks, Electronic Clearing Service, integration with e-commerce transactions such as for booking of tickets for rail and air etc. Apart these, banks have also been entered into the business of selling third-party products such as mutual funds and insurance products to the retail customers. With E-Banking, the brick and mortar structure of the traditional banking gets converted into a click and portal model thereby giving real shape to the concept of virtual banking.

GROWTH OF COMMERCIAL BANKS IN KERALA

Kerala can reasonably claim to have successfully tackled the first generation problems like illiteracy, low girls enrolment in schools, high infant mortality rate, high maternal mortality rate, low expectation of life at birth, and related indicators of under development at the societal level. The National Geographic has referred to Kerala as one of the ten paradises in the world. The UN had projected Kerala as a role model for education, health care and social welfare.

Kerala has an excellent banking infrastructure. As on March 31st, 2006 there were 49 Commercial Banks and 2 Regional Rural banks having a total of 3588 branches spread over the State as a whole. The average population per bank branch is 9,000 where as the all India average being 16,000. During 1969-2005, the growth of commercial banks branches was far below the national average (8 fold) and recorded only 5.5 fold increase with a compound growth rate of 5.8 per cent. It occupies the eleventh slot with respect to the number of bank branches (5.1% of total branches).

In Kerala most of the branches are in semi urban areas, the rural areas having only 10.7 per cent of the branches. The rural branches in the State represent only 1.1 percent of the total rural branches in the country. It is estimated that about 5 per cent of the total deposits in the country are mobilized by the commercial banks of Kerala. The per capita deposits in Kerala is 50 per cent higher than the national figure. The growth of advances in Kerala over a period of ten years was 300 percent while it was 450 percent at national level. The credit deposit ratio of Kerala is 6 per cent less than the CD ratio at the all India level.

STATEMENT OF THE PROBLEM

The Indian banking industry has undergone major changes after liberalization and globalization reforms in 1990. The entry of new private sector banks and foreign banks in 1993 posed a challenge to the monopoly enjoyed by the nationalized banks and old private sector banks. The banks cow compete with one another to offer value- added services to customers to widen their client bases. E- Banking enables the customers to perform the basic banking transactions by sitting at their office or at homes through PC or LAPTOP. Customers are being provided with additional delivery channels which are more convenient to customers and are cost effective to the banks. The new private sector banks and foreign banks expanded the usage of banking services through Automated Teller Machines, credit cards, debit cards, internet banking, telephone banking, mobile banking, home banking, electronic fund transfer etc.

Customers are the life blood of any business. In banking industry quality of customer services hold primary significance. The major objectives of Indian banks both private sector and public sector banks is now to attract a large customer base by offering more delivery channels, giving more importance to customer relationships, maintaining and enhancing customer relationships. It is against this background, the study was carried out to find out the awareness level of customers on various banking services and their level of satisfaction on various services in the light of financial sector reforms in the country.

IMPORTANCE OF THE STUDY

Modern banking operations touches almost every sphere of economic activity. The traditional Indian commercial banks faced major challenges in the form of competition from foreign banks and new generation private sector banks. The present study is an attempt to examine how far the old and new generation banks in Kerala are succeeded in popularizing their new banking services. The study also helps in understanding the level of satisfaction of customers of banks on various delivery channels. The level of customer satisfaction is revealed by an increase in dealings between the bank and its customers. The customer will select the bank only where they are satisfied. Without satisfying the customers no bank can grow in the competitive business world. The present study may be useful to banks in understanding and improving the awareness of customers on various banking services. The findings may helps banks to improve their customer base and to diagnose deficiencies in the present services. In view of the growing significance of banking services in the light of information technology revolution and globalized scenario the researcher feels that the present study can throw light on the problems of customers and banks and hence will be of use for policy formulation in this sphere.

OBJECTIVES OF THE STUDY

Following are the objectives framed for the study.

(1) To study and analyze the awareness of customers on various banking services provided by commercial banks of Kerala in the post liberalization regime.

(2) To evaluate the level of satisfaction of customers on various services provided by the banks.

(3) To offer valuable suggestions on the basis of the study.

METHODOLOGY

The study is designed an empirical one based on survey method. Data have been collected from both primary and secondary sources. The main thrust of the study is determining the awareness of customers on new banking services and also to measure the level of satisfaction of customers on various services provided by commercial banks. For the purpose of examining the awareness and level of satisfaction on various banking services at the micro-level, a multi-stage random sampling technique was resorted. In the first stage district were selected, in the second and third stages banks and customers were selected respectively.

PRIMARY DATA

Primary data had been collected from 60 customers of Four Commercial Banks in Kollam city. Data had been collected by administering, a structured interview schedule.

SECONDARY DATA

Secondary data had been collected from text books, periodicals, newspapers, research journals, hypertext etc.

SELECTION OF SAMPLES

In Kollam city, there are 21 banks with 41 branches. Of these 41 branches 12 are branches of private sector banks and 29 are the branches of public sector banks. Of the 12 private sector bank branches 4 are branches of new generation banks and 8 are branches of old private banks. From the old private banks and new generation banks one branch each and from the public sector banks two branches were selected at random by using lottery method. In total Four Commercial Bank branches in the Kollam city was selected for study. The banks selected for study are Federal Bank, UTI Bank, State Bank of India and State Bank of Travancore.

In order to collect information from the customers in each selected branch fifteen customers were selected at random. The investigator stationed in front of the branches to collect information from the customers. The customers were interviewed systematically, by the investigator in front of the branches at dates convenient to the researchers. The customers who were willing to answer the questions and prepared to spend sufficient time for this purpose were identified and interviewed.

MEASUREMENT OF VARIABLES

(I) Measurement of Level of Awareness of Customers on New Banking Services Introduced as a Result of Financial Sector Reforms.

For measuring the awareness level of customers on new services, Ten important banking services \ products were identified. The variables are identified by the researchers on the basis of available literature and discussions with banks officials. All questions in the schedule are qualitative in nature. Customers would mark '0' for no awareness, '1' for awareness and '2' for full awareness. The following are the variables identified by the researchers for the study.

Automated Teller Machine (ATM)

ATM is a modern technology introduced that enable the customers to have access to money round the clock and also throughout the year. It enables the customers to withdraw their money 24 hours a day, 7 days a week and 365 days a year. The system is known as 'Any Time Money' or 'Any Where Money', because it allows the customers to withdraw money from the bank from any where round the clock even on Sundays and National holidays. The ATM enables a customer to withdraw and deposit cash and cheque, check account balance, print mini account statement, transfer funds between own accounts, payment of utility bills, refill prepaid mobile card etc.

By the end of 1990, Indian private and public sector banks have come up with their own ATM networks under the initiative of the Indian Bank Association in Mumbai. The Bank of India is the first nationalized bank to provide ATM facilities to the customers in Mumbai. 21,147 ATMs were installed in India by commercial banks at the end of March 2006. Nationalized banks accounted for the largest share of installed ATMs, followed by the new private sector banks, SBI group, old private sector banks and foreign banks. Since the services are available 24 hours, the customers are easily satisfied. ATMs have brought about a great change in the service to the customers. It is against this back ground the researchers identified that it is an important variable to study the awareness and satisfaction level of customers.

Tele Banking

Modern banking is more information based, speedy and boundary-less due to the impact of E-Revolution. Telebanking is an innovative form of electronic banking introduced by banks by which banking services or products are provided to its customers through a telephone. A customer can access their account from the telephone anytime at any place across the country with the same Telebanking Pin they desire. Customers can perform a number of transactions from the convenience of their own home or office, in fact from anywhere they have access to a phone. Telebanking service is available 24 hours a day, 7days a week otherwise called "bank round the clock". This is one of the most convenient mode of transacting banking business. By the introduction of this facility customers can operate their account on any where in the country during banking hours. This facility is also becoming immensely popular among customers and has been given due importance in this study.

Internet Banking

Internet banking otherwise called on-line banking is nothing more than traditional banking services delivered through an electronic communication backbone, viz, Internet. It removes the traditional geographical barriers as it could reach out to customers of different countries. It is one of the efficient and cost effective delivery mechanism of banking services. Through internet Banking, banks offer extensive range of products and services which vary widely both in their content and sophistication. With the internet banking facility the customer of the bank is just a click away. The customers can check their account status, fund transfer, make bill payments, place online requests for new cheque books, review term deposits etc. In addition, it enables the customers to conduct online trading, mutual fund purchases and online shopping, and payments to services such as insurance, electricity, telephone and mobile services across the country. Banking products and services such as deposits, remittances, credit card etc. as well as all important banking information's can be made available with easy access to customers on Internet. Customers can make use of these services with no restricted office hours, no queues, no tellers, and no waiting. In view of the above facts, Internet banking facility is considered to be an important variable in this study.

Credit Cards

Credit card is a convenient medium of exchange. A credit card is nothing but a cute card made of plastic. The card contains an identification by means of a signature and in certain cards a small photo. The card authorizes the holder to charge goods or services to his account on which he is billed. Credit card is otherwise called 'plastic money'. Credit cards are designed to avoid the use of either cash or cheque. They can use in those establishments which have agreed to accept them. The credit card organizer makes payment to the concerned establishment and once a month sends an invoice to the credit card holder for all his purchases in the previous month. Banks issue different types of credit cards and credit limit of each card varies.

In India Central Bank of India was the first bank to introduce the credit card known as Central Card in the middle of 1981. Credit cards have found widespread acceptance in the metros and cities and not popular in small towns and villages. With the introduction of credit card system, the concept of everywhere and any time banking becomes a reality. Convenience and easy acceptability of credit cards and technological advancements have resulted in a continuous rise in credit card-based mode of payments. The use of credit card mode of payment increased enormously both in terms of volume and value from the previous year 2005. This facility is also becoming immensely popular since 1990 among the customers and has been given due importance in this study.

Mobile Banking

In traditional banking, customers has to visit the branch of the bank in person to perform the basic banking transactions. Mobile banking is becoming one of the customer-friendly facility, which could have far reaching implications in the financial sector. Mobile banking brings the bank to the cell phone of a customer. On-line banking is now moving to the mobile world, giving everybody with a mobile phone access to real time banking services, regardless of their location. In India banks having the facility of mobile banking services is at present providing only a limited number services to their customers. The potential for mobile banking is boundless, with the scope of introduction of more and more new services or products. With Mobile banking, the concept of anytime, any where banking is literally at the fingertips of the customer. Mobile alerts such as debits and credits to the account, registered bill payment, inquiries like balance inquiry, last few transaction statements, demat account details, mobile banking password change etc. are made available to the customers through mobile phone at a nominal charge by the bank. It is against this background that mobile banking facility is taken as an important variable for measuring the level of awareness of customers.

Utility Bill Payment

E-banking opens new vistas for providing enlarged, efficient, economic and quality service to the customers. With electronic banking, clients are able to deal with banks and get a host of requests serviced through their desk top computers or through telephone. It facilitate the immediate payment of utility bills of customers such as electricity, water, telephone, mobile bills, payment of insurance premium, tuition fees, hostel fees of wards etc. Payment of utility bill is a novel technique adopted by banks in 1994 to attract customers. Hence it is considered an important variable to assess the awareness level of customers.

Banking Ombudsmen

Banking Ombudsmen Scheme was announced in June 1995 to protect the interest of customers as well as to redress their grievances, which provides quick and inexpensive facility. The main object of this scheme is to resolve complaints of customers relating to the provision of banking services and to facilitate the satisfaction or settlement of such complaints. This scheme is applicable to all commercial banks and scheduled co-operative banks operating in India. The procedure for redressal starts with the lodgment of a complaint. Any person who has a grievance against a bank may make a complaint in writing to the Banking Ombudsmen either by himself or through his authorized agent. On receipt of the complaint as well as the information from the bank concerned, the Banking Ombudsmen shall try to promote a settlement of the complaint by means of an agreement between the complainant and the bank through conciliation or mediation. The concept of Ombudsmen is gaining important and it is indeed a land mark event in the history of Indian banking. Against this background the researchers considered Ombudsmen scheme to be an important variable.

Insurance Products

Customers are being provided with additional delivery channels which are more convenient to customers and are cost effective to the banks. Commercial banks in association with insurance companies offer insurance products to its customers. It offers personal accident insurance cover, house-hold articles, jewelry, cash and other valuable covered against fire, robbery, flood, riots, medical insurance product with cash less hospitalization and cash payment to meet incidental expenses, travel insurance, burglary, fire etc. This facility is also becoming immensely popular among the customers and has been given due importance in this study.

Investment and Financial Advisory Services

Financial advisory services or personal finance solutions are provided by commercial bank to its customers. Through financial advisory services banks understand the investment requirements of their customers and design tailor-made financial solutions. Beyond merely advising the customers, the banks also help to invest in a variety of instruments including mutual funds, RBI bonds, bonds of financial institutions, fixed deposits, insurance products, capital gain tax saving bonds etc. The banks also supply daily and weekly market roundups and quarterly newsletters to its customers. This is an innovative scheme introduced by commercial banks and the researchers considered an important variable for study.

Electronic Fund Transfer

RBI started Electronic Fund Transfer (EFT) system in 1996. The system facilitated transfer of funds from one center to another across banks. The advantage of this system is that it facilitates transfer of funds on the day next to the day of transfer. At present an upper limit of Rs. 25,000 has been set for individual transaction. This is also considered an important variable for study by the researchers.

(II) Measurement of Level of Satisfaction on Banking Services

For measuring the level of satisfaction of customers on various banking services, Ten variables were identified by the researchers. Five variables were selected from Five variables were selected from Table 1, which discloses the awareness level of customers on new banking services. The variables ranked 1 to 5 in Table 1 were selected. Five other variables were selected from traditional functions and customer facilities provided by commercial banks to attract and retain customers.

Variables ranked 1st to 5th in Table 1 are (1) ATM facility, (2) Bill payment, (3) Financial and Investment Services, (4) Credit Card and (5) Insurance products. Five other variables selected by the researchers for measuring the level of satisfaction are (1) Loan Processing Period (2) Cheque Processing Period (3) Employees Attitude, (4) Customer Conveniences and (5) Employee-Customer Relationship.

The customers of selected banks were required to indicate their level of satisfaction they derived from each variables. The customers expressed their level of satisfaction by stating as 'Excellent', 'Good', 'Satisfactory', 'Unsatisfactory' and 'No opinion'.

Traditional Functions and Customer Facilities

Loan Processing Period

The second important traditional function of a bank is advancing of loans to its customers. Loan processing period refers to the period taken by a bank for sanctioning loans. The period taken for sanction of loans vary from bank to bank depends on the nature of loan, nature of securities offered, formalities and documents required etc. Customers expect a quick sanction. But the bank need a reasonable time for sanction due to the procedural formalities. Undue delay in sanction of loans compels the borrower to follow up the loan application with frequent visits to the bank. Timely sanction of loan is considered to as an important variable for measuring the customer satisfaction.

Cheque Processing Period

The commercial banks today enjoy the privilege of printing money in the form of cheques. The cheque currency is very popular in all places of commercial importance. In modern business world, the use of cheque to settle debts is found to be more convenient than the use of cash. A banker has an obligation to clear the cheque submitted by a customer with in a reasonable time. The variable 'cheque processing period' represent the time taken by the banker to clear the cheque submitted by a customer. Generally bankers take relatively some time for clearing the outstation cheques, but the customer expects a quick clearance. It is against this background the researchers found that this variable is considered to be an important one for evaluating the customer satisfaction.

Attitude of the Employees

Every employee of a bank has a significant role to play in the success of the banking business. The attitude of the employees towards the functioning of the bank becomes very essential to attract new customers, to retain existing customers and to create a goodwill about the bank in the minds of the customers. The integrity, punctuality, loyalty and the way of behaving to the customers is great significance in the present competitive world. Hence this variable is given due importance by the researchers for measuring the customer satisfaction.

Customer Conveniences

The customers of the bank needs some minimum facilities at the bank premises at the time of availing banking service. These facilities are sufficient seating arrangements, furniture, pens, pins, drinking water facility, parking facility of vehicles, toilet facility, lighting facility, cleanliness etc. By providing these facilities customers can transact their business with out any discomfort. Customer convenience facility is considered an important variable by the researchers for measuring the customer satisfaction.

Employee-Customer Relationship

Today, the objective of a bank is to attract and retain large customer base. This object can be attained only maintaining a good customer relationship management, which implies the art of attracting, maintaining and enhancing customer relationships. Maintaining long term customer relationship is possible only by offering innovative and quality services to its customers. The researchers identified this variable an important one for the growth of the banking industry and hence due importance is give for analysis.

Distribution of Respondents According to the Level of Awareness of New Banking Services

The awareness level of customers about different banking services is ranked and depicted in Table 1.

From Table 1 it is clear that the customers of UTI Bank and Federal Bank are equally aware about "ATM facility" and ranked first. The second rank for awareness goes to customers of SBI and third to SBT. The survey further reveals that customers of new generation banks and private banks were more aware about ATM facility than the customers of nationalized banks. The awareness of customers about "Tele-Banking" facility, the table shows that the customers of UTI Bank have the highest level of awareness followed by Federal Bank. SBI get rank number 3 and the least rank for awareness goes to SBT.

The Table 1 further depicts the opinion of customers of selected banks about "Internet Banking". The customers of UTI Bank to a great extent are aware about this facility. Second rank for awareness of internet banking goes to customers of Federal Bank. But the customers of SBI and SBT are not well aware about this innovative facility. Regarding "Credit Cards" the customers of Federal Bank and SBI ranks first and second respectively for awareness. The customers of SBT are least aware about this service. It is clear from the table that the customers of all the selected banks are not well aware about the facility of "Mobile banking".

Table 1
Awareness Level of Customers on New Banking Services

Banking Services	*State Bank of India*		*State Bank Travancore*		*Federal of Bank*		*UTI Bank*		*Total Score*
	Total	*Rank*	*Total Score*	*Rank*	*Total Score*	*Rank*	*Total Score*	*Rank*	*Rank*
ATM Facility	28	II	27	III	30	1	30	I	115(1)
Tele-Banking	12	III	11	IV	21	II	22	I	66(8)
Internet Banking	11	III	11	III	15	II	21	I	58(9)
Credit Cards	20	II	12	III	24	I	20	II	76(4)
Mobile Banking	6	III	5	IV	11	II	16	I	38(10)
Bill Payments	18	III	13	I	27	I	25	II	83 (2)
Banking Ombudsmen	15	III	13	IV	18	II	21	I	67(7)
Insurance Products	22	I	16	III	18	II	I8	II	74(5)
Investment & Financial services	22	II	11	IV	19	III	25	I	77(3)
Electronic Fund Transfer	15	III	12	IV	20	II	22	I	69(6)

Source: Primary Data.

The awareness level of customers regarding the "Payment of various utility bills" the customers of Federal Bank ranked first for awareness. The second rank for awareness goes to the customers of UTI and the third rank to SBI. The customers of SBT are least aware about this facility.

Table 1 further indicates the awareness of customers about the grievances and redressal mechanism. It is observed that customers of all banks are least aware about the "Banking Ombudsmen scheme". The awareness of customers about "Insurance products", the table shows that the customers of SBI have the highest level of awareness followed by customers of Federal Bank and UTI Bank. The least rank for awareness goes to SBT. Regarding "Investment and Financial Services" customers of UTI Bank and SBI are more aware than the customers of Federal Bank and SBT. The table further reveals the degree of awareness of customers about "Electronic Fund Transfer". The study discloses highest degree of awareness of customers about this facility goes to UTI Bank and second place to Federal Bank. The lowest degree of awareness goes to SBT.

The awareness level of customers about banking services, it is clear from Table 1 that the variable 'ATM' facility obtained a good response from customers and ranked first. The customers of both public sector and private sector banks are well aware about this facility. 'Bill payments' ranked second also attracted a good number of customers due to its high level of awareness. The third rank for awareness of new banking services goes to the variable 'Financial and Investment Services'. Variables viz. 'Credit Card' and 'Insurance Products' ranked fourth and fifth. 'Banking Ombudsmen' ranks Seventh and 'Electronic Fund Transfer' ranks Sixth due to the general ignorance about the services offered by the banks. 'Telebanking' (ranks 8th) 'Internet Banking' (ranks 9th) and 'Mobile Banking' (ranks 10th), also attracted only limited number of customers due to the low level of awareness of customers about these services.

Distribution of Respondents According to the Degree of Level of Satisfaction of Customers on Various Banking Services

For measuring the level of satisfaction of customers on various banking services ten variables were identified by the researchers. The responses of the sample customers of the selected banks on each variable were shown in Table 2.

Table 2 reveals that banking services introduced since globalization, it is noted that all sample customers were expressed their level of satisfaction relating to the variable like 'ATM'. All customers also expressed their satisfaction level on banking services like 'Loan processing', 'Employees attitude', and 'Employee-Customer Relationship'. Out of 60 sample customers 28 have ranked the variables viz. 'ATM excellent',13 as good and 7 as satisfactory and 12 as unsatisfactory. Regarding 'Employees attitude' the scores are 27,16,11 and 6 and for 'Loan Processing' these numbers are 25,13,9 and 13. Out of 60 customers 19 have no opinion on 'Credit Card' and 18 expressed excellent and 10 as good. The variable namely ' Bill Payment', 18 customers have no response while 17 expressed it as excellent. Twenty customers ranked the variable 'Insurance Products' as excellent and 11 have no opinion.

Table 2 further reveals Sixteen customers have no opinion on the variable 'Investment and Financial Services' due to the low level of awareness. Another variable 'Cheque Processing' have opined by 53 customers (24 expressed as excellent and 14 as good). 'Employee Customer Relationship' also received a good response 22 expressed as excellent and 14 as good.

Table 2
Variable Wise level of Satisfaction of Customers on various banking services

Variables	*Excellent*	*Good*	*Satis-factory*	*Unsatis-factory*	*No-opinion*	*Total Customers*
ATM	28	13	7	12	-	60
Bill Payment	17	12	9	4	18	60
Credit Card	18	10	7	6	19	60
Insurance Products	20	13	8	8	11	60
Investment and Financial Services	19	12	6	7	16	60
Loan Processing Period	25	13	9	13	-	60
Cheque Processing Period	24	14	10	5	7	60
Employees Attitude	27	16	11	6	-	60
Customer convenience	21	13	9	14	3	60
Employee- Customer Relationship	22	14	12	12	-	60

Source: Primary Data.

The survey further reveals that among the ten variables selected for the study the biggest number of respondents expressed the variable as excellent are ATM Facility (28), Employees attitude (27) and Loan processing period (25). Largest number of customers expressing no opinion are the variables like Credit card (19), Bill payment (18) and Investment and financial services (16). It may be due to the general level of ignorance of the customers about these services.

CALCULATION OF SATISFACTION INDEX

The customers of selected banks were required to indicate their level of satisfaction they derived from each variables selected by the researchers by stating 'excellent', 'good', 'satisfactory', 'unsatisfactory' and 'no opinion'. For the purpose of further analysis, these qualitative grades were converted into quantitative terms. Researchers allot '0' point for 'No Opinion', 1 point for 'Unsatisfactory', 4 points for 'Satisfactory', 6 points for 'Good' and 8 points for 'Excellent'. These values when multiplied by the respective frequencies would give the total satisfaction and the same divided by total frequencies would give the Total Satisfaction Index.

Distribution of Respondents According to Variable Wise Level of Satisfaction, Satisfaction Index and their Positional Rank.

Table 3 depicts the variable wise Satisfaction Index and their Positional Ranks.

Table 3
Variable Wise Satisfaction Index and Their Positional Rank

Variables	*TotalScore of Satisfaction*	*Satisfaction Index*	*Positional Rank*
ATM	342	5.70	2
Bill Payment	248	4.13	9
Credit Card	238	3.97	10
Insurance Products	278	4.63	7
Investment and financial Services	255	4.25	8
Loan Processing Period	327	5.45	3
Cheque Processing Period	321	5.35	4
Employees Attitude	362	6.03	1
Customer Convenience	296	4.93	6
Employee-Customer Relationship	320	5.33	5

Source: Primary Data.

The satisfaction index (Table 3) of the variable 'Employees Attitude' work out to 6.03 and received first rank. During survey a good number of respondents opinioned specifically about the changes in the attitude of employees of the banks due to financial sector reforms and the entry of new generation banks foreign banks. The second rank for satisfaction index goes to the variable 'ATM' and third rank to 'Loan Processing Period'. Regarding 'Cheque processing period, customers give fourth positional rank. 'Employee customer relationship' ranked 5th and 'Customer Convenience' ranked 6th.

The Table further depicts that of the five new services selected for study, ATM attracted a good number of customers and the remaining four variables received only a low response. 'Insurance Products' (rank 7th) 'Investment and Financial Services' (8th rank) and 'Bill Payment' (9th rank) do not attract customers due to the general level of ignorance about the services offered by the banks or due to the non-availability of services in certain banks. The variable 'Credit Card' (10th rank) attracted only limited number of customers due to non-availability of the service in the bank or fear of service charges, hidden charges etc.

It is observed from the study that a good number of customers of banks in Kollam city are ignorant about the new services/products provided by the bank to its customers as result of the financial sector reforms. Banks are not spending much time for educating and popularizing these products to their customers. Some of the customers having little awareness about the products ignorant about the features, merits or benefits of the facility.

It is noted that bank staff of the public sector banks have little contact with its customers when compared to the new generation and private sector banks. Majority of the customers are satisfied about the cheque clearance facility and employees attitude. A section of the customers are not satisfied about the banker customer relationship and existing customer convenience facilities in the selected banks especially vehicle parking, drinking water facility, stationery etc. Delay in sanction of loan is also opined by the customers.

SUGGESTIONS

While keeping in view the forgoing findings of the study, certain suggestions are made by the researchers which would be useful for bankers and policy makers.

The customers of new generation banks and old private sectors banks are fully satisfied about the ATM facility. But the customers of nationalized banks are not fully satisfied about this facility because they are not having the facility of deposit of cash and cheque through ATMs. By providing these facilities banks can attract more customers and would increase the scope for better utilization of banking services.

To give an awareness to the customers about new banking services and new products, it is advisable to conduct customers meet or customer relationship programmes periodically, in which they can directly interact with their customers and to educate and illustrate them about their new products and services. Besides the employees of the bank have to take the initiative of informing the customer regarding the new schemes even though the customer does not inquire.

Many customers are ignorant and fear about the interest rate, bank charges, service charges etc. applicable to the new services offered by the bank to its customers. Before launching a new service or product the banks should give necessary information to their prospective customers regarding the specialties, and benefit of the scheme to its customers, charges applicable etc. by sending brochures to their customers and by putting details on the notice board at prominent places in the bank.

In a competitive business environment in order to widen and retain the customer base, the banks should initiate steps to improve the personal contacts with their customers. The banks must concentrate on the quality of personnel and its continuos development.

In nationalized banks some customers are concerned about the delay and keep standing in queue during peak hours for deposit and withdrawal of money. It is advisable for the banks to practice the customers to use compulsorily the ATMs for withdrawal of money up to a certain limit.

CONCLUSION

The study reveals that the strategies followed by the Indian banks are still inadequate and not obtained the expected results. Further research studies in this direction will definitely identify the correct causes for low level of awareness and poor satisfaction of the banking services. The systematic planning and introduction of customer oriented and customized products and services by the Indian banks will help them to compete and succeed in the competitive banking scenario.

REFERNCES

Banking Statistics for Kerala, "State Level Bankers Committee", Canara Bank, Thiruvananthapuram.

Dr. Benson Kunjukunju and Dr. S. Mohan (2002), "Institutional Finance and Rural Development", New Century Publications, New Delhi.

Economic Review (2004), "Kerala State Planning Board", Thiruvananthapuram.

Gordon, E. (Prof.) and Dr. K. Natarajan (2003), "Banking Theory and Practice", Himalaya Publishing House, Mumbai.

Maheshwari S.N. and Dr. R.R. Paul (2000), "Banking Theory Law and Practice", Kalyani Publishers, New Delhi.

Sathya Swaroop Deasish (2003), "Service Quality in Commercial Indian Banks in Delhi", *Indian Journal of Marketing*, pp. 41-50.

Selected Websites

www. sbi.co.in.

www. rbi.org.in.

www. utibank.com.

www. federalbank. co. in.

Name of the Bank Branches Selected for the Study

State Bank of Travancore, Kilikollur.

State Bank of India, Kollam.

Federal Bank, Kollam.

UTI Bank, Kollam.

AGRICULTURE–INDIA'S BACKBONE INDUSTRY AND ITS PLIGHT IN THE WAKE OF GLOBALISATION

*Ms. Pushap, P.**

India has been a land of AGRI+CULTURE, for agriculture has been part and parcel of Indian Culture since ages. Agriculture, farmers and India grow together owing to multifaceted link and interlink. Not a day goes by in the life of 1 BILLION Indians without an agriculture product being consumed–be its original raw material or the so called, fashionable processed foods of RTE, RTU, RTC, RTS (Ready–To–Eat/Use/Cook/ Serve) forms which are the order of the day for millions of working women as well as high income group families. " Eat–to–Live/Live to Eat" we survive and upkeep our growth and maintenance by the farmers' produce and our existence is unimaginable without this sector. 72% of our population is involved directly or indirectly in this noble profession of "producing for someone unable to produce for himself/ herself."

India has been an agrarian economy, for its contribution to our GDP is highest among all sectors of growth and employs huge number of people being the number ONE employment creator of India. Indian farmers are "sons of soil" who toil in the land and sun to protect the growth of not only our population, but also other sectors of India by providing necessary raw materials. Today Indian agriculture sector has come a very long way from the ship-to-mouth scenario of 1960s to self sufficiency, food security with adequate buffer stock to export of food grains scenario.

Having crossed these milestones of TRANSITION, the globalization of business trade in the last decade of the 20th century with the international mantras of World Trade Organization (WTO), General Agreement on Trade Related Services (GATS), Trade Related Intellectual Property Right (TRIPS) to Doha talks in 2001 created unprecedented

* Selection Grade Lecturer, Department of Nutrition and Dietetics, Seethalakshmi Ramaswami College, Trichy, Tamil Nadu.

demand in all sectors of trade including agriculture. There are voices of experts and economists that manufacturing and services sectors are the boom sectors of globalization impact while the largest sector of the world agriculture is the worst hit sector. Experts are of view that these international mantras being enforced by the developed countries to free the clutches of poverty and struggle of world farmers including India seem to be moving in the opposite direction. For, today the drivers of global agriculture are the strong forces of the international market, global agreement on agriculture, free trade, subsidy rationalization and so on. After 11-15 years of global free trade, voices across the world including developed nations accuse these mantras of developed nations for the deterioration of agriculture sector of Least Developed Countries (LDCs) and Developing Countries (DCs) including India–the largest player in agriculture sector of the world. Voices accuse the tactics of rich countries like USA and EU to dominate the LDCs and DCs, for agricultural policies of LDCs and DCs are fabricated in such a way to meet global challenges of WTO. Unable to withstand it, poor countries started suffering as they couldnot export the farm products either due import of products at much cheaper rate than their native rate (remember Vidharba's Cotton episode?) or due to domination of multinational companies (MNCs) in poor countries. On the other side rich nations are restricting the import from LDCs and DCs raising the issues of Human Rights, meagre labour welfare measures, phytosanitary qualities, poverty, quality standards, child labour in production process etc. Due to these anti poor strategies, in the last few years of the 21st century farmers have begun to feel the heat of liberalization trade and its challenges thrown by WTO regime of rich nations.

Indian farmers' plight never reached the mass of Indians as it happened now for a change. Almost all media–TV, National News Papers, Journals, National Forums and apex bodies of India–Supreme Court, Parliament and Legislatives portrayed the plight and sad end of "sons of soil" of India. There are villagers ready to sell their villages in the utmost distress. It is pertinent to point out here that though there are claims that the manufacturing and services sectors have boosted Indian economy, they do not touch the entire national population directly as agriculture sector does it.

After 11-15 years of transitional journey through the roads of international mantras it looks as if the agriculture sector of India is in a turmoil, for even India's apex forums represented by custodians of Indians endorsed the 100s and 1000s of farmer suicides since 2001 especially due to mounting debt in the hands of private money lenders in the absence of institutional credit facilities. As our farmers are sons of soil utilizing maximum land under cultivation to feed us all, it is our earnest duty to traceout the reason and causes for the present plight of farmers so as to lend our soothing hands to revitalize and rejuvenate them by reverting their plight. This paper is a small attempt in that direction.

OBJECTIVES

As objectives guide us in the right path of analysis, the following were the objectives put forth.

1. To traceout the role of Indian agriculture sector as a multifaceted industry of Indian Economy.
2. To know about its role in helping India to ensure macro and micro level food security to its people.
3. To findout whether Indian agriculture sector has augmented the goodies of WTO's free trade regime since its inception in 1995 and if so how far it has reaped the benefits.
4. If India has failed to do it, what are the crisis it has put through.
5. To highlight the status of Indian agriculture sector and farmer in the 21st century.

METHODOLOGY

Data, information and facts projected in the mass media–books, journal, national news paper, national seminars, TV as well as in the apex forums of India have been used to analyse the trends of past and present scenario of Indian agriculture sector and its status in the 21st century. Secondary data obtained were treated with suitable, simple statistical tools to give the results or interpreted with personal views and personal field exposure to arrive at consensus. This paper has been divided into 3 part–first one deals about Indian Agriculture sector's multifaceted role in our national economy. Second on the plight of agriculture including India in comparison with select other world countries and the CRUX of the paper– the plight of Indian agriculture and farmers today in the last part.

I. INDIAN AGRICULTURE SECTOR–MULTIFACETED INDUSTRY OF INDIAN ECONOMY

In countries like India agriculture has been and will continue to be the lifeline of the Indian Economy owing to its multivaried role as is evident from the below given illustration.

Illustration I
INDIAN AGRICULTURE–MULTIFACETED INDUSTRTY

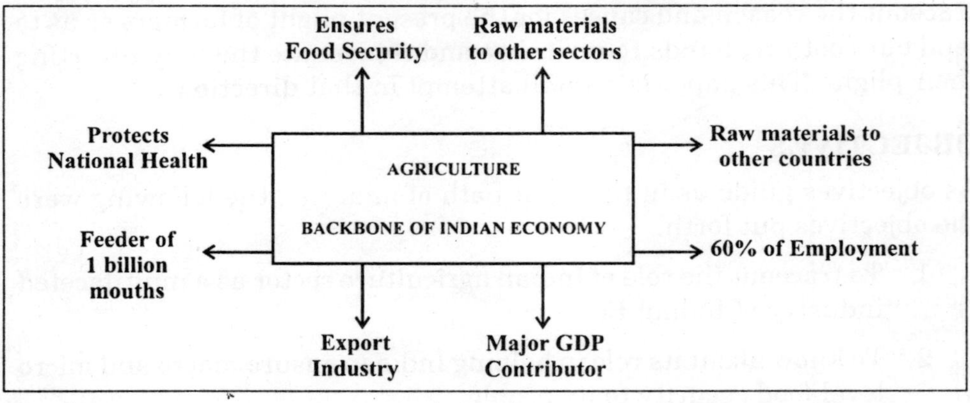

Indian agriculture being nick named 'BACKBONE" industry of Indian economy is apt as is evident from the above given illustration. It is the biggest sector with maximum contribution to national GDP, the largest private enterprise of employment in India. Its contribution to national GDP is one fourth today (decline is another story dealt in later analysis) and sustains the livelihood of about 2/3rd of its population. The below given Tables 1 & 2 justify these facts.

The two tables bring to limelight 2 contrast facts that is at one hand the trend of Indian Agriculture sector's contribution to national

Table 1
Indian Agriculture and National GDP

Years	*% Contribution to National GDP*
1950-60	56.0
1960-70	47.8
1970-80	42.8
1980-90	36.4
1990-01	28.6
2001-02	26.0
2002-03	24.5
2003-04	26.0
2004-05	23.0

Source: Dhingra, I.C., (2006).

GDP is on the decline from 60% in 1950s to. 23-26% in 2000s. Experts like Mishra, S.K., Puri, V.K (2006) and Swaminathan, M.S. (2005) are of opinion that in countries like India, for sustainable growth agriculture industry should not be sidelined, for the share of agriculture in national income is often taken as indicator of economic development not only due to its share in GDP but due to its multivaried role in touching 1 Billion population interms of employment, food and nutrition security and resultant health status of Indians and so on. They are of view that unless it gets reverted, the repercussions would be severe on the economy of India and may jeopardise our state of economy. Table 2 projects a contrast fact, for though there is decline in agriculture sector's share to GDP its employment share in total number of worker has been on the upward trend since 1957 ie from 19.7% in 1951 to 1/4th total employment scenario today. As per India year book 2002 by Hindu, agriculture sector employs maximum of 237 million workers of the 397 million total employment potential of India. Of the 397 million employed in organized and unorganized sector, only 28 million are in the organized sector while the huge junk of 369 million are in unorganized sector, of which 237 millions (64%) find employment in agriculture and allied activities as is evident from the below furnished Table 3.

Table 2
Proportion of Agricultural Labour to Total Number of Workers

Years	*% in Total Work force*
1951	19.7
1971	26.33
1981	26.15
1991	26.20
2001	26.09

Source: Dhingra, C.I. (2006).

Table 3
Indian Agriculture Sector and Employment Potential

Industry	*No. of Workers employed (in Millions)*	*% Share*
Agriculture	237.56	59.84
Mining and quarrying	2.27	0.57
Manufacturing	48.01	12.09
Electricity, gas, water supply	1.28	0.32
Construction	17.62	4.45
Trade	37.32	9.40
Financial Services	5.05	1.27
Transport, storage andCommunication	14.65	3.70
Community, social and Personal Services	33.20	8.36
Total Employment	397.00	100.00

Source: India Book of year 2002 by Hindu.

The above table endorses the fact that agriculture sector of India is he prime industry with huge employment potential among all sectors.

As per Swaminathan, M.S. (2005) agriculture sector of India continues to provide employment to millions and also supplies raw materials to various types of industries in India and abroad. The sustainability of agriculture is thus vital for the growth and development of various sector in India. Same view has been expressed by Mishra, S.K. and Mishra, S. (2001). As per National Sample Survey Organization (NSSO) report of 1999-2000, this sector enjoys the status of biggest employment provider. Thus it is apt and not exaggeration that agriculture sector is the backbone industry of India, for employment is the CRUX of all parameters of national economy and growth.

Another worth while role of agriculture is its sole role in ensuring food and nutrition security and thus the health security to Indians. It is the impound duty of our country to feed the population by ensuring adequate food to eat, for that is one of the most vital Fundamental Human Rights as per our constitution. In this mission of India, our farmers and agriculture sector have been on pace with our population growth since 1960s eventhough we had to import a bit of food grains now and then owing to decline in production as is obvious from the below given Table 4.

Table 4
India's Food Grain Scenario Over the Years

Year	*Area(million hectares)*	*Production in million metric tonnes*
1950-51	97.32	50.52
1960-61	115.58	82.02
1970-71	124.32	108.42
1980-81	126.67	129.59
1990-91	127.84	176.39
2000-01	119.80	196.10
2001-02	121.90	212.00
2002-03	111.50	184.10
2003-04	124.20	212.00
2004-05	–	206.50

Source: Dhingra, I.C. (2006).

It is obvious that Indian food grain production has been on a steady increase with declining trend now and then owing to drought. Out of 304.2 million hectare, 170 million hectares is under cultivation (56%) and compares very well with world average's 32%, USA's 40% and Brazil's 10%. Though we compare well in this parameter, our per capita availability of land is highly insignificant ie 0.40 hectare compared to 54.62 in Australia, 42.85 in Canada and 4.32 in USA. Inspite of it, our agriculture sector is the mainstay of our economy and employment as seen already. Not only that, India has also reached world class level in the 21st century in its food production from its ship-to-mouth scenario of 1960s as is crystal clear from the below furnished table.

Table 5
India's Food Production and Global Rank in the 21st Century

Food Product	*Production in Million Tonnes*	*Status at Global Level*
Foodgrains	210	III
Fruits and Vegetables	150	II
Milk	91	Highest
Tea	820	Highest

Source: Association of Food Scientists & Technologists (India) 2005.

Cashew & Coconut	–	I Largest
Sugar & Fish	–	II Largest
Tobacco and rice	–	III Largest
Coffee	–	VII Largest
Pulses	–	I
Oilseeds	–	V
Cotton	–	IV
Jute	–	I

Source: Ramkishen, Y. (2004) & Dhingra, I.C. (2006).

As per Association of Food Scientists & Technologists (India) 2005 India ranks III, II and Highest at the world level in food grains, fruits and vegetables and milk and tea production utislising184 million hectares of cultivated land. In the opinion of Ramkishen, Y. (2004) India is I, II and III largest producer of coconut+cashew nut, sugar+fish and tobacco+ rice. From import level in 1960s to world ranking scenario of our agriculture growth speaks volume about its tremendous growth rate. The unstinted effort and manual labour put in by our farmers has to be duly acknowledged with pride at this juncture. In the opinion of our scientist turned President Abdul Kalam, A.B.J., (1998) India's projected house hold demand for future food production in tune with anticipated population growth is going to be yet another new challenge confronting our agriculture sector and is projected in the below given table.

It is to be pointed out that India's population at the current annual growth rate of 1.7% with 3.2 Fertility Rate would be 120 crores and 135-140 crores in 2010 and 2020 respectively and would become no. I populated country superseding China (its FR is 1.2 now). With India's world class current status in agriculture production (Table 5) our president is optimistic that the increased demand of 2010 and 2020 though a challenge, our farmers are exceptionally entrepreneurial and would prove it as they did it again and again in times of crisis. With available necessary technology we can meet the challenge or we are capable of developing such technologies is his view. Such is our agriculture industry's potential in upholding the economy of our country through noble profession though unfortunately an unorganized sector inspite of its huge employment potential.

Table 6
India's Projected Household Demand for Food

Food Products	*Actual Household Demand in million metric tonnes*	
	2010	*2020*
Foodgrains	266.4	343.0
Milk	153.1	270.0
Edible Oil	9.4	13.0
Vegetables	117.2	168.0
Fruits	42.4	81.0
Meal, Fish, eggs	12.7	27.0
Sugar	17.3	22.0

Source: Abdul Kalam, A.B.J., Vision, 2020 (1998).

Thus from the 1960s' food import scenario to food grain self sufficiency status of 1970s and 1980s to self sufficiency with adequate buffer stock and export scenario of 2000s, Indian agriculture sector has crossed many milestones in its growth journey. Today India enjoys food security at National level owing to this tremendous growth trajectories of agriculture industry. At this juncture, it is necessary to bring it to limelight the hardwork put in by farm community of India who help the nation in this mission of ensuring food and nutrition security to its citizens. As per Ramkishen, Y. (2006) Per Capita Food Availability (PCFA) of our country increased from 350 gm in 1951 to about 500 gm today. It speaks volume about the role of agriculture sector in ensuring food security– the basic FHRs. From the facts analysed so far in a nutshell, the inevitable role of agriculture sector and our farmers deserve to be right royally declared as "multifaceted industry" in the complex Indian economy.

Does it mean India is free of malnutrition problem owing to macro food security? No.! It does face persistant malnutrition problems inspite of national food security position. Who to be blamed for such a scenario? Agriculture sector? Farmers? or others? A quick peep into it to find out the causes for our mal nutrition profile is inevitable here.

INDIA'S PERSISTANT MALNUTRITION PROBLEM–WHO TO BE BLAMED?

Inspite of India's food security at macro level, its mal nutrition scenario is yet a curse on the shining face of India owing to multivaried causes such as population explosion, poverty, unemployment, Per Capita Low Income (PCI), Per Capita Monthly Expenditure (PCME) and Per Capita Food Availability (PCFA) resulting in hunger, starvation and malnutrition. It is aptly putforth by our president Abdul Kalam A. B.J. (2006). "SO LONG THERE IS POVERTY, THERE WILL BE SOME SORT OF TERRORISM," for poverty, hunger and starvation are terrorism against human mankind in the opinion of UNO.

Malnutrition in India is an evil child of poverty, unemployment, reduced Per Capita Income (PCI), Per Capita Monthly Expenditure (PCME) and the resultant food insecurity at Micro level. The below given table depicts the malnutrition profile of India in a nutshell.

Table 7
Nutrition & Health Status of Indians

Mal Nutrition / Health Problem	*Prevalance* *Nin 1999*	*NFHS 1998-99*
PRESCHOOL CHILDREN		
Protein Energy Mal nutrition	30%	–
Bitot's Spot	3%	–
Iron deficiency anaemia	50%	74.3%
Under weight (Wt for age)	53%	47.0%
Stunted growth (Ht for age)	65%	45.5%
ADULTS		
Chronic Energy malnutrition	50%	35.8% (women)
Anaemia general Population	50%	51.8% (women)
Anaemic Pregnant Women	70-90%	–

Source: NIN Manual 1999, NFHS Report, 1998-99.

The above table reveals the wide prevalence of malnutrition in India. Not only this, experts like Sainath, P. (2005), Das, P. (2004), Bang, A. (2005), Menon, P. (2004), Badavam, L. (2005) and Katakam, A. (2005) brought to lime light 100s and 1000s of death of children due to malnutrition related issues in India. Amidst plenty of food grain production and macro food security why this grim scenario? Experts like Swaminathan, M.S. (2005) and Indian organizations like NIN and NNMB revealed the causes of malnutrition in India as poor PCI, reduced PCME and PCFA, corruption in PDS and lower wages. It is pertinent to pointout here that as per NSSO report 2004, the PCME is Rs. 565 and Rs. 1500 for rural and urban poor households and with monthly expenditure of this meagre amount no wonder that the malnutrition profile of India is highly unsatisfactory.

The CRUX of these views and facts have been endorsed by our supreme court in a historical verdict as early as 2001 a year which witnessed many starvation deaths in Orissa, Andra Pradesh and Maharastra due to poor purchasing power inspite of 50 million tones of food grains being stocked in godown. Verdict "mountains of grains Vs oceans of hunger" goes this way–even if the food grain had to be given free, it should be done as no person should be deprived of food merely because he/she has no money, for the constitution assures "right to life" to all irrespective of any discrimination including economic condition. Abdul Kalam, A.B.J. (1999) stresses the fact that the unfortunates who died and die of starvation are not victims of underproduction but of circumstances and poor administration response and not because the country does not have the food to feed them.

All these facts focus only tip of the iceberg situation of India's malnutrition profile. Thus in the eyes of experts the malnutrition problem though agriculture and food production related, neither farmers nor Indian agriculture sector to be made responsible for this ugly state of affair, for they have done their share with utmost concern. From ship-to-mouth food scenario of 1960s our Agriculture sector reaped tremendous production over the past 3 decades and now is confronted with excess of food stock, bulging warehouses with gigantic unsold stock of 60 million tonnes, rotting of grains etc. Amidst such a scenario, periodic reports of starvation death does not hold good for a democratic country like India.

WTO AND INTERNATIONAL AGRICULTURE TRADE

With the wake of WTO on Jan. 1, 1995 Liberalisation, Privativation and Globalisation (LPG) have come to occupy the buzzwords in all walks of life in the international arena. We are told constantly that the only path to prosperity and economic development in LDCs and DCs is by adhearing to free market principle so as to lift the poverty stricken population of the world. Today LPG mantra is seen as a pathway to speedy economic transition to the status of developed economy and is seen synonymously as "DEVELOPMENT & PROSPERITY." Since WTO's 1995 regime agriculture–that is nothing to do with trade got pushed compulsorily on the list of international free trade and the rules like the pattern of investment a country should pursue, the type of technology and services it must promote, the agriculture support it has to maintain, the patent system it must implement, the plant protection regime it has to adopt etc are dictated by developed nations through WTO.

In the initial stages without knowing the repercussions LPG, TRIPS, GATS, WTO–all attracted enormous interest during 1990s. But currently these are on the centre of heated debate about their possible benefits, costs and impacts particularly in LDCs and DCs. Amidst this scenario there are voices in the international arena from economists, experts and well wishers of developed nations like Madeley, J. (2005) Ha-joon-chang (2005), Monbiot, G. (2005), Jan Pronk (2005), Hiddleston, S. (2005) and Geldof, M.R. (2005) that WTO and Millennium Development Goals–2015, GATS, TRIPS are impoverishing millions, makes matter worse, slows down world's economic growth, increased inequality, unemployment, poverty, gap between haves and have-nots, exploitation of poor countries by rich nations in the name of trade and aid and to top it, it has resulted in cheap food import from rich countries and driven many farmers in LDCs and DCs into "BANKRUPTCY". 11 years of free trade policies instead of improving the economic state of LDCs & DCs only worsened the matter. These accusing voices could be better understood from the below given 3 case studies of agriculture scenario in a nutshell in the LDCs and DCs of the world.

CASE I **:** World Bank and International Monetary Fund have made lending to GHANA on condition of opening up its agriculture market for free trade but after few years of doing so, now Ghana's domestic rice production is collapsed unable to withstand the cheaper global price. Now US provides 40% of Ghana's rice import is the story of Ghana. (Madeley, J. and Monbiot, G. (2005).

***CASE II*:** According to Gresser, E. (2006) American tariffs on goods from LDCs and DCs of Asia are 10-25 times higher than those imposed on rich countries. Also European tariffs and subsidies exclude farm product produced in the middle east, Latin America and Asia from the market. To quote–"Morocco and Tunisia Olive-Orchard managers make the world's best extra virgin olive oil, but EU olive oil subsidies pay Spanish,Greek and Italian growers $2.5 billion per year to produce more than DOUBLE the value of world's olive oil trade and has resulted virtually in no Moroccan/Tunisian olive oil in American super market.

***CASE III*:** As per Chowdry , A (2006) cotton is a critical crop in many African nations especially Benin, Burkina, Faso, Chad and Mali all countries classified as LDCs.But the ability of these producers to reach the US market is hampered by massive subsidies and domestic support prices for US cotton production reported to be $4.2 billion in a year.

Though the US has committed to ending cotton export subsidies by the end of 2006, it would be very small in comparison with support in the form of domestic subsidies.

From the foregone case studies by experts it is clear that the LDCs and DCs are exploited by developed countries in the name of free trade. Rajagopal, B. (2006) has expressed that WTO is pro rich and no longer represents poor or developing countries; its rules force third world countries into unfair global economy; rich countries also refused full market access to the poor countries in order to protect their domestic farmers and industries as a result much bigger issues for developing countries are not even touched. This statement speaks about the dual role of WTO and rich nations.

WTO AND INDIAN AGRARIAN CRISIS

Anti WTO voices are also raised and heard in Indian subcontinent especially about the plight of Indian Agriculture sector (IAS). Ramkishen, Y. (2004) feels that India is challenged to face the provision of WTO agreement on its agriculture sector and will face challenge in loosing patents on agri products (Basmati and neem story), removal of meagre subsidy on crops and agri products.

IAS-SIDELINED IN THE GLOBALAISATION ERA

India has been a country of agrarian economy, for its contribution to nation's economy has been highest since 1950s. But with the wake of free trade since 1990s, it has been sidelined for its perceived limited impact and the booming impact of services sector on economic growth of India as is evident from the below furnished Table 8.

Table 8
Major Sectors of India and Their Share to Indian GDP

Sector	*Period*		
	1950s	*1990s*	*2000s*
Agriculture	60%	35%	24%
Manufacturing	–	–	19%
Services	–	–	57%

Source: Abdul Kalam's Vision 2020.

It is clear that the IAS-the life blood of India's GDP during 1950s has been shifted to the insignificant position in the free trade era of 2000s. Experts are of opinion that 60-70% of work force is in IAS and economic development of other sectors do not allow a greater absorption of rural poor. Many Indians still survive as marginal or landless farmers and this problem requires special attention to have a balanced economy. It is pertinent to point out that inspite of IAS being sidelined, it still retains the position of large employment producer. Being so, what is its share from GDP to its progress? This fact is depicted in Table 9.

Table 9
GDP Share of India to Various Sectors

Sector	*% GDP Share*
Agriculture	3-4%
Education	4%
Health	1-2%
Telecom	16%

Source: Secondary.

The above table depicts the fact that the prime sector of India gets negligible share from GDP for its growth and development. An industry whose contribution to Indian population-46 telephone for every 1000 persons (Gurusamy, M 2006) gets 4 times greater GDP share than the sector which is lifeline for 60-70% of the population. Our agriculture minister voiced for this disparity and displeasure. Punnathara,C.J (2006) stresses the fact that over the past 1.5 decades services and industrial sectors of India have been amply rewarded for stimulating 8% growth. But 2/3rd of population continue to depend on agriculture and India to sustain its growth model, real and effective demand has to grow from agriculture sector. A recent news in THE HINDU (4/3/06) focused the concern of our Government of India in assuring larger investment to remove sluggish growth of manufacturing sector, for greater productivity of that sector seems to play a vital role in poverty eradication. Its unfortunate that 1000s of farm suicides could not fetch such a soothing concern from the caretaker to the agriculture sector.

Recently Davo's participants opined that the booming growth of India has been benefited most of the Indian economy namely IT, auto and ancillaries, pharmaceutical, ITES, metals, minerals, banking sector and textile sector which are seem to be the boom sectors today. Its unfortunate Davo's representatives forgot to mention the biggest sector of India– IAS. Can India survive with these boom sectors alone? This shows that how IAS is side lined in the free trade regime. It is high time of Indians to think about our life line sector with much concern.

Madaswamy (2002) aptly putforth that TRIPS agreement of WTO will have more disastrous effect on economy especially in the vital sector of agriculture. While Guruswamy, M. (2006) emphasized that though the share of agriculture to the GDP has been dropping steadily which is now pegged at 21.2%, it employs huge 255 millions of labour force. To reach DOUBLE DIGITS growth, agriculture has to grow at 4% by 2010 atleast. Acharya, K.V. (2006) stresses the fact that "there is no need for us to become globally competitive when the rural sector needs us here most".

CAN OUR COUNTRY SURVIVE WITH TWO SECTORS SIDELINING IAS?

In the opinion of many Indians including our president Abdul Kalam, A.B.J. (1998) the answer is NO! As per Chandrasekar, C.P. (2006) there is sharp variation in the growth rates between agriculture on the one hand and manufacturing and services are not able to offer employment that can draw the large number languishing in rural India and enable them to share the joys of urban buoyancy. According to him if income grew in these 2 sectors–employment stagnates or barely doing well and many are poor.

Our scientist president Abdul Kalam opines that India cannot hope to build its future on the manufacturing and services sector alone though they are and will be a major component of an economy. Also India can't afford not to build its strength in Agriculture, for reasons of multifaceted role in the complex economy of India. Nor can it afford the other 2 sectors' strength for reasons of economy and national security. The need of the hour for India is that the manufacturing and services sector if developed properly along with the backbone agriculture sector alone can ensure new jobs to more people leading to individual and national prosperity. Sainath, P (2005) vehemently expresses "a farmer can live without a HOUSE and a CAR. Can a HOUSE OWNER and a CAR owner of urban elite live without agricultural produce?" Its high time for the think–tank of India to think not globally but really.

Our finance minister justified this fact quoting "Urban English speaking middle class is not "ALL INDIA". India is Bihar, Orissa, Andrapradesh and others where people still are starving and committing suicide. He himself endorsed many a time that farm growth less than 4% would impede our target goal of 10% GDP and unless agriculture grows at 4% whatever combination and permutation we may try, we can not sustain 10% growth rate. Hussain, S. (2002) and Alexander, M.J. (2006) almost voice similarly saying ICT, BPO, Call centers, Premier educational institutions have not only begun to offer world class services but boosted high rate of exports, for as per world bank's July 2005 report India's economy has ranked as the world's 10th largest. Really a proud

India indeed! But with all these growing figures, are India's poor (30 crores) included in this changed and changing scenario? Unfortunately the answer is No! Behind the India's social Development Report 2005's 260 million BPL citizens, there are human faces, human pain and suffering and of that the lot could be agricultural farmers and labourers.

AGRARIAN CRISIS AND DECLINE IN EMPLOYMENT

Already it has been seen that agriculture tops the list of 'employment to total number of worker (Table 3) and still it retains its premier position amidst its decline to GDP share. But if we look at it in isolation current agrarian crisis has exerted negative impact on agricultural employment opportunity. As per Dr. Mahalingam, N (2005) in Tamilnadu alone 275.5 lakh persons are dependent on agriculture for sustenance but 200 lakhs people engaged in agriculture per year remain unemployed/ underemployed during most part of the year, for the available irrigated and rainfed agriculture land of 23.10 lakh and 35.82 hectares of land respectively are capable of providing sustainable employment to only 67.58 lakhs of people. Agro enterprises are the only priority in his view to be promoted in large number to process the agro products into Value Added Products (VAPs) to absorp this unemployed mass. It is pertinent to pointout AFST's (India) view that the boost in agriculture production has resulted in surplus and wastage yet our processing levels have remained low. Even in Philippines and China VAPs is 45% and 23% respectively where as we are way behind with a meagre 7% of value added food produce, where as our capacity in VAPs is capable of employing 13 million persons directly and 2.5 times indirectly of it. Thus employment potential due to VAPs is extremely larger compared to manufacturing sector as a whole. Realising this potential only the ministry of Food processing industry has a vision document aiming at DOUBLING and TREBLING the market size of food processing by 2009-13 and 2014-15 respectively.

At this point of current agrarian crisis this is a handy solution as per NATIONAL POLICY FOR FARMERS 2006 to be adopted in view of NCF's Report for India's 2 evils–POVERTY AND UNEMPLOYMENT are directly associated with agriculture sector. Lesser its GDP contribution greater would be the increase in these 2 evils and vice versa. Therefore VAP is an opportunity of TWO-IN-ONE, goody–good export opportunity to fetch dollars and sizeable employment generation especially to rural mass.

In the view of American President George W. Bush globalisation had resulted in people loosing jobs and is painful-said so during his recent visit to India. For this his mantra for India was to make people get educated to grab the 21st century's job potentials. 60-70% of Indians are agri based and will this mantra of American president suitable for India? What would happen to our agriculture? who will feed 1 billion mouths if it works out?. The repercussions would be unimaginable. Patnaik, U. (2005) emphasises that it is time for KUMBAKARNA to wakeup, for rural India is in an acute jobless distress and is bound to turn into a TURMOIL if not addressed at once. It is high time our policy makers pay adequate concern to India's backbone to make India stand firmly and steadily in the international arena to face future challenges.

CRISIS IN INPUT COST, OUTPUT, MINIMUM SUPPORT PRICE AND EXPORT

Are we heading towards jobless growth and diminishing farms?– questions Guruswamy, M. (2006). For India has more land under cultivation than China, yet we produce far less. India's Rice, Wheat and Sugar combined production is 226 million tonnes compared to 261 million tonnes of China for the same for the three commodities. If we do not accelerate our production the repercussions would be severe on the economy of India.

Nammalvar, Director of Tamilnadu Natural farming Centre, Tanjore (Sun TV, 25.2.06) highlighted with concern the crisis India is facing due to shift from natural farming to modern chemical farming. It killed earth worms which is now a product of cottage industry manufacturing product and sold at Rs. 750/kg and farming of 1990s and 2000s paved way for not only increase in input cost but also resulted in contradictory decrease in output. Also 100s of farmers endorsed their revert to natural farming and emphasized that chemical farming reduced beneficial bacteria of soil from 400 lakhs per gram of soil prior to 1980s to meagre 1.25 lakhs of current figure. Also natural farming yield is higher–out of 22 marakkal land the output yield is 40 kgs of rice but with chemical cultivation out of 27 marakkal land the output is just 33 kgs of rice. It is apt to express the view of Prince Charles of England which coincides with the view of Tamilnadu farmers–"It is tragic that the wonderful country side of Punjab is no longer in a position to support the families who had toiled there for generations and as a farmer myself, I'm convinced that only natural farming is a genuine alternative with real commercial opportunity for farmers." A developed nation's VIP's view should get heard in the minds of our policy makers.

Another fundamental issue of IAS is its move from farmer self sufficiency to state/nation/market dominated regime. The seed bill 2005 of WTO is a threat to India, because it curbs the right of farmers to develop and innovate their own seed savings. Using their own seed has been the culture of Indian farm communities and it illegitimately prevents their right in decision making (Kothari, A 2006). Similar view was also expressed by Revathi of TN natural farming centre, Tanjore. The need of the hour to point out here is the study report of centre for Science and Environment which found out VERY HIGH levels of pesticide in the blood samples drawn from 4 villages of Punjab. The blood samples showed 15-605 times higher residues as compared to samples of people in US especially the organochlorine pesticide resides and the study called for urgent action to regulate pesticides use (Hindu 8.6.05). A liveshow in KAIRALI TV (8.8.2004) highlighted the role of ENDOSULPHAN, a prohibited pesticide of the west being used for spraying Cashew nut farms in the high prevalence of cancer rate, birth deformity and mental retardation of children and adults in KASSARKODE of Kerala. A medical camp conducted in 2001 categorically blamed endosulphan being the culprit. A study by FAO (1997) states that 80% of cancer cases of the 21st Century are attributed to environmental factors–especially right in the "HOME-SWEET HOME". Environmental protection agency says that chemicals in today's food are 3 times more likely to produce cancer than outdoor air-borne pollutants. A survey by CSE a decade ago revealed that 70% of all pesticides used in India were either banned or severely restricted in the western countries and had been identified by WHO as HAZARDOUS. Yet in India pesticides industry continues to grow virtually unchecked, for India's pesticide use accounted for 100 tonnes in 1960s to 41,000 tonnes of use in 2003-04. It coincides with the alarming rate of blood cancer and bowl cancer in Indians as per the opinion of expert doctors. Cancer an alien word in Indian history till 1980s is spreading like forest fire among both sexes and India's current cancer prevalence rate is 20 lakhs case and by 2025, it would increase by 50-60 million cases as per the forecast of WHO. Use of fertilizer is another cause for increasing rate of cancer. Another culprit of cancer is fertilizers. India's fertilizer use was 72.61 Kg/ hectare during 1960s but escalated to 185.81 Kg/hectare in 2003-04. Thus it is clear that chemical warfare on Indian soil not only increased input cost and contradictorily reduced output cost but also pose a severe health hazard to people. Its unfortunate that India once preached to the world "Food is Medicine; Medicine is Food" now has the fate of "FOOD IS POISON" due to chemical warfare on soil.

LOOPHOLES IN MSP

Of the many causes for Maharashtra's farmsuicide, selling their products especially cotton for much lower price (Rs. 1600 / quintal) against assured

MSP (Rs. 2700/quintal) is said to be the crux of agrarian crisis and farm suicide and it led to VICIOUS cycle of debt trap and farm suicide. Also in Kerala and Andra Pradesh, farmers are subjected to this kind of exploitation. According to Vasudevan, P. (2006) farmers of Kerala are forced to sell paddy at Rs. 4-5 / Kilo against the MSP of Rs. 7/kg. The irony here is that the MSP itself was coined to save farmers from exploitation by middle men and private traders. It is also apt to pointout that recently 4,000 kg of tomatoes were sold free of cost in MYSORE in protest against the price of tomato crashing to 50 paise a kg. Can a farmer take back the input cost at this rate. It is highly ironical and ridiculous that the same journal flashed the auction sale of a cup of coffee being made by a leading actor of a Tamil film industry to Rs.25,000. Where is India heading towards? Stray thoughts come to the minds of many.

CAN IAS COMPETE IN THE OPEN MARKET FREE TRADE?

Indian farmers' spokespersons recently argued with Director General of WTO that "why rice should be grown in Europe by giving hefty subsidies to enable those producers to compete with much cheaper and cost effective rice raised by South Asian Farmers?". It was learnt that EU is protecting the rice farming of SPAIN, for it is a habitat for wild birds and hence needed to be protected. What any irony? EU is worried about wild birds' survival but not the livelihood survival of farmers in India and Asia. A stakehold of cotton farmer of Maharashtra described to WTO's DG that WTO is engaged in neo-colonialism by highlighting the fact that $3.5 billion subsidy is given to cotton growers of US as a result cotton price had fallen sharply in the international market affecting cotton farmers in DCs and LDCs including India, for developed nations provide very huge subsidy to big farmers and all that led to decline in Indian agriculture and suicides to their subsidy. The crux of this episode is WTO's DG accepting the highly illegitimate stand of developed nations–"the existing comparative advantages enjoyed by developed world in agriculture is unfair and needed to be corrected by flashing subsides"– this one statement is foolproof for the WTO's role in creating agrarian crisis in the 21st Century in the fashionable concept of free trade to lift poor out of poverty.

In addition to the above strong views of farmers' spokes persons, the below given few tables illustrate our inability in competing in the international free trade. Below given table projects our production rate/ hectare in comparison with select global countries.

Table 10
Comparison of India's Production with Global Countries

Crop	*Yield / Hectare*							
	World Average	*India*	*China*	*USA*	*Australia*	*Italy*	*Ireland*	*Netherland*
Rice	3895	3002	5807	-	8813	-	-	-
Wheat	2698	2743	3295	-	-	-	7556	-
Jowar	-	1196	-	3704	-	5949	-	-
Maize	18,638	1841	-	4504	-	-	-	25,000
Cotton	600	347	-	1937	-	-	-	-
Pulses	4769	608	-	1963	-	-	-	-
Groundnut	-	931	-	2828	-	-	-	-

Source: 1. Sivanappan, K.R. (2005) Survey of Indian agri. Industry.
2. Dhingra, I.C. (2006), 3. Singh, P.B. (2002).

The above table depicts our production/hectare for select crops in comparison with World average at one hand and with other World countries at the other side. Only in wheat production we are above world average production and for all other crops our production is far below world average. If we look at it at the otherside our production is very low–as low as 1/4 to 1/5 as compared to the yield/hectare of select global countries. As per Singh, P.B. (2002) the most serious threat to IAS is from international competition, for production and prices of farm produce in the global market and Indian market are moving in the opposite directions.

Can India stand next to the sophisticated farm machine, rapid progress in biotechnology and huge subsidies offered to farmers of developed nations? The below given table is an eye opener for Indians to realize that they are giants in subsidy offer.

Table 11
Agricultural Subsidy by Some Developed Nations

Country	*Subsidy to Agriculture US $ Billion*	*No. of Full time Farmers*	*Area under Prod. of crops (Hectares)*	*Area / Farmer (Hectare)*	*Subsidy / Hectare $*	*Subsidy / Farmer $.*
USA	97.3	37,74,000	17,70,00,000	55.80	5457.0	30,655
Japan	56.8	32,36,000	43,36,000	1.34	13,099.6	17,552
Switzerland	6.2	1,78,000	4,23,000	2.38	14,657.0	34,831

Source: Singh, P.B. (2002).

It is clear that the farmers of the above mentioned 3 countries get a subsidy of minimum 17,552 US $ (Rs. 7,89,890) to a maximum of 34,831 US $ (Rs. 15,67,395) per farmer. Can IAS or its farmers with the average farm size in India being 1.41 hectares with 62% of farmers holding less than 1 hectare go next to these countrys' farmers in competition? It is learnt that in India the subsidy given to farmer is just 3% and developed nations want that to be crashed in the name of WTO and free trade. Is there any logic behind it? Indians need to think. It is also worth while to mention here that a litre of milk fetches just Rs. 8.46 litre on an average for an Indian farmer but the same 1 litre of milk fetches Rs. 38.48, Rs. 16.86, Rs. 11.48, Rs. 10.26 and Rs. 9.90 for farmers of Japan, EU, Australia, USA and Newzeland respectively. This is another fact highlighting our reduced output cost for our farmers compared to developed nations. It is highly ridiculous that the natural resources to be available free of cost as per our Fundamental Human Rights–Water has become a commercial product and it is sad that India unfortunately stands I in bottled water industry compared to other world countries. As per Kothari, A. (2006) a bottle of water's production cost is Rs. 4.25 but sold higher than the price of milk (Rs. 8.46) to Rs. 12/-. Highly drought prone Indian States' bottle water Industry is growing at the highest rate in the world. The annual growth rate for 1994-2004 is 25.0, 8.2, 8.8, 20.0, 15.4, 3.6, 4.4, 4.2, 16.5 and 6.2 percentages for India, US, Mexico, China, Brazil, Italy, German, France, Indonesia and Spain respectively.

Where do we stand in the parameter of agricultural products' export? It is abysmally at very low position again. The rate of export of Indian agricultural products was just Rs. 284 crores (596 million US $) in 1960-61 but substantially increased to Rs. 32,805 crores (7210 million US $) in 2003-04. It looks encouraging but if we see its share in India's total export, it is on the steady decline–from 14.43% in 1990-91 to a peak of 20.50% in 1996-97 to a very low 11.50% in 2004-05. In the 300 billion US $ world total agriculture trade, our share is so far less than 1% only.

The foregone analysis brings to limelight the 2 contradictory facts that at one hand we are far below developed nations in all agriculture related parameters but we are at the top in No. I position in selling the natural free of cost resource WATER. How are we going to face free trade of WTO mantra?

III. AGRARIAN CRISIS, FARM INDEBTEDNESS AND FARMER SUICIDES

IAS is in a crisis today. NSSO report on rural indebtedness released in 2005 June found out that 1 in 2 farm households are in debt. and mostly it was the money borrowed for use on the farm–only 10% of the debt was incurred for marriage or other social purposes. The survey also brought to limelight that 1 in 4 farmers did not like what they were doing because it was not profitable and 4 out of 10 given a chance would like to take up some other career. (George Bush's mantra). This report view is endorsed by Sharma, D. (2006) who highlighted the fact "Indian Villages are in despair and ready to sell their villages and 6 villages in Punjab were already up for grabs". The collapse of rural credit, soaring input cost, and falling output prices were the causes for farm distress in India as per Swaminathan, M.S. (2005) and urges "not to measure farmers' progress in terms of production in tonnes" but "measure on the rate of growth of farmers' incomes". As per this yardstick Maharastra's VIDHARBA is a "DISASTER ZONE"–he endorsed it so. Similar view–agrarian crisis gripped Vidharba, for official data suggests that by 2003 around 55% of farm households in Maharastra were in debt as focused by Sainath, P. (2005). NSSO's 2005 report also projected the fact that really 48.6% of the 90 million farm households are caught in debt trap. In Andra Pradesh 57 out of 100 indebted households are beholden to private money lenders and inspite of efforts to stream line and increase institutional credit, small farmers still depend upon money lenders for a variety of reasons. This fact looks true, for 32.7% of farmers depend on money lenders for credit (Dhingra, I.C., 2006).

Discriminatory policies seem to be another culprit for farm indebtness and suicides. Famous Vidharba region's suicides are due to reduced import cotton price and reduced MSP to farmers of Vidharba. For the last 2 decades inspite record production and over flowing of granaries, the living conditions of farmers have not improved and the farm community has been on the back-foot fearing sluggish growth, no increase in investment, fall of exports and deprivation of a reasonable price for their produce (Parsai, G. 2001). It is in India that non-essential credit is cheaper–car loans come cheaper than crop loans (Business line, 20.3.06). New Agriculture policy 2000 of India is still to materialize to revert the acute agrarian crisis. The below given one table is testimony to the pathetic agrarian crisis of our mother land.

Table 12
Farm Suicides in India in the 21st Century

Region of India	*Period / Year*	*No. of Cases*
Maharastra's Yavatmal	2001	17
Maharastra's Yavatmal	2001-2004	132
Maharastra's Yavatmal	Upto July 2005	29
Maharastra's Vidharba	Upto Nov. 2005	120
Maharastra's Vidharba	Dec. 2005–Feb. 2006	200
Maharastra's Vidharba	March 2006–May 2006	93
Karnataka	Mid 1990s to 2004	852
Kerala's Palakkad and Wayanad	Since 2001 to 2006 May	Over 1500

Source: Sainath, P. (9 episodes 2005 & 2006).
Menon, P. (2004); Hindu dated 29.12.05, 2.12.05, 13.4.06.

It is evident that the sector which helps the nation to ensure food security and eradication of mal nutrition from the face of India itself looks not only worn out, emaciated and malnourished but dieing. Maharastra's vidharba region's suicides was also endorsed by the studies conducted by Indra Gandhi Institute for Development Research and Tata Institute for social science (on behalf of Bombay High Court) of Maharastra. Swaminathan, M.S. (2005) also highlighted the farm suicides of India since 2001. A cross section of delta farmers of Tanjore, Tamilnadu opined recently that in the past 4 years 1000s of farmers had sold their land as agriculture gave them a return of less than 5% per annum as against a minimum requirement of 12% and successful drought of the past 4 years made many delta farmers "PENNILESS". Another grim fact is that in the most bustling and richest Punjab, as per Social Development Report, 2006 people in villages near Ludhiana are made to work for Rs.15 per day or Rs. 1500 per month where the minimum daily wage is Rs.92 and this sad situation is due to debt of landless farmers. To repay their debt to creditors they work for such a low pay to pay off debt. There are about one lakh workers "Prone–to–bondage" in agriculture. It speaks the plight of landless farmers (Zaidi, A. 2006).

Dhingra, I.C. (2006) quotes "India is poised to become an economic super power but the widespread poverty and farm suicides stairs us right on the face". As per our constitution, IPC and laws, all Indians are "EQUAL" without any discrimination. Does it mean repayment of loan dues to nationalized and co-operative banks of India too. It looks "not so".

An episode on Bhavani farmers of TN for not having repayed few thousands of co-operative bank loans were publically arrested and was a painful scene to witness even men crying leave alone the women who were also arrested. (Sun TV, 6/7/2005). A daily news paper of Tamilnadu Dinamalar (25.6.2002) flashed in the front page headlines–"Govt. has no intention of writing off farmers' loan dues; has extended both the period of loan repayment and seizing of property in case of future delay". Its unfortunate that the backbone of India are treated differently compared to manufacturing sector loan borrowers. Hindu editorial's view (12.1.2006) holds apt here to pointout–"since the early 1990s successive governments have given up billions of rupees in revenue annually in the form of tax breaks for the wealthy. Thousands of crores of rupees of public money borrowed by the rich and the powerful have also been written off as "BAD DEBTS". The treatment for rich being so, the farmers for few thousands of loan are squeezed. A Bombay industrialist when asked to repay Rs. 2000 crores of bank loan, refused to do so and obtained supreme court stay order; (Junior Vikadan, July, 2004) Are we all equal before Indian law?

In short we can infer from the above analysis that agrarian crisis of India is not only acute and epidemic but in a state of farmers ready to either commit suicide or sell their villages to abandon the profession of agriculture to venture into some other worthwhile, profitable career. Can India proceed with this kind of mind of farmers–it requires urgent remedies to revert IAS and its farmers to their previous pride.

FINAL WORDS

There is a general feeling among the public that trade liberalization in agriculture in India could create problems for its large and predominant poor agriculture farmers who are like mustard seeds next to developed nations' farmers. Roosevelt in 1945 proclaimed–"The point in history at which we stand is full of promise and danger; the world will either move toward 'UNITY' and widely shared 'PROSPERITY' or will move 'APART' and trade negotiations offer a chance for a more unified world." Another American a century ago quoted "Tariffs almost everywhere were ways of shifting tax burdens from the rich to the poor" or "taxing want rather than wealth".

The world's poor ofcourse would see hope for fairer trade from WTO but rich nations deprived of new markets for their hefty production could easily influence WTO to fulfill their needs. What Roosevelt anticipated as second option 6 decades ago unfortunately has become TRUE today. Many experts of India opine that a country like India whose backbone economy is agriculture should not open its doors to sharks to eat away our rich genetic wealth and the government needs to keep agriculture and food out of WTO and increase import duties on all agriculture products to stop the flow of highly subsidized international imports. International experts are also of the view that DCs and LDCs should fight for their rights with the WTO, otherwise these nations have to form a special organization similar to EU, Asia-Pacific region, ASEAN, SAARC etc.

Its worthwhile to quote the view of Nayyar, D. (2006) "how about a development bank funded by leading developing countries like World Bank? or a monetary fund exclusively for developing nations like IMF? or indeed emulate institutions like EU? She wants India not a "superpower" in the shade of others but a real superpower under the sun and this statement really holds valuable amidst this big agrarian crisis of India. (16.3.06 The Hindu).

In the words of our president Abdul Kalam unless 6,00,000 villages of India are transformed, transformation of India to either a 'super power' or 'developed nation' is like "KURUKSHETRA" only. Innovative measures are needed at this juncture than mere more allocations to revive this situation to boost agriculture sector from the current sluggish growth scenario and farm suicide episodes. In the words of Maharastra's Home Minsiter, Patil, M.R.R. (2006), "If committees and laws could have solved problems India would have become a paradise on earth long ago".

To conclude it, Nelson Mandela's words are apt–"POVERTY, HUNGER, DISEASE and DEATH cannot be fought with weapons. They can be only by HUMAN WILL. It worries that our world is becoming a GLOBAL VILLAGE only for exchange of GOODS and INFORMATION and not a place of Shelter, Livelihood, Security and Dignity for all who live in it. The divide between the world's RICH and POOR is not merely the result of Economic consequences or Market force. It is also the result of CLOSED HEARTS and NARROW MINDS. Prosperity without an EQUITABLE distribution of resources is neither JUST nor SUSTAINABLE in the long run and PROGRESS without SOCIAL JUSTICE is not a REAL HUMAN PROGRESS". Let WTO propaganda countries realise this fact and do JUSTICE for poor countries so as to have a BALANCED world.

To Put it in a nutshell, "Liberalisation and globalisation of
Indian Agriculture should be
Human Rights based and
Must favour the
Fundamental Human Rights of the
60 crores of population
whose life is AGRICULTURE".

REFERENCES

Abdul Kalam, A.B.J. (1998), "India 2020", *Viking*, New Delhi.

Association of Food Scientists & Technologies India (2005), Report, September.

Badavam, L. (2005), "Dying Young" *Frontline*, September.

Chandrasekar, C.P. (2006), "A Heady Mix for Whom", *Frontline*, March.

Daavincy, K. (2006), "Poovulakin Kadaisi Kaalam", *Weekly Series in Kumutham Reporter*, February.

Dhingra, I.C. (2006), "The Indian Economy", Sultan Chand & Sons, New Delhi.

Gresser, E. (2006), "Will Developing Nations", Hopes be Realized?", *The Hindu*, March, 27th.

Kottari, A. (2006), "A Threat Stalled", *Frontline*, April.

Mahalingam, N. (2005), "Problems and Prospects of Rural Enterpreneurship", Sakthi Group of Companies, Chennai.

Menon, P. (2004), "Loan as Leverage, An Agrarian Crisis", *Frontline*, November.

Mishra, S.K. & Mishra, S. (2001), "Globalisation of Indian Agriculture", from Batra, G.S. and Dingwal, R.C. (et) Book Globalisation and Liberalization, Deep and Deep Publications.

Misra, S.K. and Puri, V.K. (2006), "Indian Economy", Himalaya Publishers, New Delhi.

Rajagopal, B. (2006), "Poor Nations Need a Change in Strategies to Guard Trade Interests", *The Hindu*, April, 17th.

Ramkishen, Y. (2004), "New Prospective in Rural Marketing", Jains Publishing House, Mumbai.

Sainath, P. *The Hindu* (dated), 25.6.05, 29.12.05, 2.12.05, 16.8.05, 1.4.06, 18.2.06, 28.6.05, 16.3.06.

Swaminathan, M.S. (2005), "3 Pronged Strategy Needed" *The Hindu Survey of Indian Agriculture*.

Swaminathan, M.S. (2006), "Towards Biodiversity in Agriculture", *The Hindu*, March, 31st.

Sun TV, "Let us Meet, Let us Think", 25.2.06.

The Hindu (dated) 30.8.2004 ; 26.1.05, 5.5.05, 16.5.05, 1.6.05, 28.6.05, 25.6.05, 27.7.05, 17.7.05, 9.7.05, 5.8.05, 16.8.05, 6.10.05, 18.11.05, 2.12.05, 14.12.05, 29.12.05, 5.1.06, 12.1.06, 12.1.06, 21.1.06, 31.1.06, 18.2.06, 9.2.06, 25.2.06, 5.3.06, 23.3.06, 3.3.06, 25.3.06, 28.3.06, 1.4.06, 11.4.06, 14.4.06.

SUSTAINABLE FISHERY RESOURCE DEVELOPMENT IN MAHARASHTRA

P. S. Kamble & Vidya Chougule***

INTRODUCTION

Each and every country in general and each and every individual in particular desires and attempts to achieve economic development. Because it facilitates provision of satisfying a variety of wants of human beings in considerable number. Likewise, it also enables to transform under developed economy into developed or significantly developed one. Resources plays a vital role in achieving economic development in absence of which, it is impossible. But development exhausts and depletes resources especially natural or environmental resources. Initially no attempt was made so as to think of impact of development on resources. This led to propound the concept of sustainable development. It is very important and urgent need of the hour to think of sustainable development in the case of each and every productive activity due to over exploitation, misutilisation of especially environmental or natural resources such as fisheries because of ecological balance along with social welfare maximisation of human beings. In this backdrop, the present paper attempts to examine the sustainable development of fishery resources in Maharashtra.

NATURAL/ ENVIRONMENTAL RESOURCES

Resources in general and natural or environmental resources in particular play a significant role in economic development of the economy by extending services necessary in the production of goods and services. For example, land, water, minerals, fisheries etc. It is a fact that in absence of resources, production of goods and services and thereby economic development is impossible. They are natural resources because

* Reader, Department of Economics, Shivaji University, Kolhapur.
** Research Student, Deptt. of Economics, Shivaji University, Kolhapur.

of free gift of nature. Resources are classified into different categories such as material and energy resources. Material resources may be further divided into metallic and non-metallic materials. It is usual to distinguish between renewable and non-renewable resources. This is a clear distinction than the classification into exhaustible and non-exhaustible resources.[1] But no much attempts were made to think of environmental aspect of resources in their exploitation and utilisation as well while achieving economic development through natural resources. This resulted in the development of the concept sustainable economic development in general and sustainable resource development in particular.

CONCEPT OF SUSTAINABLE DEVELOPMENT

The term sustainable development was brought into common use by the World Commission on Environment and Development in its report called "Our Common Future". Brundtland (1987) Commission, which defines sustainable development as "Development that meets the needs of the present generation without comprising the ability of future generations to meet their own needs."[2] According to Mutofa K. Tolba (of UNEP) the concept of sustainable development implies[3]:

1. Help for very poor because they are left with no option other than to destroy their environment.
2. Idea of self-reliant development, within natural resource constraint.
3. The idea of cost effective development, using differing economic criteria to the traditional criteria.
4. The great issues of health control, appropriate technologies, food, self-reliance, clean water and shelter for all.
5. The notion that people centered initiatives are needed.

Gilbert and Braat[4] define sustainable development as "a pattern of social and structural transformation which optimizes the economic and other social benefits available in the present without jeopardizing the likely potential for similar benefits in the future."

There are three basic components of sustainable development: economic, social and the environment component. The economic component of sustainability requires that societies pursue growth paths that generate optional flow of income while maintaining their basic stock of man made capital, human capital and natural capital. This requires:

(a) increasing production of goods and services, (b) satisfying basic needs or reducing poverty, (c) improving equity. The social dimension of sustainable development is built on the twin principles of justice and equity. Wealth, resources and opportunity should be equitably showed. All citizens should have access to minimum standards of security, human rights, and social benefits such as food, health, education, shelter and opportunities of self-development. The environment component requires sustainable resource use, efficient sink function and maintenance of stock of natural capital.

FISHERY RESOURCES IN MAHARASHTRA

Maharashtra has a coastal length of about 720 kms. Rivers about 3.2 thousand kms. length and canals of about 12.8 thousand kms. length. The area suitable for marine fisheries is 1.12 thousand kms. and for brackish water fisheries it is 18.6 thousand hectares, the continental shelf extends upto 180 meters of depth having area of 1.12 lakh sq. kms. Out of this area, fishing takes place only upto 72 meters in depth i. e. 30 to 40 fathoms. The potential fish catch from marine area has been estimated at 6.3 lakh tonnes per year. against this, the production during 2003-04 was 4.20 lakh tonnes.[5]

It is a fact that the production of marine fisheries in Maharashtra has been increasing persistently. but it has not achieved its optimum capacity of fish production. The marine fish production rose continuously from 1.19 lakh tonnes in 1961 to 3.25 lakh tonnes in 1991, 3.95 lakh tonnes in 1999[6] and lastly to 4.20 lakh tonnes in 2003-04.

PROBLEMS OF SUSTAINABLE FISHERY RESOURCE DEVELOPMENT

Since 1972, the total world catch of fish has increased by about 509 percent, but it is based on a rather small number of species. Of 220 species of marine and freshwater fish accounted for 38 percent of the 1995 total world catch (of 112.9 million tonnes) and three species–anchoveta, Chilean jack mackerel, and Alaska Pollack accounted for 16 percent of the world total, or 18.3 million tonnes. Nor are the fish catches distributed evenly. China is the biggest fishing nation by far. counting catches of marine and freshwater fish and farmed fish, in 1996 it produced almost 32 million tonnes, which is 26 percent of the world total. between them, and in descending order or of production, China, Peru, Chile and Japan produce 45 percent of the world's fish. Apart from China, the world's largest fishing nation, Peru, Chile, India, Indonesia, Thailand and the

Philippines are among the top 12.[7] While the stock was declining it was widely believed that over fishing was the cause of the depletion, but it is more likely that the fluctuation was mainly natural due to natural population changes. Fish farming is also traditional that has been practised for many centuries in some parts of the world.

Coral reefs are under constant threat of destruction in most locations of the world. It was estimated that about 58 percent of reefs are at risk due to human interference. These are in addition to serious problems of loss of over fishing was recognized as a problem of management of fishery resources even at the beginning of the twentieth century. Food and Agricultural Organisation (FAO, 1997) observed that the annual growth rate in the harvest was about 7 per cent, and this is no larger sustainable. The top 200 species account for about 77 per cent of the world's fish production. During the mid 1990s, about a third of these were showing declining yields, and more were still developing. This suggests that a reduction of at least 30 percent of the fishing effort was required to rebuild the resources (FAO, 1997)[8] Marine fisheries constitute an important segment of the economy in several countries like Canada, Norway and Iceland. Estimates of world marine production, based on total harvest, was about 82 million tonnes in the 1990. It is important to note that another 27 million tonnes are discarded every year. The rising demand for fish due to an expanding human population, and the increasing shortfall in the supply depicts expected market features: rising fish prices, and thus rationing out the poorer sections of the society from their consumption baskets. This far from conducive to equity in food consumption, considering the assessments that fish remains among the most desirable food item for nutrition and health values and any effective denial of the poor can aggravate their malnutrition problems and the consequences.

According to Independent World Commission on the Oceans (1998), in addition to other pollutants like discarded nuclear submarines, petroleum hydrocarbons released into the oceans each year amount to about 2.5 million tonnes, and that this trend shows no sign of slowing, thus adversely affecting the sink's assimilative capacity.

POLICY IMPLICATIONS AND MEASURES FOR SUSTAINABLE FISHERY RESOURCE DEVELOPMENT IN MAHARASHTRA

The foregoing analysis clearly and adequately reveals problems and necessity of sustainable fishery resource development in theoretical as well as practical perspective. That analysis is applicable to sustainable fishery resource development in Maharashtra also. The analysis adequately provides policy implications and demands to suggest suitable measures whereby sustainable fishery development can be materialized. There is an urgent need for achieving optimum level of production of fisheries, which is lacking in Maharashtra. In the case of other coastal areas and nations, it is necessary to control over fishing by reducing fishing efforts. For sustainable development of fisheries attempts should be made to adopt modern fish farming along with due protection to the fish species declining. This also enables in increasing yields from fishing of fishery resources. As a result, the problem of high and rising prices of fisheries can be tackled. As fish plays a very vital role in the balanced diet of the human being, the denial of poor people from consumption of fisheries demands to pay due attention. It is socially unjust as well as the important problem of malnutrition can be severe. for this, the rationing of some fish food for the poor population could be a measure. Likewise, it is also important to take into consideration the earnings of fishermen and the contractors or wholesalers. It seems more benefits of fishing are being derived by the wholesalers.

Due care of pollutants by nuclear submarines, petroleum hydrocarbons have been polluting oceanic water and posing a serious threat to fishery resources and their sustainable development. The role of government in sustainable fishery development is of vital importance. But at the same time, people's consciousness and their active participation is desirable and most welcome. It will be of vital importance to impart education and knowledge regarding sustainable development of fisheries through Agriculture Colleges, Universities and more importantly by local bodies.

Besides this, the FAO (1997) measures are useful in sustainable development of fisheries. These measures consist of: Rehabilitate the over harvested and degraded regions, Underdeveloped areas of fishing are exploited further at an enhanced but sustainable rate, Discarding and wastage are significantly reduced.

Likewise, provisions of the U. N. Convention on the Law of the Sea 1982 are also useful. They are conservation and Management of Straddling Fish Stock and Highly Migratory Fish Stocks, Development and use of selective environmentally safe and cost effective fishing apparatus and techniques, Allocation of resources for ensuring the effectiveness of multi species management of the commercial fishery sector.

CONCLUSION

Resources in general and environmental resources in particular plays a vital role in rapid and all round economic development of the economy. But unless the sustainable development of environmental resources is achieved the goal of economic development can not be materialised. Hence, the concept of sustainable economic development has been emerged out and it is more relevant one. Fisheries is an important natural or environmental resource which plays a vital role in sustainable economic development and welfare of human beings especially in the coastal areas. This necessitates to achieve sustainable development of resources like fisheries. It is very important and need of the hour to achieve such development of fisheries in the state like Maharashtra, which is one of the developed states in India.

REFERENCES

Hanley, Shogren and White (2004), "Environmental Economics in Theory and Practice", Macmillan, Delhi, pp. 216-217.

Karpagam, M. (1999), "Environmental Economics", Sterling Publishers Private Limited, New Delhi, p. 179.

Ibid., p. 180.

Rao, P.K. (2001), "Sustainable Development: Economics and Policy", Blackwell Publishers, Oxford (UK), p. 89.

Directorate of Economics and Statistics (2004-05), "Government of Maharashtra", *Economic Survey Maharashtra*, Mumbai.

Bureau of Economics and Statistics, Government of Maharashtra, *Statistical Abstract of Maharashtra*, Mumbai.

Allaby, M. (2002), "Basics of Environmental Science", Routledge, London, pp. 228-232.

Rao, P.K. Above cited, p. 48.

PRIMARY EDUCATION AND INFRASTRUCTURE IN INDIA: PROGRESS AND PROBLEMS

Harisha N., Jayasheela** &*
*V. Basil Hans****

"Learning should not be restricted to school age, nor to any other age" –UNESCO.

INTRODUCTION

Education, healthcare, water and sanitation services are collectively known as social infrastructure. They are as important as physical infrastructure for economic development. Increase in human capital, through education will be essential for enabling individuals to translate market opportunities into reality and for the increase in economic growth. In the words of Schultz, "I propose to treat education as an investment in man and so treat its consequences as a form of capital. Since education becomes a part of the person receiving it, I shall refer to it as human capital".

It is education that documents and indicates qualitative growth of a county's population. It promotes individual growth and builds bridges between people and their institutions. Education has become even more important today than before. An illiterate person cannot participate in the new knowledge-based society driven by information technology and globalization. Knowledge as infrastructure is one of the practical issues under Intellectual Property Rights in the globalized world.

Primary education pays substantial returns to society worldwide and India is no exception. In the short term it raises the productivity and earnings of workers across the economy, generates substantial additional

* Junior Research Fellow, Department of Economics, Mangalore University. Mangalagangothri, Karnataka Sate, INDIA.

** Reader, Department of Economics, Mangalore University, Mangalagangothri.

*** Professor of Economics and HOD of Arts, St Aloysius Evening College, Mangalore, INDIA

social benefits in the form of improved family health and welfare, and contributes to lower fertility and slower rates of population growth. In the medium term, rising primary education leads increasingly well-educated parents to send their children to school, with girl benefiting substantially. Primary education puts a foundation for futuristic growth; a good primary education provides the stamina and staying power for human capital formation in a sustainable manner. Therefore, providing primary education for all has become necessary. At the same time there is a great urgency to build and strengthen educational infrastructure including school buildings, drinking water, playgrounds, electric connectivity, toilets etc, in the country. This paper tries to focus on the issues pertaining to educational infrastructure in India. The objectives of the paper are:

1. To review the present primary educational situation in India in terms of enrolment and dropout rate.
2. To understand reasons for high dropout rate in India.
3. To examine the availability of basic infrastructure in primary schools of India.

The study is based on available secondary data and reviewed literature on primary education in India.

EDUCATIONAL ACHIEVEMENTS AND PROBLEMS

Despite more than half a century of planned economic development in India, a large number of people in India are illiterate. In fact, with a literacy rate of 65 per cent, we have 296 million illiterates in the age group of seven years and above, as per the 2001 census. The highest male literacy rate was 94 per cent in Kerala while Bihar had the lowest male literacy rate of 49 per cent. Among women, the highest rate of literacy was 88 per cent in Kerala, and Bihar and Jharkand had the lowest rate of 35 per cent. In other words, only one in 3 women in Bihar was a literate in 2001.In fact, between 1991 and 2001 the total number of illiterates in Bihar increased by 2.98 million. Traditionally deprived communities such as the scheduled castes and schedule tribes remain backward; only 46 per cent of males were literate and 19 per cent of women were literate in 1991.The corresponding figures for scheduled tribes were 41 and 18 per cent respectively. Among agricultural labourers in 1993-94 only 40 per cent of males and 16.8 per cent of females were literate (See Table 1).

In 1951, about 82 per cent of Indians were illiterate, while the 1991 Census had found that 48 per cent were illiterate. By 2001 the situation had further improved and the illiteracy rate fell to 35 per cent. It reveals that we have only 65.38 literacy rate. But the problem is that while we have sufficient level of enrolment, we also have a high level of school dropout rate. Low level of literacy and high level of dropout indicates the lack of infrastructure for education at this level.

Table 1
Literacy Rate in India

Census year	*Persons*	*Males*	*Females*	*Male-Female disparity in literacy rate*
1951	18.33	27.16	8.86	18.30
1961	28.30	40.40	15.35	25.05
1971	34.45	45.96	21.97	23.98
1981	43.57	56.38	29.76	26.62
1991	52.21	64.13	39.29	24.84
2001	65.38	75.85	54.16	21.70

Source: Census Survey of India, (1951-2001).

ENROLMENT VS DROPOUT

The school and pre-school enrolment in class I-V and pre-primary section in the various states and union territories of the country has been increasing over the years. At the primary stage 94 per cent of the rural population has a school within one kilometer, while at the upper primary stage 84 per cent of rural population has a school within 3 km. The states where the enrolment ratio was lower than the national average were Uttar Pradesh, Bihar, Punjab, Rajasthan, Hariyana, Jammu & Kashmir at the primary stage, and Andhra Pradesh and Orissa, at the upper-primary stage. The enrolment of scheduled castes and scheduled tribes has also increased because of the affirmative policies of the government and is now in proportion to their population. This impact is seen in case of boys and girls both at primary and pre-primary levels (See Table 2).

Table 2
Enrolment in Pre-Primary and Primary Classes (I-V) in India, 1999-2000

	Pre-Primary Enrolment	*Primary Enrolment*
Boys	1440777	64103289
Girls	123614	49509252
Total	2704391	113612541
Total Enrolment 94.90 %		

Source: Department of Women and Child Development, Ministry of Human Resource Development, Government of India.

Table 2 shows the enrolment of boys and girls in the primary education. The total enrolment during 1999-2000 was around 94.90 per cent the Table 3 reveals dropout rate of boys and girls in the primary education.

Table 3
Gross Dropout Rates 1999–2000 (Provisional)

	Class I-V	*Class I- VII*
Boys	38.67	51.96
Girls	42.28	58.00
Total	40.25	54.53

Source: India, Ministry of HRD, Department of Elementary Education and Literacy (2001) Annual Report 2000-2001, New Delhi, pp. 223-225.

Although the enrolment ratio in classes I-V was 94.90 per cent in total (boys 104.08 per cent, girls 85.18 per cent) the dropout rate was also quite high (total 40.25 per cent, boys 38.67 per cent, and girls 42.28 per cent). Enrolment ratio in class VI-VIII was only 58.79 per cent in total (boys 67.15 per cent, girls 49.66 per cent). The dropout rate from classes I-VII was 54.93 per cent in total (boys 51.96 per cent, girls 58.00 per cent). The dropout rate from classes I-X was 68.28 per cent total, and while the dropout rate for boys was 66.58 per cent, for girls it was 70.60 per cent. Thus the dropout rate in case of class I-X was more than half (68.28 per cent). This is a matter of serious concern. We need to address the questions, viz., *"why the dropout rates are high in India? Is lack of infrastructure the basic cause of the problem?*

SCHOOL INFRASTRUCTURE

There has been substantial expansion of primary and upper-primary schools in the country (See Table 4). The number of primary schools increased nearly three times between 1951 and 1991. In 1957 there was only one upper-primary school for every six lower primary schools but

Table 4
Number of Primary/ Upper Primary Schools 1990-1997

Year	*Primary School*	*Increase*	*Upper–Primary School*	*Increase*
!990	560,935	57,172	151,456	29,079
1991	566744	5809	155,926	447o
1992	571248	4504	158,498	2572
1996	598354	27106	176,772	18272
1997	618763	12,409	185,506	8734

Source: Education in India, Ministry of Human Resource Development, Department of Education, New Delhi, 1998; and Selected Education Statistics 1997-98, Ministry of Human Resource Development, Government of India.

this situation gradually improved to 3:1 by 1993. The increasing trend has continued during the last decade. An estimated 95 per cent of the rural population living in 826,000 habitations has access to a primary school within a radius of 1 km. and about 85 per cent of the population has an upper-primary school within a radius of 3 km.

As Table 4 clearly reveals, physical distance between home and school is not a major problem. (This problem exists only for minority of families, particularly in hilly regions). But there are other major problems which are discussed below.

- Lack of adequate classrooms in the school.
- Absence of an upper primary school with in the village.
- Social distance.

The inadequacy of upper primary schooling infrastructure remains a major problem. In rural India as a whole, 43 per cent of the population lives more than 1 kilometer away from the nearest upper primary school. Here again, girls are the main victims, because many a times parents are reluctant to allow their daughter to attend school in other villages. As far as social distance is concerned it is a situation of social inequality within the socio-cultural framework of development: a paradoxical situation indeed. In many areas, for instance, village is divided into separate hamlets, and children from one hamlet may be denied entry to school in another hamlet, the reason may be caste tension. Only 50 per cent of hamlets in rural India have a primary school, and in states like Uttar Pradesh, the proportion of such hamlets is as low as 30 per cent. For girls freedom of movement further enhances the problem of social distance and deprivation. As revealed by the PROBE (Public Report on Basic Education) Survey 1998, in 162 of the government primary schools following conditions are prevalent.

- Six do not have any building and classes are held in open spaces.
- Several do not have a building of their own. Instead they depend on rented rooms, Panchayat ghars, Dharmasalas, etc. In such cases teaching clashes with other uses of these premises, more often and simultaneously.
- Only 58 per cent of schools had at least two pucca rooms.
- Sixty per cent have a leaking roof. This is a major nuisance on rainy days, and sometimes prevents any classroom activity for weeks together during the monsoon.
- 31 per cent of school had no pucca classrooms, 11 per cent had one pucca classroom, 37 per cent had two, and 21per cent had more than two pucca classrooms.

The overall quality of school infrastructure is poor. In 1993 only 65 per cent of all schools had pucca buildings. About 4 per cent of the schools are in thatched huts and 0.3 per cent in tents. Further 56 per cent of schools had no drinking water facilities and 70 per cent had no toilets.

The story with regards to availability of teachers is also a lamenting one. In absolute terms, the number of teachers has expanded greatly over the last fifty years but in real terms the growth in number of teachers has fallen steadily over time from 50.6 per cent in the 1950s to 4.5 per cent in the 1960s and 2.7 per cent in the 1970s. Between 1984-85 and 1989-90 the growth rate dropped to 10.6 per cent and there was an absolute decline in the number of primary school teachers between 1990-92 and 1992-93. The fifth All India Educational Survey conducted in 1986, found that 28 per cent of all primary schools were single teacher schools and another 32 per cent had two teachers each. In some places like Rajasthan about 50 per cent of schools were single teacher schools. The shortage of teachers is reflected in the rising teacher-student ratio which is a threat for maintaining quality education or teaching-learning process. Experiential learning with inbuilt effective mentor and monitoring systems seems to elude India's primary education, today. On an average there were 41 pupils per teacher in primary schools in 1978. The ratio went up to 44 in 1986. In 1999-2000, it became 42 per cent In developing countries like China, the pupil-teacher ratio was 22. The ratio was 19.8 in Thailand, 20 in Malaysia, 36 in the Philippines, 39 in Nepal and 50 in Pakistan.

Wherever the teacher-student ratio is low, their education level is high and dropout rate low as is quite evident in case of Bihar and Kerala (See Table 5). In Bihar teacher-student ratio is 62 and dropout rate is 56.50 and literacy rate is 48 per cent. In Kerala student-teacher ratio is 30 and dropout rate is only 7.05 and literacy rate is 91 per cent. But in Manipur, teacher-student ratio is 18, literary rate is 69 and dropout rate is 76 per cent. Quality education largely depends both on teachers and teaching environment and efficiency.

TOTAL SCENARIO OF BASIC FACILITIES IN PRIMARY SCHOOL

There is a wide variation in the availability of basic facilities such as drinking water and toilets, blackboard, dusters, chalk, teacher table, library, map, globe, chart, flash cards, science kit, games equipment, furniture etc. (See Table 6). There is noticeable difference in the expansion of these facilities between the DPEP and non DPEP states. The provision of safe drinking water, the most basic facility, has not been able to keep pace with the new opening of new schools. Nevertheless there has been an overall expansion of these facilities during the period 1986-1997 across the country.

Table 5
Pupil Teacher Ratio 1997-98

India / State / UTs	*Primary*	*Upper primary*	*Secondary*
Andhra Pradesh	49	39	32
Arunachal Pradesh	36	27	29
Assam	37	24	21
Bihar	62	49	42
Delhi	39	30	28
Goa	19	15	25
Gujarat	47	41	30
Haryana	47	34	23
Himachal Pradesh	30	18	31
Jammu & Kashmir	30	22	17
Karnataka	31	52	20
Kerala	30	29	29
Madhya Pradesh	44	35	34
Maharashtra.	38	40	32
Manipur	19	19	21
Meghalaya	40	17	19
Mizoram	28	10	9
Nagaland	21	19	25
Orissa	35	33	17
Punjab	40	18	28
Rajasthan	42	33	25
Sikkim	17	19	21
Tamil Nadu	39	40	45
Tripura	18	15	17
Uttar Pradesh	42	29	39
West Bengal	57	-	-
Andaman & Nicobar Islands	21	20	22
Chandigarh	42	29	28
Dadar & Nagar Haveli	39	39	25
Daman & Diu	45	38	13
Lakshadeep.	33	18	15
Pondicherry	27	24	27
India	42	37	29

Source: India, Planning Commission. (2002). *National Human Development Report, 2001,* New Delhi, p. 215.

Basic facilities are not at all adequate in India. Only 56.14 per cent of schools have safe drinking water while remaining 44 per cent of schools have shortage of safe drinking water. Only 39 per cent of schools have urinals, and 31 per cent have separate urinals for girls. Electric connectivity has only 34.36 per cent of schools. It shows a bad picture of basic facilities in primary schools in India. Better communication for boosting education is not happening at the required degree and scale at present.

Table 6
Overall Positions of Basic Facilities in Primary School, 1996-97 (Per cent)

Year	*Safe Drinking Water*	*School With Urinals*	*Separate Urinals for Girls*	*Lavatory*	*Separate Lavatory for Girls*	*Electric Connectivity*
1986	46.59	15.00	4.86	06.37	2.90	–
1993	44.23	18.93	8.66	10.86	5.12	–
1994	41.73	20.64	12.83	–	–	19.16
1997	56.14	39.49	31.20	–	–	34.36

Source: India Education Report, 2002, National Institute of Education Planning and Administration, p.173.

As per the PROBE Survey Report (1998) nearly 74 per cent of the schools have blackboards, which have helped to deliver the goods for the students. Nearly 9 per cent of the schools have blackboards but they are not in use, 17 per cent not available at all. Playgrounds: 48 per cent available and functional, 8 per cent available but non-functional and 44 per cent not available. Maps and Charts: 41 per cent available and functional, 16 per cent available but non-functional, and 44 per cent not available. Teaching kit: 33 per cent available and functional, 2 per cent available but non-functional, 55 per cent not available. Toys: 25 per cent available and functional, 14 per cent available but non-functional, and 61 per cent not available. Libraries: 23 per cent available and functional, 5 per cent available but non-functional, and 72 per cent not available. Musical instruments: 15 per cent available and functional, 16 per cent available but not functional, 69 per cent not available at all. These facts and figures are an ample proof for low standard of basic facilities in primary schools.

On the basis of the above analysis we can infer that the availability of teaching-learning materials has considerably improved in all projects but the basic facility is not adequate. In overall primary education infrastructure India stands at very low position compared to other countries in the world.

EXPENDITURE ON PRIMARY EDUCATION AND INFRASTRUCTURE

The allocation for education and educational infrastructure also has been increasing over the years significantly. The plan out lay on education has increased from Rs. 151.20 core in the First Five Year Plan to Rs. 43, 825 cores in the Tenth Five Year Plan (2002-07). The Expenditure on Education as a percentage of GDP also rose from 0.64 per cent in 1951-52 to 3.74 per cent in 2003-04. Right from the beginning, Government gave priority to elementary education rather than higher education. In the First Plan, Government spent Rs. 870 million on primary education, with 58 per cent of the total expenditure. In the Tenth Five Year Plan it reached Rs. 2, 87,500 million with 65.7 per cent of the total expenditure.

GOVERNMENT POLICIES AND PROGRAMS TO PROMOTE PRIMARY EDUCATION AND INFRASTRUCTURE

The Parliament has passed the 86th Constitutional Amendment Act, 2002 to make elementary education a Fundamental Right for children in the age group of 6-14 years. The components of Indian primary education system (programme) are as follows.

Sarva Shiksha Abhiyan

The scheme of Sarva Shiksha Abhiyana (SSA) was launched in 2001. The goals of SSA are as follows: (1) All 6-14 age group children in school/education guarantee scheme centre/ bridge course by 2003. (2) All 6-14 age children complete five-year primary education by 2007. (3) All 6-14 age group children complete eight years of schooling by 2010. (4) Focus on elementary education of satisfactory quality with emphasis on education for life. (5) Bridge all gender and social category gaps at primary stage by 2007 and elementary education level by 2010; and (6) Universal retention by 2010. During 2004-05 the SSA approved 44719 new schools, appointment of 210431 new teachers, construction of 50,044 toilets and provision of drinking water for 44,322 schools and free text books for 3239155 teachers, against annual district elementary education plan for 598 districts. A sum of Rs. 438647 crore has been released by Central Government to the States/UTs.

Education Guarantee Scheme and Alternative and Innovative Education

Education Guarantee Scheme and Alternative and Innovative Education (EGS and AIE) is an improved component of elementary education. Alternative Education interventions for specific categories of very deprived children e.g. child labour, street children, migrating children, working children, children living in difficult circumstances and older children in the 9+age group especially adolescent are being supported under EGS and AIE all over the country.

Mid-Day Meal Scheme

The National Program of Nutritional Support to Primary Education (NPNSPE) popularly known as the Mid-Day Meal Scheme was formally launched on 15 August 1995. Under the scheme central assistance is provided to states for the following (a) 100 gram of food grains per child for school day where there is a meal program, alternatively three kg per child per month for 10 months and (b) admissible transport subsidy for transport of food grains from the nearest FCI depot to the school subject to a ceiling of Rs.50 per quintal. During 2004-05, 10.88 crore primary school children were brought under the scheme. A total of 26.66 lakh metric tonnes food grains was allocated to various states/UTs against which 15.28 lakh MTs of food grains was actually lifted by them up to December 2004.

District Primary Education Programme

The centrally sponsored scheme of district primary education programme was launched in 1994.The programme component includes construction of classrooms and new schools, opening of non-formal/alternative schooling centres, appointment of new teachers, setting up of early childhood education centers etc. Under this scheme so far more than 1,60,000 new schools have been opened, including almost 8,400 alternative schooling (AS) centres. The AS centers cover nearly 3.5 million children, while another two lakh children are covered by bridge courses of different types. About 1,77,000 teachers, including Para-Teachers/Shiksha level and 29,725 centres at cluster level have been set-up.

Operation Blackboard

The scheme of operation black board (OBB) was launched in 1987-88, with the aim of improving human and physical resources in primary schools of the country. Provision of at least two reasonably large rooms, at least two teachers and essential teaching/learning materials for every existing primary school was the component of this scheme.

Lok Jumbish Project

An innovative project "Lok Jumbish" with assistance from Swedish International Development Agency (SIDA) was launched in Rajasthan to achieve education for all through people's participation. The first phase of project was implemented during June 1992 to June 1994, at a cost of Rs. 14.03 cores, second phase between July 1994 to June 1998 at a cost of Rs. 96.92 cores, and third phase was implemented from July 1999 to

June 2004. The project received assistance from Department for International Development (DFID), UK during the phase and project cost was Rs. 400 crore. However, in phase III 102 blocks were covered with 561 clusters taken-up for operationalization and 14,559 villages in which environment building was done.

Shiksha Karmi Project

The Shiksha Karmi Project (SKP) aims at universalization and quality improvement of primary education with attention given to girls. The project at present covers 3,650 villages in 150 blocks in Rajasthan. The project provides primary education to 2.76 lakh children in day schools.

Lansdale Programme

Lansdale programme is a collaborative effort of the Government of India and Five UN agencies-UNDP, UNICEF, UNESCO, ILO and UNEPA-to provide supports to the ongoing efforts towards achieving Lansdale programme. The programme covers 139 blocks, including 10 cities in 30 dist cts of nine states with a total project outlay of Rs. 103.13 core. The programme, which was to conclude on 31st December 2002, was extended for two years.

Navodaya Vidyalaya

The National Policy on Education 1986 envisaged setting up of model schools, one in each district of the country. Navodaya Vidyalaya is a fully residential co-educational institution providing education up to senior secondary stage. The scheme, which stated in 1985-86, has grown to 513 schools (as on 31 March 2005) covering as many districts in 34 States/UTs with over 1.68 lakh students on rolls as on 31st March 2005. More than 30,000 new students are admitted every year.

Kendriya Vidyalaya

The Government approved the scheme of Kendriya Vidyalaya Sanghatan in 1962, on the basis of recommendations of the Second Pay Commission. Initially 20 residential schools in different states were taken over as central schools. At present there are 931 Kendriya Vidyalayas (as on 17 June 2005) out of which three are abroad i.e. one each in Kathmandu, Moscow and Tehran.

MAJOR FINDINGS OF THE STUDY AND POLICY PRESCRIPTIONS

The following findings have come out in our study.

1. *Enrolment rate and dropout rate are high in primary education in India.* The enrolment ratio in class I-V is 94.90 per cent and the dropout rates are as high as 40.25 per cent. It clearly shows the problems in primary education.
2. *School building infrastructure is inadequate in India and it is one of the reasons for high dropout rate.* Still 5 per cent of rural population have to go more than 1 km for primary education and 15% population have to go more than 3 km for upper primary school. And 35 per cent of schools have no pucca buildings and in some regions there is scarcity of buildings.
3. *Teacher student ratio is high in India.* In case of primary education in India in some places like Rajasthan about 50 per cent of schools were single teacher schools and student teacher ratio in India is 42. Compared to other countries including developed countries it is very low.
4. *Basic infrastructure in primary education is poor in India:* There is scarcity of toilets, safe drinking water, playgrounds and library and electric connectivity. So lack of basic facilities is also one of the reasons for high dropout rates in India.
5. *There is uneven progress in the infrastructural facilities.* As far as the primary educational infrastructure is, concerned in India it is unequal. In some states like Kerala, Delhi, Goa, Gujarat, Mizoram, infrastructure it is well developed. Teacher student ratio is low. In some parts like Bihar, Jarkhand it is very poor.
6. *Government has taken several measures to improve the situation; it has launched several programs to improve primary education in India.* Some of these initiatives are National Technology Mission, District Primary Education Program, Nutrition support for primary education, Lok Jumbish and Shiksh Karmi in Rajasthan, Bihar Education Project (BEP). National Open School, Sarva Shiksha Abhiyan and other state specific initiatives.

In the light of the macro analysis of infrastructural facilities in primary education sector in India–position and problems, we make the following suggestions for improving the performance of both students and teachers.

- *Strengthen basic facilities in primary schools.* Governments–central, state and local-have to take initiatives to improve the basic facilities like drinking water, toilets and play grounds and library and furniture.
- *Effectively implement the polices.* There is a need to implement effectively the government policies in primary education level, for example Child Labour Prohibition and Regulation Act, which will improve the enrolment rate and reduce the dropout rate.
- *Increase the percentage of public expenditure on education infrastructure.* The percentage of public expenditure on primary education in total expenditure was 3.9 in 1998-99 and in 2004. It should be increased substantially in order to avoid sub-standard education.
- *Encourage private sector participation in primary education in a meaningful way.* To improve the infrastructure facilities in primary school level and to enhance the quality, private participation in the primary educational level is needed. Individuals and organizations should play a pro-active role in systemic growth of primary education in a systematic way. Value-based and inclusive education (incorporating gender equity; quality consciousness; awareness of rights and duties; communication with purpose and performance; and effective, environment-friendly, accessible and affordable infrastructure) should be the basic agenda of primary education, at the earliest.

CONCLUSION

Universal elementary education is possible only when infrastructure of universally acceptable standard is provided and is utilized effectively. Government has to concentrate on providing infrastructure like pucca school buildings, and basic facilities like blackboards, toilets, drinking water, playgrounds and libraries etc. And government has to realize that education is one of the best investments for developing countries. Reaching the Millennium Development Goal of increasing literacy rates by one-half by 2015 will then be easier.

REFERENCES

Government of India (2002), "The Indian Child: A Profile", Department of Women and Child Development Ministry of Human Resource Development, New Delhi.

_________(2006), *"India 2006"*, A Reference Annual, Research Reference and Training Division, Ministry of Information and Broadcasting, New Delhi.

Hans, V.B. (2000), *"A Handbook of Economics of Development"*, Mangala Publications, Mangalore.

Hans, V. Basil (2006), "Intellectual Property Rights and India–Issues and Imperatives", *The Journal of World Intellectual Property Rights*, Vol. 2 No. 1-2, pp. 229-239.

Parikh Kirit S. and R. Radhakrishna (ed.) (1999-2000), *"India Development Report"*, Oxford University Press.

_________ (2002), *"India Development Report, 2002"*, Oxford University Press, New Delhi.

R. Govinda (ed.) (2002), *"India Education Report"*, Oxford University Press.

The PROBE Team (1998), *"Public Report on Basic Education in India"*, Oxford University Press.

UNESCO, (2003), "Reaching Education", *EFA Global Monitoring Report 2002*, UN Chronicle, No. 2.

The World Bank (1995), *"Economic Development in India–Achievement and Challenges"*, The World Bank, Washington D.C.

HEALTH FOR ALL IN INDIA AND HUMAN DISTRESS

*W. N. Salve**

INTRODUCTION

Education and health are key inputs in the development of human resources. Health is an equally important constituent of well being and foundation of prosperity and development of social sector in a country. (Chopra, 2004) Education, health, family welfare, sanitation, water supply, shelter, environment, health security, health care expenditure all these factors constitute the basic social sector.

Health is wealth, this old adage is important today and it is relevant for all countries in the world. Good health is an essential requirement for the enjoyment of every aspect of life. Therefore, the health of the people is an index of the prosperity and well being of a country. (Shyamala, Mathuraja, 2004) The UPA government of India is trying to increase government expenditures on health and education to implement its commitment of growth with a human face (Jhunjhunwala, 2006).

OBJECTIVES OF THE STUDY

The objectives of the study are follows:

1. To examination the health status of poor and under privileged class in India.
2. To know the National health policy regarding the goal health for all in India.
3. To analyze some basic indicators of human development relating to health.
4. To provide necessary suggestions as remedial measures.

This paper is based on primary and secondary data published in different reports of the government and non-government agencies.

* Shri Venkatesh College, Ichalkararij, Maharashtra.

WHAT IS HEALTH?

Firstly, we shall try to discuss the concept of health. Health is a broad concept in development of the society. Health does not mean merely adjust of individual to extend environments physical and social (Madan,1976) health is defined by the World Health Organization (WHO) as a state of complete physical, mental and social well-being and not merely absence of disease or infirmity. This definition was accepted by all the signatories to the Alma-Ala declaration on health, which was adopted by the thirty first world assembly in 1978. The declaration gave the call for all nations about health for all by 2000 A.D. and accepted that primary health care was a key to attending this goal (Mahadevia, 2000).

In the UNO charter of human rights prepared in1948, the right to basic education and primary health care has been recognized as human rights. India had signed the UN conversion on human rights (Chopra, 2004).

According to the Article 47, under Directive principles of state policy in the Indian constitution, the State Public Health Department, which has the responsibility of primitive, preventive, curative and rehabilitative care has been playing a vital role in evolving a machinery to create conditions congenial to the promotions of positive health. Therefore, every child born in India must have an assurance of good health, education and prosperity.

HEALTH STATUS IN INDIA

There is a very close relationship, which exists between water, sanitation, health, nutrition, and human well being. Health is a multi-dimensional phenomenon. The basic needs approach considers health as a basic need along with food, clothing shelter and education. In developing countries, such as India, there are number of factors that affect the peoples health status, from the health status factors point of view, Mahadevia (2000) has classified varies factors, some of them listed below:

1. Poverty, food security, food pricing and malnutrition.
2. Environmental pollution and degrading.
3. Occupational health problems.
4. Household hold economy and wages.
5. Economic development represented by per capita income, urbanization and industrialization.

6. Social development, especially literacy rates.
7. Prices of private health care system and public health care delivery system.

There is a very close relationship between poverty, environment and health factors. In India, about 26 per cent of the rural and urban population is below the poverty line. They live in make shift houses. About 70 per cent of rural households and 60 percentages of urban households do not have access to safe sanitation. Around 20-30 per cent of urban residents live in slums (Sarma, 2005) .

According to the Ninth Five Year Plan draft, urban migration over the last decade has resulted in rapid growth of urban slums. In some cities in India, the health status of urban slum dwellers is worse than that of rural population.

As a result of high incidence of poverty, large sections of population are under nourished. As far as literacy is concerned the average rate of literacy at the national level is still 65%. Female literacy is even lower, around 54%,female literacy in rural areas is only 47%.in many parts of the country, it is common to find that male and female workers and even child workers migrate from rural area to construction sites in cities and towns, in search of daily wages employment. These workers are forced to live in sub-human conditions. Poor people tend to live in unhygienic environmental conditions and are at high risk of infections and at high risk of infections and diseases. They are trapped in the vicious cycle of malnutrition, low birth weight female infants, malnourished adolescents, malnourished pregnant and lactating mothers and low weight. (Mahadeva, 2000).

Rajasekaran (2006) says that Eighty to Ninety percent diseases are due to malnutrition and poverty and poor living conditions. The health problems in India are different from those in the west. India is heading from an explosive increase in HIV infections. It is estimated that about 40 million India's will be infected by HIV virus by next two decades. According to World Health Organization Report June 2006, as much as 24% of all global diseases are caused by environmental exposures and can be averted. The report estimates over 33% of diseases in children under five is caused by environmental exposures. The four main diseases influenced by poor environments are diarroea, lower respiratory infections, various forms of unintentional injuries, and maleria. Preventing environmental risk could save as many as four million lives a year, mostly in developing countries (The Times of India, June 18, 2006).

PUBLIC HEALTH INDIAN SCENARIO

The government of India adopted the new Economic Policy, and Economic Reforms were launched in 1991, almost one and a half decades ago. As far as health expenditure in India is concerned, public expenditure contributes a significantly small percentage of health care expenditure. It was 17.9 percentage of the total in 2001, which was less than other developing countries (Bhat, Jain, 2006).

From the Table 1, we can see that expenditure on health as percentage of total GDP declined in India from 1.3 % in 1990 to 0.9% in 2001. In most developed & developing countries, it differs from 5% to7%.

Table 1
Expenditure on Health as Percentage of Total GDP of Selected Countries (As %of GDP)

Country	*Public Expenditure on Health (1990)*	*(2001)*
Bhutan	N.A	3.6
Bangladesh	1.4	1.5
Maldives	N.A.	5.6
India	1.3	0.9
Nepal	2.2	1.5
Pakistan	1.8	1.0
Srilanka	1.8	1.8
China	2.1	—
Indonesia	0.7	—
Thailand	1.1	—
Malaysia	1.3	—
Korea	2.7	—
Australia	5.8	—
Japan	5.2	—
New Zealand	5.9	—
South Africa	3.2	—
Canada	9.0	—
USA	13.3	—
France	9.1	—
Germany	9.1	—
United Kingdom	6.6	—

Source: University News, 37 (34), August 23, 1999, " Socio-Economic Indicators". Economic and Political Weekly, April 2, 2005.

At the time of budget 2005-06, the government of India had emphasized on poverty alleviation in the UPA governments Common Minimum Programs (CMP) and repeated assurances given by the Prime Minister Dr. ManMohan Singh that his government would deliver reforms with a human face. The Finance Minister Shri. P. Chidamberam had announced in the budget speech 2006-07 that the allocation for the department of health and family welfare has been increased by 22.0% to Rs. 12546 crore (The Economic Times, 1 March, 2006).

The government of India faces the key challenges of increasing public spending from less than one percent of GDP to 2-3 per cent over the next years. Shivkumar (2005) says that India's health record, relatively speaking and in an absolute sense is extremely poor. According to human development report 2004, Bangladesh in 2002, reported a lower infant mortality rate of 51 deaths per 1000 than India (64 deaths per 1000 live births) in 2002. India's IMR was much higher than IMR for Malaysia (8), Shrilanka (7), China (20) and Thailand (24). Similarly India's maternal mortality ratio (MMR) is higher than other developing countries. India's health status, which revels poor performance as compared to other countries of the world. On an average per capita per day caloric intake in India (2496) is quite low as compare to china (2897), Canada (3119), and Malaysia (2977). (Chopra, 2004, Murty-2004).

Besides, the number of doctors and nurses per lakh population in India are lower as compared to other countries of the world.

HUMAN DISTRESS

India is committed to the goal health for all and in the last four decades, a wide network of primary health centers and sub centers has been created, yet most of the states in India are far away from this goal (Roy, Kulkarni-2004). Many surveys as well as National Family Health Survey, NHFS-1 and NHFS-2 shows that either the services do not reach the disadvantaged sections of the society or from those sections do not utilize the available services. Roy and Kulkarni (2004) examined the social inequalities in health and nutrition in India.

Health achievements among communities classified as belonging to scheduled castes and scheduled tribes tend to be consistently below national average (Shivkumar, 2005). The importance of improving the health status of the Indian people as well as need for equitable, efficient and high quality healthy services has been pointed out in both the tenth five year plan as well as in the National Health policy NHP 2002. (Alpana sagar, 2003). However, 26% of the population is below the poverty line in India. These poor people are struggling for basic health services. Table 2, shows backlog of major human deprivations regarding health in South Asia during 1995-2010.we can see from this Table that 140 million people are denied access to basic health care, 234 million are without safe drinking water. There are 63 million malnourished children under the age of five. India's health status is poor as compare to other countries in South Asia. The population of country is still having poor health standards due to inadequate medical care, lack of nutritious diet, poverty and unhygienic conditions. It has been observed from human development report that, 640 million people are deprived of basic sanitization facilites, 88 % of all pregnant women aged between 15 and 49 suffer from anemia. In mega-cities like Bombay, 57% of the population lives in slums. 29% million adults are still illiterate. 45% million children were out of primary schools in 1995 (University News, March 30, 1998).

Table 2
Backlog of Major Human Deprivations Regarding Health in South Asia During 1995-2010 (in millions)

Health	*India*	*Pakistan*	*Bangladesh*	*Nepal*	*Srilanka*	*Bhutan*	*Total Asia*
No access to basic health care:1995	140	63	66	N.A.	1.3	0.6	271
additional population to be provided basic health care: 1995-2010	286	66	52	9.5	4.3	0.8	419
total no. of people to be provided health care during 1995-2010	426	129	118	9.5	5.6	1.4	690
Safe Water							
no access to safe drinking water:1995	234	71	26	12	7	N.A.	350
additional population to be provided safe Water: 1995-2010	286	66	52	9.5	4.3	0.8	419
total no. of people to be provided safe water during: 1995-2010	520	137	78	22	11	0.8	769
Nutrition							
no. of malnourished children:1995	63	9	13	1.7	0.7	N.A.	87

N.A.: Not available
Source: University News 36 (17), April 27, 1998

Nearly one third of children under 1.6 are forced into child labor.44% of the total population lives in absolute poverty. Nearly one-third of the world's poor live in India (University News, April 13, 1998).

As per census data, 2001, only 36.4 percent of total population has latrines within or attached to their houses. However, in rural areas only 21.9 percent of population have latrines within or attached to their houses. Women in rural areas often suffer from lack of privacy harassment and need to walk large distances to find a suitable place for defecation in the absence of house hold or appropriate (Saxena, Prakash, 2006).

Indian women face traditional taboos, based on cultural practice and religious belief, against consulting doctors (Shyamala, Muthuraja, 2004). Malnourishment is high in the tribal areas, it is mainly due to lack of food security and water security for the people in drought prone areas in India. Most of the agricultural laborers landless laborers and marginal farmers ,laborers belonging to scheduled castes and tribes migrates from drought prone areas to sugar factories in Maharashtra and other states in India. Seasonal migrants workers live in a temporary shelters at the periphery of large. Sugarcane areas. They get drinking water from unprotected source and they live on polluted soil, which dangerous to health of people. They suffer from various types of sickness like Diarrhoea, Dysentery and Vomiting, Measles, Bronchits, Chicken-Guinea, Worms, Scabies, Typhoid, Teething, Jundice, Fever Tetanus, Cough, Cold-Influe, Toothache etc. Contract basis seasonal migrant workers agree not covered by the industrial hygiene programs in the sugar factories under the factories Act, (Salve, 2004). Informal sectors employment, including that of migrant workers, is generally excluded from protective legislation (Ashrit, 2006).

The government of India has introduced the Universal Health Insurance (UHI) scheme, targeting the poor in 2003. Social Health Insurance Scheme (SHI), that has been recentaly launched for the workers in the unorganized sectors. However, it does not cover contract basis workers, seasonal migrants workers, agricultural workers in the unorganized sector (Gupta, Trivedi, 2005). The General insurances corporation has a mediclaim policy, which is admittedly not successful. Currently, the health care system in India suffers a serious paradox, a very high expenditure without a matching outcome, often, low quality service, difficulties in accessing health care by the poor and under privileged, misplaced subsides, etc. are considered responsible for this mismatch. (Choudhary, 2004).

The national common minimum program announced by the UPA government, under scores the urgent need to increase the levels of public spending on health from 0.9 percent of GDP to 2-3 percent over the next five years. It calls for extending health insurances coverage for the poor, stepping up investment to control communicable diseases and providing leadership for the control and prevention of AIDS. In response, the prime minister has announced the setting up of a National Rural Health Mission (NRHM) (Shivkumar, 2005).

However, in India, public health care provision has not been successful in building health security into the lives of the poor. Public health services are weak and inefficient (Ahuja, 2005). The poor and vulnerable groups have no access to public sector insurance. WHO estimates that about 80% of all sickness and diseases are due to lack of safe water and sanitation and evidences relating to higher incidence of communicable diseases such as diarrhoea,cholera,maleria etc. in the country. Lack of or inadequate sanitation impacts the local economy by adversely affecting, for instance productivity loss due to sickness and over all quality of life. (Saxena, Prakash 2006).

CONCLUSION

Health is a broad concept and health status of the Indian people, therefore is related to a number of factors. Expenditure by government on public facilities affects health status; the government of India has been trying to introduce health insurance schemes, for the low-income segments. However, most of the people belonging to scheduled castes and scheduled tribes are illiterate and ignorant, they are not aware of public health insurance schemes of the government of India.

From the foregoing discussion, following measures can be suggested.

1. Health should be recognized as a fundamental human right of the citizen of India.
2. There is an urgent need for public action in building health security into the lives of the poor. Health security to the poor is priority social need.
3. There is the need for an expansion of health insurance mechanism in the country, especially to cover the low-income households, and contract basis workers, seasonal migrant workers in unorganized sector.
4. Rural health-facilities should be expanded and extended vigorously through a network of community health centers and sub-centers in order to improve their accessibility and availability.
5. Educational and health care programs must be implemented effectively.
6. Adequate attention should be paid to the common man as a citizen of the country in order to achieve the goal health for all in India.

REFERENCES

Ahuja Rajeev, Narang Alka (2005), "Emerging Trends in Health Insurances for Low Income Groups", *Economic and Political Weakly*.

Alpana Sagar, Imrana Qudeer (2002), "Alternative Economic Survey 2002-03", *Rainbow*, New Delhi.

Ashrit Radha, R. (2006), "Health Status of Working Women", *Yojana*, March.

Bhat Ramesh, Jain Nishant (2006), "Analysis of Public and Private Healthcare Expenditures", *Economic and Political Weekly*, January 7.

Chopra Vipla (2004), "Basic Education and Healthcare in India", See Edited Vol. Murty. S.

Gupta Indrani, Trivedi Mayur (2005), "Social Health Insurance", Redefined *Economic and Political Weekly*, September 17.

Jhunjhunwala Bharat (2006), "Government Expenditure on Health Services", *Teacher's Movement* Vol. 8.

Madan, G.R. (1976), "Indian Social Problems", Delhi, Allied.

Mahadeva, Darshini (2000), "Health for all in Gujarat", *Economic and Political Weekly*, August 26, September 2.

Murty, S. (2004), "Education, Health and Housing in India", Some Aspects, Edited Vol. *RBSA Publication* Jaipur.

Rajasekaran (2006), "Radical Changes Required in Medical Education", *University News* 44.

Roy, T. K. Kulkarni, Sumati, Vaidehi Y. (2004), "Social inequalities in Health and Nutrition in Selected States", *Economic and Political Weekly.*

Salve, W. N. (2004), "Health Status of Seasonal Migrants in Maharashtra", See Edited Vol. Murthy, 2004.

Sarma E.A. (2005), "Social Sectors Allocations", *Economic and Political Weekly*, April 2.

Saxena Shipra, Prakash Anjal (2006), "Sanitation and Health", *Yojana*, June.

Shyamala, S. Muthuraj. C. (2004), "Gender and Health in India-Strategies and Challenges", Edit Murty, 2004.

Shyamalaya, S. Muthuraja. C. (2004), "Health for All in India Myth and Reality", See Edited Vol. Murthy, S. 2004.

Shiva Kumar A. K. (2005), "Budgeting for Health", *Economic and Political Weekly*, April 2.

Others:

The Times of India, June 18, 2006.

The Economic Times, March 1, 2006.

University News, 36 (13), March 30, 1998.

University News, April 13, 1998.

University News, April 27, 1998.

University News, August 23, 1998..

PROBLEMS AND PROSPECTS OF DAIRY COOPERATIVES IN INDIA

P. S. Kamble, A. S. Suryavanshi** & Lalita Jagtap*

INTRODUCTION

Agriculture is the main occupation of more or less each and every developing country in the world. Likewise, it is also the main occupation in India. Even though, the share of agriculture in GDP of India shows a falling trend, its significance as a means of livelihood is indebatable today also. It is more than 60 percent today. Agriculture coupled with the allied activities like dairy, poultry, etc. can play a very pivotal role in achieving rapid and all round economic development of the economy in general and rural economy in particular. Such agro allied activities developed in the cooperative sector has a special importance. Because cooperative sector has a very important place in socio-economic development of the economy, which facilitates participation in development as well as socio-economic development of the poor section of the population, necessary for social welfare maximisation of the people, especially in rural areas.

India has an old and rich heritage of cooperative sector, which has played a very vital role in socio-economic development of the Indian economy in general and rural economy in particular. The development of economic activities like textile mills, sugar factories, credit facilities, marketing, poultry, dairy and so on. The role played by them in the development of agro allied activities in India is so much important. The new economic policy popularly known as economic reforms programme has brought about the number of changes in economic policy in general and policies of sub sectors in particular. This has led to significant changes in economic activities, productive sectors and their development as well. We see the positive, negative repercussions on the economy of India. In

* Reader, Department of Economics, Shivaji University, Kolhapur.
* Research Students, Deptt. of Economics, Shivaji University, Kolhapur.

this backdrop, it will be of vital importance to study dairy cooperatives growth, problems and prospects. It is against this background, the present paper endeavours to examine the growth, problems and prospects of dairy cooperatives in India especially in the new economic policy regime.

OBJECTIVES

The important objectives of the present study are enlisted below.

1. To study the role of dairy cooperatives in economic development of India.
2. To examine the growth of dairy cooperatives in our country.
3. To analyse development of dairy cooperatives states wise as well as at macro level.
4. To find out or identify the problems or challenges before Indian dairy cooperatives.
5. To reveal policy implications as well as measures to tackle the problems before the dairy cooperatives in India.

HYPOTHESIS

Following is the hypothesis of the present study.

"Cooperative sector is an important productive sector in India as far as its role in socio-economic development of India is concerned. It has no alternative even in the era of economic reforms also. But due care and attempts should be made in that direction in the case of agro allied cooperative activities such as dairy cooperatives."

DATA BASE AND RESEARCH METHODOLOGY

The present study will attempt to examine the growth, problems and prospects of dairy cooperatives in India with reference to economic reforms period specially. It mainly relies on the secondary data. The secondary data necessary and required is collected from the publications, reports and official records such as Animal Husbandry Department's. Basic Animal Husbandry Statistics, CSO Statistics, Economic Survey, Cooperative Quarterly, Dairyman, Report of National Dairy Development Board (NDDB) etc.

The collected secondary data is classified and tabulated in the light of the objectives and hypothesis of the present study. The processing of data is so much necessary for revealing trends, relationships and inferences. Hence, the collected data is processed by using the necessary and suitable statistical tools such as Compound Growth Rate (CGR),

Simple Growth Rate (SGR), Mean, Standard Deviation (SD), Correlation, Regression, ANOVA and others. For this, the use of computer software packages such as SPSS, EXCEL has been made.

DAIRY COOPERATIVES IN INDIA: A MACRO PERSPECTIVE

The Indian dairy industry acquired substantial growth during the Eight Plan, achieving an annual output of over 69 million tonnes of milk.[1] As dairy cooperatives is a national level economic activity, it's progress can be reviewed at national level i. e. in macro perspective. It is presented in Table 1 by employing some important parameters.

Table 1
Dairy Cooperatives in India in a Macro Perspective

Item	*1980-81*	*1990-91*	*2003-04*	*2004-05*
No. of Dairy Cooperatives	13284	63415	109674	113152
Members (in thousands)	1747	7482	11994	12326
Milk Procurement (in thousand Kgs per day)	2582	9702	17483	20070
Liquid Milk Marketing (in thousand liters per day)	2783	9046	14875	15828

Source: National Dairy Development Board, Annual Report, 2004-05.

India's milk output has not only placed the industry first in the world. But also represents sustained growth in the availability of milk and milk products.[2] It is observed that the growth of number of dairy cooperatives was higher than 100 percent as indicated by CGR (Compound Growth Rate) during the period of 23 years from 1980-81 to 2004-05, showing more than 4 percent growth on an average. During the same period, the growth in members of dairy cooperatives was considerable (88 percent), but not in the proportion of growth of number of dairy cooperatives. Dairy cooperatives have done a commendable work in milk procurement, which showed 96 percent growth during the period into our consideration. Their attempts in liquid milk marketing is considerable, but not to the extent expected (77 per cent). The mean value of number of dairy cooperatives, members, milk procurement and liquid milk marketing stood at 74881.25, 8387.25, 12459.25 and 10633 respectively. The standard deviation of all these parameters shows it was higher for number dairy cooperatives (46907.29). After that milk procurement (7923.04), liquid milk marketing (6031.13) and members of cooperatives (4947.55) showed their more difference from the mean values. The study of correlations between all these parameters showed strong relations between them. Their Pearson correlation coefficient stood at .99 (0.05 significant level). This is a clear indication of all the parameters used to examine the progress of dairy cooperatives in India during the period 1980-81 to 2004-05 played a very vital role in the progress of dairy cooperatives in India in macro perspective. Likewise, the partial correlation between milk procurement and milk marketing shows a strong correlation (.98) between them.

Milk production has a special importance in the progress of dairy cooperatives in India. It also determines the per capita availability of milk in our country. Hence, it is of vital importance to examine the trends in the production of milk and its per capita availability.

Table 2
Milk Production and Availability in India

Year	*Production Per (Million Tonnes)*	*Capita Availability (Grams per day)*
1991-92	55.7	178
1995-96	65.2	197
2000-01	80.6	220
2001-02	84.4	225
2002-03	86.2	230
2003-04	88.1	231
2004-05	90.7	229
CGR	7.91	4.07

Source: State/Union Territory Animal Husbandry Departments, 2004.
SGR: Compound Growth Rate

It is revealed that during 1991-92 to 2004-05 milk production showed growth of 7.91 per cent CGR. But per capita availability of milk has been adversely affected by rapidly growing population of India. As a result, it showed only a considerable growth of 4.07 per cent (CGR) during the same period. Milk production remained at the mean value of 78.70 million tonnes with 215.79 grams per day average availability of milk per capita. Their deviation (Standard Deviation) from the means was 13.14 million tonnes and 20.37 grams per day per capita during the same period. The analysis of variance (ANOVA) of both milk production and per capita availability of milk stood at 1035.96 and 2491.42 between groups respectively. Likewise, milk production and its per capita availability showed a very strong correlation showing .99 coefficient of correlation. More or less the same degree of partial correlation we found between milk production and the per capita availability of milk.

DAIRY COOPERATIVES IN INDIA: A STATE WISE ANALYSIS

From the point of view of assessing the state dairy cooperatives in India, its state wise analysis as a special importance. This facilitates in examining centralisation or decentralisation of the dairy cooperatives in India during the period into our consideration i.e. 1980-81 to 2004-05. It also enables in highlighting other dimensions of dairy cooperatives in India. Table 3 presents the state wise growth of dairy cooperatives in India.

Table 3
State wise Growth of Dairy Cooperatives in India

State	*1980-81*	*1990-91*	*2003-04*	*2004-05*	*SGR*
NORTH					
Haryana	505	3229	4219	5172	90.23
Himachal Pradesh	-	210	293	387	45.73
Jammu & Kashmir	-	105	-	-	-
Punjab	490	5726	6892	6893	9289
Rajasthan	1433	4976	9643	10852	86.79
Uttar Pradesh	248	7880	18104	18272	98.64
EAST					
Assam	-	117	65	66	-77.27
Bihar	118	2060	4657	5023	97.65
Jharkhand	-	-	80	80	-
Nagaland	-	21	76	76	72.36
Orissa	-	736	1654	1896	61.18
Sikkim	-	134	189	194	30.92
Tripura	-	73	84	84	13.09
West Bengal	584	1223	2287	2367	48.33
WEST					
Chattisgarh	-	-	424	445	4.71
Goa	-	124	169	174	28.73
Gujarat	4798	10056	11400	11615	58.69
Madhya Pradesh	441	3865	4699	4815	90.84
Maharashtra	718	4535	18349	19192	96.25
SOUTH					
Andhra Pradesh	298	4766	5072	4561	93.46
Karnataka	1267	5621	9293	9619	86.82
Kerala	-	1016	3208	3238	68.62
Tamil Nadu	2382	6871	7631	8031	70.33
Pondicherry	-	71	96	100	29.00

Source: National Dairy Development Board, Annual Report, 2004-05.
SGR: Simple Growth Rate

It is revealed that northern states have achieved significantly rapid growth of dairy cooperatives. The noteworthy are UP, Punjab, Haryana and Rajasthan. Except Bihar, Nagaland all other Eastern states in India have failed in the development of dairy cooperatives. Maharashtra, Madhya Pradesh have achieved a significant growth in the progress of dairy cooperatives. In the Southern states, Andhra Pradesh and Karnataka are in leading position. Gujarat has failed in making dynamic the process of dairy cooperatives growth. On an average, Uttar Pradesh

(11126), Maharashtra (10698), Gujarat (9465), Rajasthan (6726) and Karnataka (6450) have performed well in the context of growth of dairy cooperatives in India. On the contrary, Assam has failed in the development of dairy cooperatives (-77.27 percent). And the states like Chhattisgarh, Tripura, Goa, Sikkim have shown a very dismal performance. Members of the dairy cooperatives play a very vital role in the development of any cooperatives in general and dairy cooperatives in particular. Hence, it is so much important to study the growth of members state wise.

Table 4
State wise Growth of Members

State	*1980-81*	*1990-91*	*2003-04*	*2004-05*	*SGR*
NORTH					
Haryana	39	184	230	239	83.68
Himachal Pradesh	-	17	21	20	15.00
Jammu & Kashmir	-	2	-	-	-
Punjab	25	304	402	409	93.88
Rajasthan	80	340	534	565	85.84
Uttar Pradesh	18	392	824	845	97.86
EAST					
Assam	-	2	3	3	1.00
Bihar	3	100	240	254	98.81
Jharkhand	-	-	2	2	-
Nagaland	-	1	3	3	66.66
Orissa	-	45	122	130	64.61
Sikkim	-	4	7	7	42.85
Tripura	-	4	4	4	-
West Bengal	20	66	172	184	89.13
WEST					
Chattisgarh	-	-	19	20	5.00
Goa	-	12	19	19	36.84
Gujarat	741	1612	2360	2428	69.48
Madhya Pradesh	24	150	231	239	89.95
Maharashtra	87	840	1582	1621	94.63
SOUTH					
Andhra Pradesh	33	561	756	762	95.66
Karnataka	195	1013	1737	1909	89.78
Kerala	-	225	706	733	69.30
Tamil Nadu	481	1590	1988	1998	75.92
Pondicherry	-	17	32	32	46.87

Source: National Dairy Development Board, Annual Report, 2004-05.

It is seen that the Northern states have greatly succeeded in increasing the number of members of dairy cooperatives except Jammu & Kashmir and Himachal Pradesh during 1980-81 to 2004-05. After that, Southern states have contributed considerably in the growth of membership of dairy cooperatives. In the state wise growth of membership of dairy cooperatives Bihar (98.81%), Uttar Pradesh (97.86%), Andhra Pradesh (95.66%), Maharashtra and Punjab (93.88%) were in leading position. At the same time Assam, Tripura, Chhattisgarh, Jharkhand, Jammu & Kashmir and Himachal Pradesh have shown a very poor performance in enhancing their membership. Dairy cooperatives perform an important function to assure reasonable price and income for their members is procurement of milk. Hence, it can be considered as a major indicator of development of dairy cooperatives in India.

Table 5
State wise Trends in Milk Procurement

State	*1980-81*	*1990-91*	*2003-04*	*2004-05*	*SGR*
NORTH					
Haryana	33	94	331	367	91.00
Himachal Pradesh	-	14	25	28	50.00
Jammu & Kashmir	-	11	-	-	-
Punjab	75	394	745	780	90.38
Rajasthan	138	364	1036	1470	90.61
Uttar Pradesh	64	382	814	958	93.31
EAST					
Assam	-	4	4	4	-
Bihar	3	95	296	482	93.37
Jharkhand	-	-	6	6	-
Nagaland	-	1	2	3	66.66
Orissa	-	41	127	164	75.00
Sikkim	-	4	9	7	42.85
Tripura	-	3	2	3	-
West Bengal	31	52	324	326	94.49
WEST					
Chattisgarh	-	-	18	18	-
Goa	-	16	43	51	68.62
Gujarat	1344	3102	5102	5857	77.05
Madhya Pradesh	68	256	294	392	82.65
Maharashtra	165	1872	2680	2698	94.19
SOUTH					
Andhra Pradesh	79	763	950	1055	92.51
Karnataka	261	917	2043	2700	90.33
Kerala	301	1106	1664	1981	84.80
Tamil Nadu	-	26	54	51	49.01
Pondicherry	-	185	614	669	72.34

Source: National Dairy Development Board, Annual Report, 2004-05.

Like all other parameters, in the context of milk procurement Northern states of India have achieved a tremendous progress in the milk procurement by dairy cooperatives during the period 1980-81 to 2004-05.

As usual, Northern states were so much ahead even in milk procurement compared with other category of states. At national level, West Bengal (94.49%), Maharashtra (94.19%), Bihar (93.31%), Uttar Pradesh (93.31%) and Andhra Pradesh (92.51%) have done very well in the procurement of milk. Conversely, Jammu & Kashmir, Assam, Jharkhand, Tripura and Chhattisgarh showed a very dismal performance in this context. On an average, Gujarat (3851.25 thousand kgs), Maharashtra (1853.75), Karnataka (1530.25), Tamil Nadu (1263) and Rajasthan (752) achieved ranks in descending order. The same states showed higher volume of deviation in milk procurement from mean (SD).

Only collection of milk is not sufficient but marketing of milk is very much essential for the development of the dairy cooperatives as well as their economic viability. This necessitates to review liquid milk marketing by the dairy cooperatives state wise in India. It is shown in Table 6.

As far as region wise liquid milk marketing is concerned, Northern states were ahead as usual. They have achieved a rapid growth in the marketing of liquid milk. Eastern states were so much behind in this activity. The states like Uttar Pradesh, Haryana, Maharashtra, Rajasthan, Punjab achieved rapid growth in the sale of liquid milk. On the contrary, the states such as Jammu & Kashmir, Assam, Jharkhand, Chattisgarh, Himachal Pradesh showed a very poor performance in the marketing of liquid milk. On an average, the marketing of liquid milk of the leading states in India stood at Delhi 1447 (thousand liters per day), Mumbai 1083, Karnataka 1042.50, Maharashtra 819.50, Andhra Pradesh 624.25, Kolkata 588 respectively. The standard deviation (SD) of all the states in India reveals that the performance of the states such as Delhi (680.62 thousand liters per day), Maharashtra (740.13), Karnataka (664.67), Andhra Pradesh (450.74), Rajasthan (459.25) was considerable in the sale of liquid milk during the period into consideration.

The success and future of dairy cooperatives is greatly affected by the progress in the production of milk. Hence, growth in milk production can be considered as a parameter of assessing growth of dairy cooperatives. It is simple that rapid growth in the production of milk will facilitate in the development of the dairy cooperatives in India. The necessary data about this parameter is presented in Table 7.

It is observed that during the period 2000-01 to 2004-05, the states such as Orissa (31.72%), Uttaranchal (31.57%), Nagaland (26.08%), Sikkim (23.91%), Arunachal Pradesh (23.86%) were in leading position that achieved a significant growth rate in the production of milk. On the contrary, the states like Kerala (-28.64%), Karnataka (-28.64%), Tamil

Table 6
State wise Liquid Milk Marketing

(in thousand liters per day)

State	*1980-81*	*1990-91*	*2003-04*	*2004-05*	*SGR*
NORTH					
Haryana	2	80	153	214	99.06
Himachal Pradesh	-	15	15	16	6.25
Jammu & Kashmir	-	9	-	-	-
Punjab	7	139	496	501	98.80
Rajasthan	12	136	855	874	98.62
Uttar Pradesh	1	326	436	425	99.76
Delhi	697	1051	1937	2103	66.85
EAST					
Assam	-	10	8	7	-42.85
Bihar	8	111	288	293	97.26
Jharkhand	-	-	163	173	5.78
Nagaland	-	1	4	4	75.00
Orissa	-	65	132	151	56.95
Sikkim	-	5	7	7	28.57
Tripura	-	6	9	9	33.33
West Bengal	17	26	30	33	48.48
Kolkata	283	526	786	759	62.71
WEST					
Chattisgarh	-	-	28	30	6.66
Goa	-	36	89	90	60.00
Gujarat	39	279	296	304	81.11
Madhya Pradesh					
Maharashtra	18	363	1421	1476	98.18
SOUTH					
Andhra Pradesh	19	552	898	1028	98.15
Karnataka	166	889	1518	1597	89.60
Kerala	-	223	738	801	72.15
Tamil Nadu	109	405	511	578	81.14
Pondicherry	-	22	53	59	62.71
Chennai	245	662	695	751	67.37

Source: National Dairy Development Board, Annual Report, 2004-05.

Nadu (-2.63%), Delhi (3.96%), Chhattisgarh (6.49%) showed a very dismal performance in promoting the production of milk. On average basis, Uttar Pradesh (85993.80), Punjab (8164.40), Rajasthan (7873), Arunachal Pradesh (6426) and Maharashtra (6230) performed well in enhancing the production of milk. The same states show their better performance in this activity when their values of standard deviation are taken into account.

Milk has a special importance in the balanced and nutrient diet of the human beings. It is the per capita availability of milk, which facilitates

Table 7
State wise Milk Production in India

(in 000 tonnes)

State	*2000-01*	*2001-02*	*2002-03*	*2003-04*	*2004-05*	*SGR*
Andhra Pradesh	80607	84406	86159	88082	90715	11.14
Himachal Pradesh	5521	5814	6584	6959	7252	23.86
Arunachal Pradesh	683	682	705	727	739	7.57
Assam	2489	2664	2869	3180	2974	16.30
Bihar	45	45	46	48	57	21.05
Goa	5312	5862	6089	6421	6745	21.24
Gujarat	4850	4978	5124	5221	5222	7.12
Haryana	761	756	773	786	870	12.52
Jammu & Kashmir	1321	1360	1389	1414	1422	7.10
Karnataka	4599	4797	4539	3857	3917	-17.41
Kerala	2605	2718	2419	2111	2025	-28.64
Madhya Pradesh	4761	5283	5343	5388	5506	13.53
Maharashtra	5849	6094	6263	6379	6597	10.93
Manipur	66	68	69	71	75	12.00
Meghalaya	64	66	68	69	71	9.85
Mizoram	14	14	15	15	16	12.5
Nagaland	51	57	58	63	69	26.08
Orissa	876	929	941	997	1283	31.72
Punjab	7777	7932	8173	8391	8554	9.08
Rajasthan	7455	7758	7789	8054	8310	10.28
Sikkim	35	37	45	48	46	23.91
Tamil Nadu	4910	4988	4622	4752	4784	-2.63
Tripura	77	90	79	84	86	10.46
Uttar Pradesh	13857	14648	15288	15943	16512	16.07
West Bengal	3471	3515	3600	3688	3790	8.41
Delhi	291	294	296	299	303	3.96
Chhattisgarh	777	795	804	812	831	6.49
Uttaranchal	1025	1065	1079	1188	1195	14.22
Jharkhand	910	940	952	954	1330	31.57

Source: Basic Husbandry Statistics, 2004.

in getting balanced and nutrient diet for the people. Therefore, it is of vital importance to assess the state of per capita availability of milk state wise. This will enable us in examining the opportunities to have a balanced diet in the context of milk. It is shown in Table 8.

The efforts of some of the states in India led to a rapid growth in the per capita availability of milk during the period from 1990-91 to 2004-05. In this context, the attempts made by a few states like Arunachal Pradesh, Tripura, Orissa, Jammu & Kashmir, Goa were considerable one. The noteworthy thing is that they did not have much dairy cooperatives development. Conversely, the states having dairy cooperatives development could not promote to that extent the per capita availability

Table 8
State wise per Capita Availability of Milk

(gms per day)

State	*1991-92*	*2000-01*	*2001-02*	*2002-03*	*2003-04*	*2004-05*	*SGR*
Andhra Pradesh	120	194	209	231	238	250	52
Himachal Pradesh	313	335	341	339	337	378	17.19
Arunachal Pradesh	22	102	105	112	109	114	80.70
Assam	77	69	70	71	71	72	-6.94
Bihar	100	80	88	92	100	92	-8.69
Goa	65	89	91	91	93	110	40.90
Gujarat	236	280	317	321	330	344	31.39
Haryana	586	614	645	647	643	631	7.13
Jammu & Kashmir	204	348	367	365	363	364	43.95
Karnataka	149	233	249	209	190	194	23.19
Kerala	167	219	234	203	173	169	12.5
Madhya Pradesh	197	211	240	236	233	233	15.45
Maharashtra	136	162	172	172	172	176	22.72
Manipur	122	81	86	85	85	90	-33.55
Meghalaya	76	74	78	78	78	81	6.17
Mizoram	31	42	43	45	44	46	32.60
Nagaland	96	69	78	78	83	90	-6.66
Orissa	43	64	69	68	71	92	53.26
Punjab	722	854	892	895	898	917	21.26
Rajasthan	275	353	376	368	371	376	26.86
Sikkim	194	173	187	222	231	221	12.21
Tamil Nadu	164	211	219	198	198	204	19.80
Tripura	31	77	66	68	68	70	55.71
Uttar Pradesh	199	203	241	245	250	254	21.65
West Bengal	120	116	120	120	120	124	3.22
Delhi	65	56	58	57	56	54	-20.37
Chhattisgarh	-	100	105	103	102	103	2.91
Uttaranchal	-	323	344	379	365	364	11.26
Jharkhand	-	90	96	94	92	129	29.13

Source: Basic Husbandry Statistics, 2004.

of milk such as Gujarat, Karnataka, Maharashtra etc. Dairy industry in general and dairy cooperatives development in particular is affected by livestock growth. Livestock growth in India is presented in Table 9.

The significance of animal husbandry in the Indian economy arises also because of its assistance to tackle the serious problems of unemployment and underemployment for weaker sections in the country and for providing subsidiary occupation for income generations.[3]

It is observed that the growth in the livestock population during the period from 1951 to 2003 was marginal, which stood at only about 8 percent. Buffaloes play a vital role in the development of dairy industry as well as dairy cooperatives. It also plays a dominant role in the dry land agriculture particularly in the semi arid and arid areas of the country. Animal husbandry and dairy development are being used as a poverty eradication measures.[4] But the growth of adult female buffalo took place at the rate of about 20 percent during the same period, which is good thing but not desirable one. Conversely, the growth in the goat population was significantly higher that stood at 22.50 percent, which does not play any role in the development of dairy industry as well as dairy cooperatives in India. In this context, the role of cow population remains important one, but I could not get the sufficient data about that.

Table 9
Livestock Population Growth in India

(in million numbers)

Species	*1951*	*1961*	*1972*	*1982*	*1992*	*2003*	*SGR*
Cattle	155.3	176.6	178.3	192.5	204.6	185	4.06
Adult Female Cattle	54.4	51	53.4	59.2	64.4	64.5	4.84
Buffalo	43.4	51.2	57.4	69.8	84.2	97.9	17.91
Adult Female Buffalo	21	24.3	28.6	32.5	43.8	51	19.83
Total Bovines	198.7	206.8	235.7	262.2	288.8	283.1	7.71
Sheep	39.1	42.2	40	48.8	50.8	61.5	9.46
Goat	47.2	60.9	67.5	95.3	115.3	124.4	22.50
Total Livestock	292.9	336.5	353.2	419.6	470.9	485	7.87
Poultry	73.5	114.2	138.5	207.7	307.1	489	44.35

Source: Livestock Census, 2003.

Demand for the goods and services affect the development of concerned productive activities in general and industry in particular. Likewise, the demand for milk and milk products greatly influences in development of dairy industry as well as dairy cooperatives. Table 10 provides adequate data about per capita consumption expenditure as a determinant of demand for milk and milk products.

It is of significance importance that during 1970-71 to 1999-2000 total consumption expenditure of both the rural and urban population has been increased. Its increase was higher (92.81%) for urban areas than for rural (92.73%) areas. But consumption expenditure of the people in India was considerably higher on the total non-food than total food. Besides this, growth of expenditure on milk and milk products was lesser than growth of consumption expenditure on meat, egg and fish. This has adverse effect on the development of the dairy industry in general and dairy cooperatives in particular. And this was true in the case of both the rural and urban section of the population. The range of minimum and maximum of the milk and milk products, meat, egg and fish, total food, total non-food, total expenditure stood at 3.03–74.18, 1.02–26.77,

25.98–410.10, 9.33–444.10, 35.31–854.96 respectively. Their mean values stood at 25.01, 9.31, 156.09, 123.13 and 279.31 respectively. Total expenditure showed maximum value of standard deviation (296.27) showing its rapid growth, after that total non-food (144.26), total food (133.96), Milk and Milk products (24.10) and meat, egg and fish (8.74) were in ascending order. The study of correlation revealed that milk and milk products had significant correlations with total food expenditure (.992) and total expenditure (.998) but less than the item meat, egg and fish especially to total food expenditure.

Table 10
Per Capita Consumption Expenditure on Broad Groups of Items

(*in Rs.*)

NSS Round	*Milk & Milk Products*	*Meat, Egg & Fish*	*Total Food*	*Total Non-Food*	*Total Expenditure*
25th (1970-71)					
Rural	3.03	1.02	25.98	9.33	35.31
Urban	5.01	1.90	34.04	18.81	52.85
38th (1982)					
Rural	8.45	3.40	73.73	38.71	112.45
Urban	15.15	5.92	96.97	67.06	164.03
46th (1990-91)					
Rural	19.04	7.08	133.34	68.78	202.12
Urban	32.37	12.29	185.77	140	326.75
55th (July 1993 – June 2000)					
Rural	42.56	16.14	288.80	197.28	486.07
Urban	74.18	26.77	410.10	444.10	854.96
SGR					
Rural	92.88	93.68	91.00	95.27	92.73
Urban	93.24	92.90	91.67	95.76	93.81

Source: Basic Animal Husbandry Statistics, 2004, Government of India.

ROLE OF DAIRY COOPERATIVES IN INDIA

India is still today an agricultural country when its role as a means of livelihood and source of employment especially in the rural areas is considered. Dairy industry is an important agro based industry and allied activity. It has been playing a vital role on various fronts such as employment generation, income generation, development of agriculture, improving standard of living, reducing inequalities, eradiation of poverty, rural development, economic development of the economy and all others. It is of vital importance to study the role of dairy cooperatives in the socio-economic development of India in general and rural India in particular.

Agriculture and livestock sector in general and dairy industry in particular cannot be separated from each other. Hence, the role of agriculture and livestock sector in creating GDP gives us an idea about their contribution in economic development of India.

Table 11
Share of Agriculture and Livestock Sector in GDP

(Rs. in Billing)

Year	*GDP Total*	*GDP Rs.*	*Agriculture % Share*	*GDP Rs.*	*Livestock Sector % Share*
1980-81	1224	425	34.72	59	4.82
1990-91	4778	1352	28.30	308	6.45
1995-96	10733	2778	25.88	650	6.06
2000-01	19030	4235	22.25	1093	5.74
2001-02	20910	4631	22.15	1186	5.67
2002-03	22495	4564	20.29	1281	5.69
2003-04	25197	5215	20.70	1315	5.22
CGR	58.17	45.32	- 8.12	57.57	- 0.27

Source: National Accounts Statistics, 2005, CSO.

In India, agriculture still remains the predominant economic activity and any fluctuations in it have serious repercussions on the whole of the economy.[5] It is seen that India's total GDP has rose at the annual compound growth rate (CGR) of 58.17% during the period 1980-81 to 2003-04. During the same period, agriculture GDP, livestock GDP increased by 45.32% and 57.57% respectively. But their relative shares in GDP show significant falls with fluctuations. However, the importance of agriculture appears to be slowly declining.[6] This reveals that agriculture as well as livestock sector have played a very vital role in the development of India.

Item wise analysis of livestock sector facilitates us in assessing the role of dairy industry in general and dairy cooperatives in particular in economic development of India.

It is revealed that the livestock sector's contribution in output generation has rose at the marginal rate of 4.87% per annum during 2000-01 to 2004-05, which shows availability of further potentialities. More or less the same growth rate was achieved by milk ground i. e. dairy industry, in generating value of output, which remained at 4.73% annually. It is an indicator of under exploitation of potentialities of dairy industry in economic development of our economy. On the contrary, the contribution of poultry industry in the development was significantly rapid, which stood at about 28 per cent during 2000-01 to 2004-05.

Table 12
Value of Output from Livestock Sector
(At current prices in Rs. crores)

Item	*2000-01*	*2001-02*	*2002-03*	*2003-04*	*2004-05*	*CGR*
Milk Group	95490	101216	105537	108978	115970	4.73
Meat Group	24702	28118	28415	28751	30401	4.47
Eggs	4587	4874	4956	5013	5567	27.92
Wool & Hair	332	320	396	374	378	4.24
Dung	11436	11356	12599	12959	13877	5.32
Silk Worm Cocoons and Honey	1524	1922	1560	1639	1687	0.44
Investment in Stock	3407	3727	4071	4772	5470	12.67
Value of Output from Livestock	141478	151533	157534	162486	173350	4.87

Source: CSO, Department of Statistics, Government of India.

Value of output shows contributions of different productive sectors as well as economic activity wise in the economic development of the economy. That value of output is influenced by the changes in the prices of their commodities. This necessitates to examine the trends in the prices of their goods.

Table 13
Index Number of Wholesale Prices
(Prices Base 1993-94 = 100)

Particulars	*1994-95*	*2001-02*	*2003-04*	*2005-06*	*CGR*
All Commodities	112.6	155.7	175.9	195.6	42.43
Food Articles	112.8	170.5	181.5	195.3	42.17
Foodgrains	114.7	173.8	176.3	187	38.66
Fruits & Vegetables	108	160	195.6	218.9	50.66
Milk	110.3	163.2	176	184.3	40.15
Eggs, Fish & Meat	116.1	186	186.4	217.4	46.59
Oils Seeds	118.5	129.3	177.8	167.1	29.08
Food Products	114.9	145.7	166.7	176.8	35.01
Dairy Products	117	187.1	196.3	206.5	43.34
Edible Oils	110.9	112.9	157.9	146	24.04
Oil Cakes	121	146.4	223.9	189.7	36.21

Source: Office of the Economic Advisor, Government of India.

It is observed that the prices of all commodities have increased at the rate of 42.43% per annum during the period 1994-95 to 2005-06. Rise in milk prices as well as dairy product prices was significant one, which stood at 40.15% and 43.34% respectively. But this growth was less than the growth in prices of fruits and vegetables, eggs, fish and meat. But it was higher than the growth in prices of oil seeds, edible oils, oil cakes and oil seeds.

Dairy cooperatives in India have been playing a pivotal role in empowering women. The participation of women in dairy cooperatives have been significantly rose from 131388 in 2000-01 to 197958 in 2004-05 registering 1.5 fold growth.[7] Dairy cooperatives have been empowering the women through financial assistance to Self Help Groups (SHGs) of women.

Besides this, dairy cooperatives play an important role in the development of animal husbandry especially in the rural areas. They have been providing employment opportunities at significant level through milk processing, sale and production and sale of milk products. They are helping especially in rural areas in the eradication of poverty. Their role in the development of small businesses is important one. They have been also playing an important role in the development of infrastructural facilities such as road, transport. They have been also contributing to educational development, the degree of development may be less. Likewise, they are also availing some necessary goods particularly produced by them.

MAJOR CONCLUSIONS AND POLICY IMPLICATIONS

The foregoing analysis and data interpretation reveals some major conclusions regarding the dairy cooperatives in India. Further, their policy implications are necessary to take into consideration to overcome the challenges and problems before them. No doubt, the number of dairy cooperatives in India has been increasing as indicated by the growth rate but it is not adequate in the era of economic reforms to meet present challenges. Hence due efforts are necessary to promote the growth of the dairy cooperatives in India. Likewise, their membership is necessary to increase, which is not to the extent desirable. At the same time, they have not succeeded in promoting the activity of marketing of milk. As it is a definite source of income or earnings, serious efforts are necessary to undertake in that direction to promote and improve their financial position. Production of milk has been increasing in India, but it is inadequate as shown by its per capita availability. This indicates under exploitation of potentialities of dairy industry in India. Hence, it is of vital importance to promote the size and level of milk production whereby inadequate per capita availability can be abolished. These further demands to undertake efforts so as to achieve the development of animal husbandry useful for dairy industry. A state wise analysis of dairy cooperatives reveals that dairy cooperative development has been concentrated in the Northern states of India such as Uttar Pradesh, Punjab, Haryana, Rajasthan. It is harmful and unsustainable for the development of dairy cooperatives in India. In this situation, the state as well as union government can play a vital role in achieving balanced development of dairy cooperatives. But for that the necessary conditions availability for animal husbandry development and dairy development should be taken into consideration. Members strengthen the cooperative movement. But only Northern states like Uttar Pradesh, Maharashtra, Punjab, Andhra Pradesh have attempted to promote the membership of the dairy cooperatives in their states. The same strategy should be adopted in other categories of states. The Northern states are ahead in increasing even the marketing of milk, which has further helped in the development of cooperatives, and its concentration in the same region. Production of milk plays a vital role in the development of dairy cooperatives. It is found that Orissa, Nagaland, Sikkim, Arunachal Pradesh have attempted well in increasing production of milk. Likewise, on average basis, Uttar Pradesh, Andhra Pradesh, Punjab, Rajasthan and Maharashtra's efforts are to be appreciated in raising milk production as well as dairy cooperative movement. These states have succeeded in promoting per capita availability of milk and all others could not avail the milk to the extent expected. This indicates the need for developing dairy industry as well as dairy cooperatives in these states, and concerned state governments have to shoulder this responsibility in this regard. It is the need of the hour to undertake honest efforts to achieve the development of animal husbandry because of marginal growth in the livestock population. But it is good thing the growth rate of buffalo population at national level was significant. Its further production can be of more use in tackling the problem of inadequacy of milk availability per capita. Growing consumption expenditure on non-food items can be an obstacle in the development of dairy industry as well as dairy cooperatives. This suggests the need for undertaking efforts so as to promote expenditure on food items in general and milk and milk products in particular. Even in the era of economic reforms the role of government and the participation of the people can play a vital role in the development of the dairy cooperatives in absence of which, it will be difficult the livelihood of the people especially poor section that depend on dairy cooperatives. Dairy cooperatives have been played a vital role in socio-economic development of the Indian economy, nationwide as well as state wise. But it has scope in performing well in the fields like health facilities, education, employment, welfare schemes, water supply etc.

CONCLUDING REMARKS

Dairy industry in general and dairy cooperatives in particular are very much important in the socio-economic development of India in general and rural Indian economy in particular. Their role is appreciable but not complete. They have to strengthen the level and scope of their role in socio-economic development of the Indian economy, especially in economic reforms era. There is no alternative to the development of dairy cooperatives in overall development of especially rural areas. For this, these institutions should be far away from politics and a pure and effective means of socio-economic development only. The efforts in this direction and ideology will offer a bright future to the dairy cooperatives, no doubt.

REFERENCES

Government of India (2004), "India 2004", Government of India Publication, New Delhi, p. 85.

Ibid., p. 85.

Datta & Sundharam (2002), "Indian Economy", S. Chand and Company Ltd., New Delhi, p. 543.

Ibid., p. 543.

Misra & Puri (2001), "Indian Economy", Himalaya Publishing House, Mumbai, p. 228.

Ibid., p. 228.

Dairy Development Report (2004-05), "Government of India", New Delhi, p. 25.

PROBLEMS AND PROSPECTS OF ESCOMS IN POWER DISTRIBUTION

*B. Siddappa**

INTRODUCTION

Power is energy is an indispensable good for the survival of the Universe. How the air is inevitable in survival of an individual, like wise the power is inevitable in order to survival of the human generation–not only present but also in future days. Its dependency is mounting horizontal and vertical lines because the survival of agriculture, industry, service, besides the domestic that we are depending upon it. Hence, the technical staff should take much care in order to provide quality and quantity of power with reasonable cost. Improvement of efficiency of the staff is only the alternative to meet the ends of the present circumstances.

In order to know the problems and prospects of the Escoms (Electricity Supply Companies) in Karnataka state the some selected indicators are to be used viz. (1) sale of power by the KPTCL (Karnataka Power Transmission Company Limited) to the Escoms (2) Metered and Unmetered power consumption of Escoms with line loss. (3) Income generation of the Escoms (4) Consumption of power excluding line loss (5) Cost of supply of power includes lines loss (6) subsidy of the Escoms. All these indicators are examined by taking the 2003-04 year data of the four Escoms of the State. The each of these indicators are examined below.

SALE OF POWER BY KPTCL TO THE ESCOMS DURING THE YEAR 2003-04

KPTCL is distributing power to the four Escoms in Karnataka State. The Escoms in turn transmitting and distributing the power to the State Universe. The KPTCL has distributed 29555 MU (Million Units) of power

* Reader, Chairperson and Co-ordinator P.G. Departments of Studies and Research, Tumkur University, Tumkur, Karnataka.

to the four Escoms during the year 2003-04. The details are given in the following table.

Table 1
Sale of Power by KPTCL to the Escoms in 2003-04

Company Name	*Power Supply in MU*
BESCOM	13758 (46)
MESCOM	5697 (1)
HESCOM	5889 (20)
GESCOM	4211 (15)
Total	29555 (100)

(Figures in the parenthesis are percentages).

The table data suggests that the BESCOM alone purchased nearly half of the power supplied by the KPTCL during the year 2003-04 followed by the HESCOMs, MESCOM and GESCOM occupied second, third and fourth place respectively.

METERED AND UNMETERED CONSUMPTION OF POWER

The metered and unmetered consumption of power of four Escoms has been given in the following table. Such consumption is including the line loss of the respective–companies during the year 2003-04.

Table 2
Metered and Unmetered Consumption of Power
Including Line Loss of the Companies in 2003-04 (in MU)

Company name	*Metered*	*Unmetered*	*Line loss*	*Total*
BESCOM	6313 (46)	3808 (28)	3637 (26)	13758 (100)
MESCOM	2815 (49)	1693 (30)	1189 (21)	5697 (100)
HESCOM	1568 (27)	2605 (47)	1716 (29)	5889 (100)
GESCOM	1162 (28)	1419 (34)	1630 (38)	4211 (100)
Total	11858 (40)	9525 (32)	8172 (28)	29555 (100)

(Figures in the parenthesis are the percentages).

It can be observed from the above table that the metered consumption of power of BESCOM and MESCOM have noticed highest whereas the HESCOM and GESCOM have noticed lowest. The metered consumption is exact accountable one whereas un-metered consumption of power is non-exact accountable one. But the figures for line loss side are opposite the case, because the HESCOM and GESCOM have highest in line loss whereas the BESCOM and MESCOM have lowest in line loss. The line loss as defined by the KPTCL itself is the loss of electrical energy due to resistance and the length of wire in circuit. The line losses are two types in nature one is the technical line loss and another one is the commercial line loss. The technical line loss is due to the technical reason and it can be reduced with the help of technical staff but the commercial line loss is due to the mismanagement, theft and other illegal activities. It can only be reduced with the improvement of the prompt service of the staff. Overall 40 pe rcent of power is consumed through the meter and 32 percent of the power is consumed through the unmetered source in Karnataka State as a whole. The remaining is the (28 per cent) line loss. The State government is worried about the line loss as it is affecting the financial structure of not only the Escoms but also the Government.

INCOME GENERATION OF THE ESCOMS

The four Escoms have collected the revenue by sale of power to the various categorical consumers in the State. The revenue collected by the four Escoms by sale of power during the year 2003-04 has been given in the following table.

Table 3
Income Generation by Sale of Power of the four Escoms in 2003-04

Name of the company	*Income (in crores of Rs.)*	*(Average revenue per unit of power) (Sale of power in MU)*
BESCOM	3558 (45)	13758/025 crores per 1 million units and Rs 2.5 per unit
MESCOM	1554 (20)	5697/0.27 crores per 1 million units and Rs. 2.7 per unit
HESCOM	1570 (20)	5889/0.27 crores per 1 million units and Rs. 2.7 per unit
GESCOM	1082 (15)	4211/0.26 crores per 1 million units and Rs. 2.6 per unit
Total	7844 (100)	29555/0.26 crores per 1 million units and Rs. 2.6 per unit

(Figures in Parenthesis are percentages).

The four companies have collected Rs. 7844 crores revenue during the year 2003-04 by sale of power. The BESCOM again collected highest revenue and the MESCOM and HESCOM stood second place and the GESCOM occupied the least place in revenue collection. The table further highlights that the average revenue per unit of power in BESCOM is Rs. 2.5 per unit, in MESCOM it is Rs. 2.7 per unit in HESCOM it is Rs. 2.7 per unit and GESCOM it is Rs. 2.6 per unit of power. In an average, four companies revenue per unit of power is Rs. 2.6 per unit.

COST OF SUPPLY OF POWER

The four companies cost of supply of power during the year 2003-04 is given in the following table.

Table 4
Cost of the Supply of Power of Four Companies in 2003-04 Including Line Losses

Name of the company	*Cost of the power, total cost divided*	*Average revenue Per unit of power by the sale of units of power*
BESCOM	Rs. 3558 crores power in Units 13758	0.25 crores per 1 million units of power and per unit cost Rs. 2.5
MESCOM	Rs. 1540 crores power in Units 5697	0.27 crores per 1 million units of power and per unit cost Rs. 2.7
HESCOM	Rs. 1554 crores power in Units 5889	0.26 crores per 1 million units of power and per unit cost Rs. 2.6
GESCOM	Rs. 1078 crores power in Units 4211	0.26 crores per 1 million units of power and per unit cost Rs. 2.6
Total	Rs. 7725 crores power Units 29555	0.26 crores per 1 million units of power and per unit cost Rs. 2.6

The above table figures suggests that the four companies have spent Rs. 7725 crores in order to supply the 29555 units of power to the different category of consumers in Karnataka. The BESCOM spent highest amount and the MESCOM and HESCOM have spent the same amount and whereas the GESCOM spent lowest amount on power when compared with the counterparts. Whereas the average cost per unit of power and the average revenue per unit of power is more or less similar in respective companies. They have balanced in their annual accounts. Overall Rs. 7725 crores have spent on power by all the four companies for distributing 29555 MU of power. The average cost of the power per unit of the power is Rs. 2.6 during the year 2003-04 which is including the cost of line loss.

WHO BEARS THE COST OF LINE LOSS?

Line loss is a serious issue. Not only to the consumers but also to the Department of Energy, Government of Karnataka. Since it is one of the technical problems but it is not without solution. Line loss means loss of electrical energy due to the resistance and the length of wire in a circuit. There are two types of line loss i.e. technical line loss and commercial line loss. The primary loss can be reduced to the zero level with the sincere effort of the technical staff of the KPTCL along with the company staff, the latter loss may also bring down to the zero level with the improvement of the staff honesty, accountability and transparency of the staff of the four companies. It seems that these two are the necessary steps to be taken by the Authorities of the State. Otherwise the line loss cost is to be borne by the State Government or the State Power Consumers. The total cost of the line loss during the year 2003-04 was Rs. 2100 crores from the four power distributing companies of the State. It can be observed from the following table and found that one of the serious problems of the line loss is the bearing of the burden of the line loss. Who bears the cost of line loss? It seems that the companies are trying to shift this burden to the consumers by submitting proposal of increasing the tariff to the KERC. If the KERC does not accept its burden it is to be borne by the Government of Karnataka through the subsidy? But the thing is whether the shifting of the line loss upon the consumers or upon the Government is justifiable? Why the Group of Sinness (GOS) of the companies are not realizing their mistakes? Though the answer is within the GOS but they may not seriously taken this sensitive issues. The Department of Energy, Government of Karnataka, can solve this issue in consultation with the senior staff of the Department of Electrical Engineering, Indian Institute of Science. Bangalore.

Table 5

Cost of the Line Loss in Four Companies During the Year 2003-04

Name of the company	*Line loss in MU*	*Cost per unit of power (Rs.)*	*Cost of the loss (in crores of Rs.)*
BESCOM	3637	2.5	909
MESCOM	1189	2.7	321
HESCOM	1716	2.6	446
GESCOM	1630	2.6	424
Total	8172	2.6	2100

UNDESIRABLE SUBSIDY

The ESCOMS are functioning with some transparent manner the necessity of Government subsidy may be bring down to the negligible level. For distribution of power to the socio-economic backward households the Rural Electrification Corporation has shared the burden and for Bhagya Jyothi/ Kutira Jyothi beneficiaries the State government bears the burden. Subsidy amount for such purpose is almost desirable. Even for small and marginal farmers also extend the benefit. But the subsidy amount for big farmers and for rich consumers is not advisable. The subsidy part of the Escoms varied from 8 per cent in Bescom to 44 per cent in Hescom. An average 21 per cent (1622=21) of the total cost of the 7725 crores. The State Government in the form of subsidy reimburse it to the Escoms during the year 2003-04. It can be observed from the following table.

Table 6
Subsidy Re-imbursed to the Escoms

Name of the company	*Subsidy amount during the year 2003-04 (Rs. in crores)*
BESCOM	279 = 8 per cent of the total cost
MESCOM	237 = 15 per cent of the total cost
HESCOM	684 = 44 per cent of the total cost
GESCOM	422 = 39 per cent of the total cost
Total	1622 = 21 per cent of the total cost

The table figures further reveals that the HESCOM and GESCOM have received highest subsidy from the State Government when compared with the remaining companies. This performance shows that these companies staff efficiency might be low, in the sense, the staff might have allowed very liberal for line loss. As a result the subsidy part of amount seems to be high when compared to the other companies besides the free supply of power to the weaker sections by the Government.

EDUCATION AND TELECOMMUNICATION

*S. N. Yogish**

INTRODUCTION

The world Education has a very wide connotation. It is hard to define. There is no single objective which can over the whole of life with this various manifestations. The two poles of our concern, the temporal and the world of spirit are widely apart. Philosophers and thinkers from Socrates to Dewey in the west and Yajnavalkya to Gandhi in the east have define education in accordance with their philosophy of life with the result that there emerged divergent concepts and definition of education. The concept of education is like a diamond which appears to be of a different colour when seen from a different angle.

In the words of Dewey "Education is the development of on those capacities in the individual which will enable him to control his environment and fulfill his responsibilities."

Thomson says "By education I mean the influence of the environment upon the individual to produce a permanent change in his habits of behaviour, of thought and of his attitude, environment has various aspects-physical, social and cultural. Education should facilitate the task of adaptation of the child to his environment.

THE USE OF TELECOMMUNICATION IN EDUCATION

Within the last decade, synergetic fusion of the progress in telecommunications, technologies with the progress in computing technologies plus accompanying developments in the cognitive sciences has accelerated the rate of change of many services and functions that are basic to the operations of a modern society during these services and functions education is beginning to undergo a dramatic transformation in terms of its design and delivery. Not only in distance education

* Reader, Department of Studies in Economics, Kuvempu University, Jnana Sahyadri, Shankaraghatta, Karnataka.

becoming a much more common and much more viable alternative to the conventional classroom-based model for educational delivery, but also within this conventional context many unconventional learning and teaching strategies based on the exploitation of possibilities offered by the new technologies are being implemented.

DEVELOPMENTS IN TELECOMMUNICATIONS

The area of technological synergy is occurring through the fusion of computer technologies and telecommunication technologies. The full automation of the telecommunication system and its increased power of data transmission as it progresses to fibre optics based ISDN (Integrated Services Digital Network) distribution methodologies is well on the way to creating a worldwide communication to all citizens (Magel, 1991, 1993). Current USA development work will soon offer on Information superhighway" of upto 500 channels of cable television to the typical household many of these available for interactive education programming. Existing ad projected satellite communication networks and developments in cellular telecommunications will offer global interactive communication facilities even to those who are not connected to cable networks (McElgum, 1991 and Velasquez, 1991).

The business community is very rapidly moving towards telecommunication-network based management systems as opposed to the previous methodologies involving group meetings. The economies to be made in a large organization by the elimination of travel to meetings are immense. It is difficult to imagine that business educational systems will resist the implementation of network based distributed methodologies.

Not only can one implement training through the synchronous teleconferencing or tele-training model, but also by the asynchronous or computer conferencing mode which is being adopted by an ever increasing number of organizations. This model can multiply the economic benefits of telecommunications based education by not only profiting from the economies of Gavel and other related costs avoidance but also from the flexibility of trainee-controlled learning which enables the trainees to utilize a networked systems during moments of relative leisure in their work and therefore not disrupting productivity. Both synchronous and asynchronous tele-conferencing are also being implemented in a growing number of projects in the field of formal education. Yet other see social and practical benefits for the participants, particularly in the case of adult continuing education or education or educational benefits to be gained at all levels and with all age groups through the adoption of network based collaborative learning strategies (see Kaye (ed.), 1992).

The worldwide education utility predicted a few years ago (Goler, 1986) has not yet appeared, but immemorable local projects are making the use of computer-mediated communication the faster growing form of technological innovation in both education and training.

CATEGORIES OF TELECOMMUNICATION APPLICATIONS IN EDUCATION AND TRAINING

There are several alternative manners in which the uses of telecommunications based educational systems can be classified. It may be useful to review these classifications, as a way of better understanding the field. Perhaps the terms that is most commonly associated with the use of telecommunication in education is teleconferencing this may take many different forms however, so some qualifying terms are required to precisely define the nature of the educational applications. Some of the common ways of classification are as follows:

CLASSIFYING ACCORDING TO THE MEDIA USED

Audio conferencing by means of several telephones in different localities, often amplified for group listening, linked together into a network that allows all the stations to both transmit and receive spoken messages.

Video conferencing systems which may allow full audiovisual message transmission between all the linked stations or may be limited to one-way video transmission from the first station supported by multi-way audio transmission between all the satellite stations.

Audiographic conferencing systems, that support a basic audio conferencing systems by some means of transmission and sharing of visual material-these may use any combination of previously mailed printed material, fax transmission, networked personal computer or special purpose slow scan television camera systems that capture and transmit still images from one station to another across the normal telephone system.

Computer conferencing systems that utilize existing networks of computers as means of collaborative decision-making and decisions on the basis of shared messages and files.

Furthermore, this overall media based distinction between teleconferencing system is rapidly becoming meaningless as the aforementioned process of technological synergy is establishing world telecommunication standards for ISDN (Integrated Services Digital Networks) that will ensure that the regular telephone system of the future will offer the full range of multimedia communication facilities to support any form of teleconferencing. Today's macro decision on what type of teleconferencing system to adopt will be replaced by the macro decision making process of detailed design of a specific application selecting the communication modality that is most appropriate for a given step in the communication process.

CLASSIFICATION ACCORDING TO THE COMMUNICATION PROCESS

One-on-one communication as in a personal telephone call or electronic mail message. Defined-group communication as in a teleconferencing that links a few selected sites or public access communication as in broad cast mass media or electronic bulletin boards and open conferences.

Synchronous communication made in which all participants have to be on line at the same time (as in the majority of audio, audio-graphic and videoconference systems of the past) or asynchronous communication made in which the messages are recorded and stored so that individual participants may interact with them at any time that is convenient (as in the majority of computer conferencing applications).

Informational communication made in which the goal is to make certain bodies of information available to potential users without direct concern for how the information will be used or whether it will be used at all, or conversational communication made in which the goal is to share view points and establish communal understanding or reach a consensus on a given issue.

The above characteristics define such aspects as the goals of the communication process. The participants in the communication, the time and place in which the communication process may occur and so on these are some of the micro characteristics that may have to be defined for any telecommunication systems that is being planned for use in a given educational context.

RECENT INSTRUCTIONAL DESIGN TRENDS AND TELECOMMUNICATION BASED EDUCATION

A stranger emphasis on education based within a paradigm that is more learner drives and less system driver means that there is a trend towards greater student autonomy and control in all aspects of the planning and the execution of the teaching/ learning process. This implies a new role for the teacher in this process. Part of this new role involves the division of responsibility for teaching between the teacher and various support resources and tools that are largely technology based. However, if the learner assumes increased autonomy and control over the learning process and the teacher becomes more a collaborator with the learner in this process, these design of the learning resources and tools must be based on a paradigm that reflects this new reality of teaching and learning.

HYPERMEDIA NETWORKS UNDER LEARNER CONTROL

The approaches to the design of learning may therefore, have to change. This need for change is being felt in the instructional design field where current interest has moved from the earlier behaviourist inspired programmed instruction methodologies towards approached which are more based on cognitive principles on philosophies of humanism and constructivism and on instructional theories such as situated cognition and cognitive apprenticeship.

The new generation of learning environments and teaching materials is characterized by an emphasis on learner control over aspects such as content, presentation, learning rate and study method. It also emphasizes engagement of the learner in the learning process both in terms of motivation and interest and in terms of increased responsibility for the outcomes of learning. A third characteristic is based on the realization that individual learners needs are ever more fragmented and ever faster changing. Therefore, it is not feasible to thin of developing standard materials for closely defined learning populations, but rather one should work toward the creation of knowledge bases in particular domains of knowledge that are so designed as to satisfy multiple learning goals for a multiplicity of learners with different characteristics.

NETWORKED MULTIMEDIA THAT REALLY WORK

Second area of important research and development related to the creation of effective learning resources for the further, individualized system is one the educational application of multimedia learning environments. The so-called multimedia revolution is in reality a computer technology drivers revolution in the availability of tools and techniques for manipulating information in a variety of media formats. However, whether this constitutes a revolution in terms of the effectiveness of education is a question that had hardly yet been addressed at all. This is not to say that there is a lack of activity in the area of educational applications of multimedia however, much of current activity is not sufficiently research-based and is therefore not contributing to the rather small amount of knowledge the designers currently possess.

A FULLER CONCEPT OF INTERACTIVITY

A third research issue related to the development of future generations of educational resources revolved around the questions of interactivity. The multimedia band-wagon is in the habit of appending interactive to the terms multimedia to describe what is being produced. However, the bulk of current productions, ranging from the simpler hypercard stacks through to sophisticated and expensive multimedia learning resources interpret interactivity merely in terms of offering many choices to the learner.

CONVERSATIONAL, MAN/MACHINE NETWORKS OF EDUCATION

An alternative approach to the creation of intelligent and adaptive telecommunications-network-based teaching systems that does not rely on artificial software solutions and does not eliminate the teacher has been the basis of a research agenda of the present author. In this manner a student may be studying learning resources which has previously been prepared and which may will be structured in a hypersect like way so that they are very much control in terms of the content and the depth of study that the learner wishes to engage in.

POTENTIAL LIMITATIONS OR PROBLEMS

Given the operational advantages, simplicity and relative economy of network-based learning with the more sophisticated hardware and software now becoming available. The key to its success falls ever more on those who develop and support this instructional made.

- Faulty involved in this method need to expand a great deal of time and energy in guaranteeing the success of a project.
- The construction of structural communication exercises is also a skilled and time-consuming task.
- The greater the number of students per class, the more the problem compounds.
- On the other hand, it is very rewarding.

FURTHER DEVELOPMENT: THE FUTURE OF NETWORKED EDUCATION

Work is now in progress to combine the user interface benefits of the Macintosh with the networking advantages of mainframe computers. The relatively sophisticated structural communication exercises are resident on the hard discs of distributed microcomputers allowing fast and graphically emerging interaction in the initial exercise. Coupling the microcomputer to a CD-ROM drive or utilizing some other forms of multimedia workstation is not ruled out as a further development student input is on the other hand, limited to short text messages, which can be easily handled by currently widely available electronic networks (such as Bit net or Internet). As broad band digital information transfer on the proposed information superhighways becomes a reality, fully interactive multimedia case presentation and further discussion may become possible.

Over the computing problems of future systems are sorted out, a phase of large scale experimentation will commence involving students scattered across several sites may be several countries or even continents collaborating on highly structured seminar and case-study assignments.

In another parallel set of experiments, structural communication environments have been made available to the undergraduate writing programme which annually processes about two thousand students. The on-line exercises in the study are composed of examples of writing-technical writing, proposal writing, persuasive writing and so on and an invitation to critically analyze the examples according to a large set of 'good writing principles' that may (or may not) be applicable.

There will also be an opportunity to compare the effectiveness and the viability of such structured approaches to tele-teaching with less structured large group conferencing approaches that are already being used to the same programme. Also there will be an opportunity to incorporate an element of voice-messaging as a means of sharing view points on a problem in addition to the typed comments that have been used so far.

The overall outcome of this multi-research agenda will hopefully point the way to improve methodologies for the exploitation of further educational telematics systems.

REFERENCES

Agarwal, J.C. "Theory and Principles of Education", Vikas Publishing House Pvt. Ltd., New Delhi, pp. 1-10.

Barker. B.O. and Goodwin R.D. (1992), "Audiographics: Linking Remote Classroom", *Computing Teacher* 19 (7) pp. 11-14.

Boppana Nagarjuna, "Economic Reforms and Perspectives, Recent Developments in India Economy", Serials Publications, pp. 371-390.

Collis B.A. (1991), "Telecommunication–Based Training in Europe: A State of the Art Report", *American Journal of Distance Education* 5(2) pp. 31-40.

Venkataiah, N. "Educational Technology", APH Publishing Corporation, 5, Ansari Road, Daryaganj, New Delhi, pp. 131-165.

THE LAW ON INDUSTIAL DESIGNS IN INDIA

Sowmya M.S. & Sreenivasulu N.S.***

INTRODUCTION

The Intellectual property law has spread over every aspect of human life. Intellectual property as the name itself suggests is the labor of human brain i.e., to say in conceiving new ideas, leading to innovations and creations. Intellectual property is all about the result of application of human idea and creativity for practical purposes. The intellectual property law is all about protection and regulation of innovations and creations. Its subject matter is formed by new ideas conceived by man. New ideas may be applied in as many ways as the human mind conceives. The new ideas can be embodied in familiar things such as books, music, art, machinery, processes, and also in sources of information. The conception and development of new idea may require the expenditure of considerable time, effort and money.

Even if the idea is intended purely for personal use, that expenditure may need recompense. In this process the creator of the new idea is a prey of being copied by others for commercial purposes, as a results, it becomes vital to protect the creator of the new ideas from being exploited, thus the protection becomes desirable. The law intents to protect the intellectual labor of a man, in the form of inventions, write-ups, designs through the grant of Patents, Copyright or Design. There are certain inventive, functional products and process which fall into the sphere of Patents. On the other hand, creative, artistic or musical works fall into the sphere of copyrights. However there are certain creative efforts marked with features that have an artistic, aesthetic and functional attraction, which does not fall neither under patent or under copyright but under a separate sphere called Designs. A Design is unlike to market

* B.A.L., LL.M., Doctoral Candidate in Law, 880, II nd Staze, Vinaya Marga, Sidhartha Nagar, Mysore, Karnataka

** B.com., LL.M, Ph.D, Faculty of Law, National Law School of India University, (NLSIU), Bangalore

constitute an invention and in most cases; the article bearing the design may not be new or innovative enough to secure a Patent. But it was thought that copyright has always had the potential to provide a source of design protection.[1] Meanwhile, in today's global design is recognized as a powerful corporate tool, and plays an increasingly critical role in distinguishing, identifying the products to which it is applied. Further designs serve the purpose of catching the eyes of the customer in the process of advertising and marketing.

WHAT IS DESIGN?

Industrial design refers to creative activity which results in the ornamental or formal appearance of a product. According to ICSID (Industrial Council of Societies of Industrial Design) "design is a creative activity whose aim is to establish the multi-faceted qualities of object, processes, service or their system in the whole life-cycles. Therefore, design is the central factor of innovative humanization of technological and the crucial factor of cultural and economic exchange." As per the definition, "design[2] must have some shape, configuration, pattern or ornamentation or composition of lines or colors." Design may be applied to articles in any form through an industrial process. It is important that the product or article to which the design is being applied has to be produced in an Industrial way. The design must be incorporated in the article itself. Design may be said, as an activity in which market information is transformed into initial ideas and design concepts and then into a specific configuration of materials and components with technical specification to manufacture a new product. Design right refers to the right to use a novel or original design accorded to the proprietor on registration. Industrial design is an applied art, whereby the aesthetical and usability of product may be improved. Design aspects specified by the designer may include the overall shape of the object, the color, textile, sounds and aspects concerning the use of the product ergonomics.

HISTORICAL EVOLUTION AND DEVELOPMENT OF LAW ON INDUSTRIAL DESIGNS

The Design must be capable of being applied to an article, in such a way that article to which it is applied appeals to the eye of the customer. Design must be judged solely by the eye.[3] If good design is to be encouraged, the persons responsible for producing design must be protected against the promiscuous taking by others of the fruits of their labor. In order to provide protection to the author / creator of the design, to promote design activity, and to promote design element in an article of production it has become necessary to evolve the legal system for providing protection to industrial designs. Paris convention for the protection of industrial property intends to offer protection to new industrial designs. The convention postulates for mutual protection f industrial designs by the member countries. For the instance if one country does not offer protection to the designs produced in the second country, the later country is not obligated to offer protection to the designs produced in the former country.[4]

India being one among the member countries to the convention enacted the Design Act, 1911, to offer protection to industrial designs. It also intended to ensure that the Law does not unnecessarily extend protection beyond what is necessary to create the required incentive for design activity while removing impediments to the free use of available designs. The magnakarta of intellectual property rights the TRIPS agreement provides for minimum standards of protection for Industrial designs.[5] India has amended its legal regime on industrial designs by enacting Industrial Designs Act 2000 where in it implemented the minimum standards on industrial designs as postulated by the TRIPS agreement. Basically the aim of design law is to promote and to protect the design element of industrial production. It is also intended to promote innovative activity in the field of industries.[6] To achieve this objective and to meet the growing demands in the field and also to implement the TRIPS agreement, the Design Act of 1911 was repealed by enacting The Design Act of 2000.[7] The new Act on industrial designs in India is intended to serve the purpose of extending protection to industrial designs as per the international standards in the light of rapid changes in technology giving rise to innovative and creative designs.

PROTECTION OF INDUSTRIAL DESIGNS

The industrial designs law intends to protect eligible industrial designs. Protection is offered only to registered designs and unregistered designs are not offered protection. Any one who intends to protect his designs from being exploited from others has to get his design registered. For the purpose of registration of designs there established a registry of industrial designs. The registry administers the registration of designs. A design shall fulfill certain requirements for registration. A Design to be register must have some conception or suggestion as to the shape configuration, pattern or ornament. The basic requirements that a design shall fulfill are as follows:

1. Appeal to the eye.
2. New and original
3. Capable of being applied to industrial articles
4. Capable of distinguishing the article to which it is applied from other article.
5. Must not been published or exploited or part of the existing knowledge in the society.

A Registered design is one which is new and its features are applied to an article and whose appearance is material. The Act aims at protecting the designs which serve the purpose of visual appeal. The appeal of the design is solely judged by the eye of the consumer.[8] The registration cannot be deemed to be effective unless the design sought to be protected is new and original. The design should not be the same as any design published or registered.

REGISTRATION OF DESIGNS

A person claiming to be the proprietor of a design[9] or the person who is proposed to use it always desires to register it. A design which is new and original, which is not previously published[10] in India or in any country, could be registered. Though the term publication has not been defined in the Design Act 2000, it solely depends upon the visual appeal. Design must be significantly different from other known design or combination of known designs and should not contain scandalous or obscene matter. The procedure for the registration of a design is simple compared to the procedure for registration of patent or trademark. The person claiming to be the proprietor/owner/author of the design or a proposed user has to file an application for registration before the controller-general of designs.[11] Under the Act there is no express bar on foreigners from applying for registration. The application shall contain the following:

1. Name and addresses of the applicant.
2. The proprietor of design has to file an application for registration of design to the Controller-General.
3. In the application, proprietor of design shall state the class in which the design is to be registered[12] and shall also file a brief statement about the novelty of the design.
4. The application presented for registration, shall accompanied by the prescribed fee and in prescribed form and in a prescribed manner.

Application filed for registration must be accompanied by a representation of design i.e., some thing in the nature of a drawing or tracing. A conception or suggestion as to the mode of principle of construction of a design is not registrable. However the mode or the principle of construction of an article may affect its shape or configuration. The conception of such a mode or principle of construction may lead to a conception as to the shape or configuration of the completed article[13] which may be registered. The Controller-General,[14] shall examine the application of design and determine whether design is capable of being registered under the Act. The Controller-General is also empowered to refuse the application for registration, if the proposed design is previously published in India or other country and if it is contrary to the public order or morality or already existed one.

The applicant, whose application for registration is refused by the controller, for the above said reasons, may make an appeal to the Central-Government, and whose decision on the matter is Final. When the controller is satisfied after all the examination, that the design is new and original, and not previously existed one, he shall accept the design and makes the entry of the same in the Register of Design[15] The Controller, as per the Act, shall gives the Number to the design and specify the class in which it is registered and also the date of filing the application for registration and the date of registration of design and such other matter, which could effect the validity of the proprietorship of a design. The Register of design is also maintained wholly and partly on Computer, under floppies or discs, which shall be under the control of the controller.[16]

PUBLICATION OF REGISTERED DESIGNS

The Controller, if finds that the applicant has fulfilled the prescribed requirements, registers the design and gives the advertisement of the same in the Official Gazette. The purpose of advertisement of registration is to let the general public know that the propertior of design claims that his design is new and original[17] and to invite objections if any from any interested person/s who could validly oppose the proprietors claim. The Controller, on any objection failed or appeared shall communicate the statement of objection to the proprietor of design or to his agent. The proprietor or his agent as the case may be, has to remove the objection within a month of communication of the objection; otherwise application for registration shall deem to be abandoned.

It is left to the proprietor of design to disprove the objection made and to prove that the designs are new and original. After the clearance of all the claims, if the Controller is satisfied he would register[18] the design and shall grants the certificate of registration to the proprietor of the design. In case of loss of original certificate, the propertior of design shall make an application to the controller, in a prescribed manner after paying the prescribed fee. The Controller shall thereupon grant them a new certificate. In this regard the Controller may seek more information from the applicant and such other evidence as he thinks fit. The Registered Design gives protection to the owner of the design for the period of ten years, which is renewable for another five years. Protection is granted only after examination of its novelty, distinctness, appeal to the eye and capability of being applied to industrial articles.[19] Registration of design excludes all persons from using the design including the Government except its registered owner.[20] The Government is bound to honor the copyright in the design. However it can use the design or acquire it or even prohibit a person from misusing it in certain circumstances.[21]

CANCELLATION OF REGISTRATION

Any Person interested may make a Petition to the controller for the Cancellation of Registration of Design on the following grounds:

1. The design has been previously registered in India.[22]
2. The design has been published in India prior to the date of registration.[23]
3. The design is not new or original[24]
4. The design is not registrable under the design Act[25]
5. It is not a design, as defined under the Act.[26]

A Petition may be presented to the High Court, without any limitation of time,[27] or where the cancellation is sought on the first two grounds, it may be presented to the Controller, within a Year from the date of registration. The Controller enjoys discretionary power under the Act with regard to the registration and cancellation of designs. The Discretionary power given to the Controller under the Act shall not be adversely exercised by him, without giving the propertior of the registered design an opportunity of being heard.

RIGHTS CONFERRED ON REGISTRATION

The registered proprietor of a design is the owner of the right in the design and he possesses copyright over the design.[28] The registered proprietor of a design is given the exclusive right to commercially exploit articles to which design is applied. The copyright over the registered design confers on its owner the exclusive right to use the design and it is termed as copy right in the design which subsists during ten years from the date of registration.[29] The design right also authorizes the proprietor to use it, including the right to make offer, put on market, import, export or to use a product in which the design is incorporated.

The registered proprietor of the design, on the expiration of the said ten years, may make an application to the controller, for the extension of the period of copy right, in the prescribed manner, after the payment of prescribed fee. The Controller may extend the period of copyright for the second period of five years from the expiration of the original period of ten years.[30] Apart from this registered proprietor has the right to protect the "design from piracy."[31] Infringement of copyright in a design is termed as "piracy of design."[32] A person responsible for infringing the monopoly of proprietor of design is guilty of piracy and liable for penalty and fine.[33] The proprietor of design can choose to assert design right in the whole or any part of his product. The design registered under the Designs Act cannot be protected by the copyright, even though it may be an original artistic work.

If a design qualifies for registration under the design Act, but has not been so registered under the Design Act, the exclusive right will subsist under the Copy right Act. If such a design is of an article which is commercially produced, the copyright over the design under the copyright will cease to exist when the article to which design has been applied has been reproduced more than fifty times by the industrial process by the owner of copyright. A Design right is transmissible by assignment, testamentary disposition or operation of law, just as any personal or movable property. When a person becomes an licensee, mortgagee, otherwise, by virtue of operation of law, assignment or transmission, to the design right he shall apply to the controller in a prescribed manner for registration of his or her title as proprietor or co-proprietor. The matter can also be brought to the notice of the controller, by assignor, mortgagor or licensor or other party to that instrument as the case may be.

OWNERSHIP OF DESIGN RIGHT

The person creating the design is the author of that design and the basic rule is that the author is entitled to be the original proprietor of design. The basic exception to the rule is that; firstly, if the design is created by the employee during the course of the employment, than the employer will be the owner of the registered design. Secondly, if the design is commissioned for money than the person who commissioned the design will be the proprietor of the design. In case, if two persons had produced the similar design and the fact of the same is communicated to the other, neither of them is alone the proprietor of a new design developed, there will be a joint authorship of the design. A specific problem may arise when the design is computer generated. A computer is not a person and cannot become the owner of the design, in such cases; the ownership is attributed to the nearest person who is involved in its creation, i.e. the person who made the necessary arrangements for the creation of the design.

ENFORCEMENT OF REGISTERED DESIGNS

The registered owner of a design is given the exclusive right to do certain things in relation to articles which embody the design and in respect of which the design has been registered. The owner has the right to make or import the designed article for sale or for hire or for the purpose of trade or business. Any person who does any of the above said acts without the consent or license from the owner of the registered design infringes the rights in the registered design. Infringement can only be avoided if the design used is substantially different from the registered design. It is not lawful for any person during the existence of copy right over the design to do the following acts without the consent or license from the registered proprietor of the design such as; to publish or to have it published or expose for sale any article of the class in question on which either the design or any fraudulent or obvious imitation has been made, to either apply or cause to apply the design to any class of goods covered by the registration or any imitation of it, to import for the purpose of sale any article belonging to the class in which the design has been registered and to which the design or a fraudulent or obvious imitation thereof has been applied.[34]

The Judicial remedy for infringement of a registered design recommended in the Act is award of damage.[35] A Suit in appropriate manner for seeking relief in the form of an injunction to stop the infringer from continuing the act of infringement immediately is also recommended.[36] The registered owner of the design can institute a suit claiming damages or injunction against infringement of his copyrights in the design. The general principal of law is that party making the charge, i.e. accusing another party for an act has to establish the occurrence of the act. The person alleging the infringement of his right has to establish the infringement. The burden of proof is thus lies on the plaintiff who brings an action for infringement to establish the fact of piracy of his design or violation of copyright in the design.[37] It is important to note that 'design is not infringed' by the reproduction of a feature of the design, which is not taken into consideration while determining the eligibility of the design for registration.

CONCLUSION

Intellectual property provides legal protection for the useful ideas conceived and developed by man. Intellectual property rights are increasingly recognized as the key economic resources in the modern times. The creator of an idea, and the manufacture of its embodiment will have an interest in gaining reward for their effort and expenditure and this is possible only if there is a protection against the risk of imitation. Design is also one of such invention of man which could be protected under intellectual property laws. The violation of intellectual property rights was not as much in the ancient times, as it is in the contemporary world. Design which appeal to the eye can be of a tremendous commercial value; it does not amount to an invention and cannot be protected under patent laws.

Besides, copyright law does not protect the idea behind the design, so there is a real need to register it under the design laws which is probably the only way to protect it from competitors from cashing in on design by using a substantially identical design. A new and original design comprising of shape, configuration, pattern or ornamentation or composition lines which could be applied to industrial articles is registrable. The person claiming such design shall have the copyright over that design. The copyright over the design gives the creator / author an exclusive right to use and exploit it. Besides, design rights give an advantage to the owner who can produce articles with a definite design having compatibility to compete in the market leading to large scale production of the article. On registration the owner enjoys monopoly over the design for a term of ten years which is renewable for another five years.

The Paris convention on industrial property which is popularly known as Paris Convention adopted in 1883, revised at Stockholm in the year1967 can be said to have brought great recognition to the design rights in the International sphere. The need of harmonization of law concerning intellectual property rights was felt at the international level at later point of time. The result being the TRIPS agreement aiming at bringing basic levels of harmony in the intellectual property laws across the world. Being a signatory to the agreement India brought necessary changes in its intellectual property laws including design law to harmonize the same with the standards set in the agreement.

NOTES

1. See: Principles of Intellectual Property Law by Catherine Colston, Cavendish Publishing Limited, P. No., 279.
2. Sec: 2(d) of The Design Act, 2000.
3. www.wikipedia, last visited 30-11-2006.
4. Law relating to Patents Trademarks Copyright Designs and Geographical Indications by Dr.B. L. Wadehra. Universal Law publishing Co. Pvt. Ltd.
5. Art: 2.1 of the TRIPS agreement obligates its members to comply with articles 1 to 12 and Article 19 of the Paris convention.
6. Art: 25.1 the TRIPS agreement obligates the member to provide protection of independently created Industrial design that is new or original.
7. The Design Act of 2000, was enacted 25th May 2000.
8. Comments made by House of Lords regarding to the definition of Design in AMP Incorporate vs Utilux property Ltd. (1972) Rpc. 103. See Samsonite corp vs Vijay Sales, (1998) 73 DLT 732; 1998(3) Raj 70 (Del).
9. Sec: 2(j) of The Designs Act defines 'Proprietor of Desig'.
10. Wimco Ltd., Bombay vs Meena metal industries, AIR 1988 Del-587.
11. Sec: 5(i) The Designs Act of India, 2000.
12. The Design Act of 2000, lays down 31 classes plus 99 goods to which Ornamental Design etc., which are capable of being registered.
13. Pugh vs Diley cycle coy 29 RPC,196 at P. No. 202.
14. Sec: 2(b) of the Design Act 2000 which defines 'Controller'.
15. The Register of Design is a book which is kept at the Patent Office, wherein the entries of Names and Addresses of the Proprietor of Registered Design are made under.
16. The information maintained in the floppies and discs shall be used in case of any dispute or doubt with regard to the information of design and back file shall be the Final.
17. "Original" in relation to a design, means originating from the author of such design and includes the cases which though old in themselves, yet are New in their application.
18. **
19. Art: 26.3 TRIPS agreement, See also Dover Ltd. vs Nurnberger celluloid.
20. Ibid: Art: 26.1 .
21. Sec: 20 of The Designs Act of India 2000.
22. Ampro Food Products vs Ashok Biscuits Works and Another, AIR 1973, AP. 17.
23. National Trading co vs Monica chawla, AIR 1994 Del.309 and also See, J.G Vaccum Flask Ltd vs Eagle Flask (p) Ltd., (1997) 70 DLT 225.

24. Metro plastic Industries vs Galaxy footwear,(1997) Raj, 110 (Del), Para 9.8.
25. Hindusthan Lever Ltd., Bombay vs nirma Pvt. Ltd., Ahmedbad, AIR 1992 Bom. 195.
26. Clause (d) of Sec: 2 of the Designs Act of India, 2000.
27. Giridhari Lal vs K. Gain Chand Jain and Co., AIR 1978 Del 146.
28. Sec: 11 of The Design Act, 2000.
29. Sec: 11(1) The Design Act of India 2000.
30. Ibid: Sec: 12 (1).
31. Ibid: Sec: 22 (1).
32. Law relating to Patents Copyright Designs and Geographical Indications by Dr., B. L. Wadehra, P. No. 463.
33. The Fine laid down for infringement of design is fifty thousand rupees.
34. Law relating to Patents Trade mark Copyright Designs and Geographical Indications by Dr. B. L. Wadehra, Universal Law Publication Co. Pvt., Ltd., Second Edition, P. No. 463.
35. Indo Asahi Glass Co Ltd. vs Jai Mata rolled glass Ltd, and Anr, 1995 PTR 89.
36. Giridhari Lal vs Gian Chand Jain and Co., AIR 1978 Del. 146 Delhi LT 132 (FB).
37. Jg Vaccum Flask Ltd. vs Eagle Flask (P) Ltd., 1996 PTR 214.

GATS AND INDIA'S EDUCATION SECTOR–ISSUES AND OPTIONS

Shoukat Ali M. Magalmani[*], *Jayasheela*[**] & *V. Basil Hans*[***]

"Scholarship is less than sense, therefore seek intelligence"
(Panchathantra).

INTRODUCTION

That knowledge is power has been acknowledged by humans over the centuries. Knowledge is the driving force in the rapidly changing globalised economy and society of the modern era. It may not be an exaggeration if we state that today "knowledge maketh a man". In the (business) economy the quantity and quality of highly specialised human resources determine their competence in the global market. Schultz treated education as an investment in man and its consequences as a form of capital, specifically human capital (Hans, 2000) Emergence of knowledge as driving factor results in both challenges and opportunities. It is an established fact that the growth of the global economy has increased opportunities for those countries with good levels of education and vice versa (Carnoy, 1999; Tilak, 2001; Stewart, 1996; Ilon, 1994). India is no exception to this global phenomenon. As part of globalisation, the economic reform packages were introduced in India in 1991. Due to the liberalisation of the economy and the introduction of a new world economic order these reform packages imposed a heavy compression on the public budgets on education sector, more specifically so on higher education. But in India education is of such critical importance to the social, cultural and economic development of society that the implications and impact of globalization in general and of services in particular on education should be properly analysed. Therefore, the objectives of this paper are:

* Principal, Besant P.V. Evening College, M.G. Road, Mangalore-575003, Karnataka.

** Reader, Department of Economics, Mangalore University- 574 199, Karnataka.

*** Professor of Economics and Head, Department of Arts, St Aloysius Evening College, Mangalore–575 003, Karnataka.

i. to make an over view of the purposes and principles of GATS,

ii. to analyse GATS and services sector in general and education (higher) in particular,

iii. to know whether India should make commitments in education services sector,

iv. to understand the different kinds of regulatory challenges posed by the GATS in the field of education services and

v. to suggest policy options in the context of liberalisation of education service.

PURPOSE OF GATS

The General Agreement on Trade in Services (GATS) is the result of the Uruguay Round (1986-1994) of negotiations and came into force on 1 January 1995, with the establishment of the World Trade Organisation (WTO) by replacing General Agreement of Trade and Tariff (GATT). The main purpose for evolving GATS was to create a credible and reliable system of international trade rules, which ensured fair and equitable treatment of all countries on the principles of non-discrimination.

GATS aims at stimulating trade and development by seeking to create a predictable policy environment wherein the member countries voluntarily undertake to bind their policy-regimes relating to trade in services. It also aims at progressively liberalizing the trade in commercial services that will promote economic growth in the WTO member countries. These commercial services are of wide variety ranging from entertainment, e-commerce, and education.

Under the framework developed through GATS, member countries are expected to put forward their specific proposals, engage in negotiations, and make their own commitments for the progressive liberalisation of trade in such services.

RULES OF GATS

The basic rules of GATS which will apply to services like education are as follows:

1. A general framework of obligations that applies to all member countries of WTO including two principles of "Most Favoured Nations Treatment" (MFN) and "National Treatment". The MFN implies that there should be no discrimination between the members to the agreement. The principle of "National Treatment"

suggested that 'each member shall accord to services and service suppliers of any other member, in respect of all measures affecting the supply of services, treatment no less favourable than that it accords to its own like services and service supplies'.

2. Each member country will have to make a request offer for a particular service to be a part of the agreement. That is, a member country can decide which service sector it would like to cover under GATS rule.

3. A member maintaining practices which may "restrain competition and thereby restrict trade in service", is directed to "enter into consultation with a view to eliminating them", when requested by another member. In case of disagreement between members, the Council for Trade in Services "shall refer the matter to arbitration", the decision of which "shall be final and binding on the member".

4. Members have to ensure that all measures are administered in a reasonable and impartial manner.

5. There shall be transparency in all policies related to barriers to market access and discriminatory restrictions by the members have to be notified.

6. Individual countries have the power to determine the degree of market access to each of the subsectors. This can include "no access at all". However, due to the most favoured nation principle all countries must be treated equally in terms of market access and national treatment for services covered in the scope of the agreement.

GATS AND SERVICE SECTOR

GATS has three parts. The first part is the Framework Agreement containing 29 Articles, second part consists of national schedules that list a country's specific commitments on access to the domestic market and the third part consists of a number of Annexures, Ministerial Decisions, Schedules of Commitment etc. Presently, the GATS covers all internationally traded services with two exceptions: services provided to the public in the exercise of governmental authority, and, in the air transport sector, traffic rights and all services directly related to the exercise of traffic rights. The WTO Secretariat has divided all services into the following 12 sectors (these 12 areas are further divided into 161 sub-sectors):

- Business service (including professional and computer services),
- Communication services,
- Construction and Engineering services,
- Distribution services (e.g. Commission agents, wholesale & retail trade and franchising),
- Education services,
- Environment services,
- Finance (including insurance and banking) services,
- Health services,
- Tourism and Travel service,
- Recreation, Cultural and Sporting Services,
- Transportation Services, and
- Other services, not elsewhere classified.

EDUCATION SERVICE IN GATS

GATS provides for four modes of supply of services: cross-border supply, consumption abroad, commercial presence, and presence/movement of natural persons.

Mode 1: Cross-border supply refers to a situation where the service flows from the territory of one Member country into the territory of another Member country. For example, an architect can send his architectural plan through electronic means; a teacher can send teaching material to students in any other country; a doctor sitting in Germany can advise his patient in India through electronic means. In all these cases, trade in services takes place and this is equivalent to cross-border movement of goods.

Mode 2: Consumption abroad refers to a situation where consumer of a service moves into the territory of another Member country to obtain the service. Example, a tourist using hotel or restaurant services abroad; a ship or aircraft undergoing repair or maintenance services abroad.

Mode 3: Commercial presence implies that service suppliers of a Member country establish a territorial presence (a legal presence) in another Member country with a view to providing their services. In this case, the service supplier establishes a legal presence in the form of a joint venture/ subsidiary/representative/branch office in the host country and starts supplying services.

Mode 4: Presence or movement of natural persons (this only refers to export of manpower) covers situations in which a service is delivered through persons of a Member country temporarily entering the territory of another Member country. Examples include independent service suppliers (e.g. doctors, engineers, individual consultants, accountants, etc.) However, GATS covers only temporary movement and not citizenship, residence or employment on a permanent basis in the foreign country.

As per the informal WTO Classification List (W/120), Education Services have been classified into five sub-sectors, namely, (a) Primary Education Services, (b) Secondary Education Services, (c) Higher Education Services, (d) Adult and Continuing Education Services and (e) Other Education Services. There is also a proposal from the United States to add two other services: Training Services and Educational Testing Services, under Other Services.

INDIA'S HIGHER EDUCATION SCENARIO

While evaluating the probable impact of GATS on Indian higher education it is necessary to take into consideration the basic facts related to the existing system of higher education. Some of these are:

- India has the third largest higher education system in the world comprising of about 330 university-level institutions, about 16,000 colleges (including some 4,500 professional institutions), over 9.5 million students and approximately 350,000 teachers. The objective is to increase enrolment to about 14 million by the end of the Tenth Five-Year Plan period, i.e. by 2007-08.
- The government is the principal contributor of higher education in the country. However, over the years its share in the expenditure on higher education has been steadily decreasing. (Tilak, 2003).
- Today, the private sector is making a significant contribution to professional education at the degree level. In 2002, there were 977 colleges providing education, at the under-graduate level, in engineering and technology, of which 764 (78.20%) were in the private sector. Likewise, out of the 1,349 institutions offering degree programmes in different branches of medicine and health sciences, 1,028 (76.20%) were in the private sector. In that year, out of the 505 institutions for management education, offering programmes leading to a Masters degree, 324 (64.15%) were in

the private sector. Additionally, there were over 400 private institutions offering post-graduate diploma programmes in different areas of management. Colleges for teacher education have also expanded considerably in the country. There were, in 2002, 1,541 colleges in this discipline of which 1,038 (67.35%) were in the private sector.The expansion of professional higher education, especially in the private sector, continues. For example, in 2004 there were 800,000 students in technical education of whom 380,000 were in degree-level programmes.

- Though the quality of education imparted by different higher education institutions in India is admittedly variable there are quite a few institutions that provide education of a quality that is comparable with that offered at the best international institutions, as for example IIM, IIT, deemed universities etc. The quality of the education provided is monitored by different statutory bodies in the professional disciplines and by accrediting agencies (e.g. NAAC).
- International players (providers) are entering the Indian 'education market' in increasing number (e.g. the B-Schools). Data for the period from January to April, 2004 show that there has been an increase in the number of advertisers from 144 in 2000 to 319 in 2004; in the number of providers recruiting students for their home campuses from 117 to 204; and in the number of providers offering programmes in India, under the commercial presence mode, from 27 to 114 (Powar, 2004). What is disturbing is that nearly a third of foreign providers were not universities, and an equal percentage of their Indian collaborators were not a part of the formal higher education system at all.
- There exists in India a parallel, non-formal stream of education in the form of training institutions that provide skill-oriented programmes while encouraging its students to register at the same time in bachelor degree programmes in the conventional universities. The NIIT is the prime example.
- The academic structure of Indian universities is similar to that of the universities in the Commonwealth (except Canada) and European countries. The basic eligibility is successful completion of twelve years of schooling (Senior Secondary Certificate Examination or equivalent programme). The Bachelor degree programme is of three years in the liberal arts and four to five years in the professional disciplines. The Master degree

programme is of two years. The doctoral degree involves a minimum of two years of work, but normally takes about four years.

- The non-formal institutions have different programmes. The best-known institution, NIIT for instance, has two 'domains'. *Domain A* is an adaptation of the university structure. *Domain B* is for those who do not aspire for a degree and includes short-term, skill-oriented courses whose value is determined by the market.

The fact of the matter is that while many universities in the developed world look upon India as a lucrative market for their educational wares (including software), India itself has a large higher education system capable of providing quality education to the developing countries. It is, therefore, necessary that the developed countries look upon India, not as an importer of education, but as a possible partner in cooperation (Powar, 2004).

SIGNIFICANCE OF GATS IN INDIAN EDUCATION SERVICES

GATS relevance to India's education services sector is seen as under:

- India has both export and import interests in education services across all GATS modes.
- India has private presence in education services which co-exists with and is in competition with public educational institutions.
- GATS provides a means to gain predictable and transparent market access conditions overseas to expand India's exports of education services.
- GATS commitments could be used to facilitate participation by foreign institutions in India and increase supply of higher education to alleviate supply constraints and declining public funds.
- But GATS could pose challenges to domestic regulation and autonomy in national education policies.

India's Import Interests

- *Mode 1*: Prospects for distance education and degrees from foreign academic institutions.
- *Mode 2*: Indian students studying in foreign universities (US, UK, Australia) Over 40,000 studying in US courses and several thousand in Europe.

- *Mode 3*: Foreign institutions entering India through twinning and franchise arrangements Indian students getting foreign degrees, doing professional courses at local branch campuses of foreign institutions in India, for example, UK-based Wigan and Leigh College, Indian School of Business tie up with Kellogg, Wharton, and London Business School. Western International University, Arizona. NIIT tie-up with ITT Educational Services, USA. Tata InfoTech tie up with Hertfordshire University, UK.
- *Mode 4*: Foreign faculty and scholars teaching can in India.

Liberal FDI policy in education services is allowed but poor enforcement of regulations and weak regulatory capacity affect ability to meet objectives of quality, accreditation, and equivalence. Recently guidelines formulated to covering granting of equivalence to degrees offered in India by foreign universities requirements of adequate infrastructure and facilities, programme. Foreign university were also asked to give undertaking via certificate that degree or diploma awarded to student in India equivalent to that awarded by home university, recognised in that country as being equivalent to that given by awarding university. Guidelines thus far poorly enforced.

India's Export Interests in Education Services

Mode 1: Prospects for tele-education in management and executive training. For example, experience with distance learning, use of new technologies as in the case of IGNOU.

Mode 2: Students from developing countries studying in Indian engineering and medical colleges. Around 5,500 students from neighbouring developing countries (2001) exchange programmes and twinning arrangements. According to India Country Fact Sheet (see Table I) in the Open Doors 2004 reports, India continues to remain the largest sending country of origin for the 3rd year, and the number of Indian students in USA climbed by 7% over the prior year, to a total of 79,736 in 2003/04, offsetting decreases from a number of other countries which experienced sharp declines. However, India's rate of increase in 2003/04 has slowed from the prior year's dramatic 12% growth. Total enrolments fell by 5% for students from China (still the second largest sending country with 61,765) Of the 74,603 students from India, 79.0% were graduate students, 17.0% undergraduate and 4.0% other.

Table 1
Number of Indian Students in USA from 1993 to 2003

Sl. No.	*Year*	*Number of Indian Students in USA*	*Indian Students as Percentage of Total Foreign Students in USA*
1.	1993-1994	34,796	7.70
2.	1994-1995	33,537	7.40
3.	1995-1996	31,743	7.00
4.	1996-1997	30,641	6.70
5.	1997-1998	33,818	7.00
6.	1998-1999	37,482	7.60
7.	1999-2000	42,337	8.20
8.	2000-2001	54,664	9.90
9.	2001-2002	66,836	11.50
10.	2002-2003	74,603	12.70
11.	2003-2004	79,736	13.90

Source: India Country Fact Sheet (2004), *http://opendoors.illenetwork.org.*

Mode 3: Setting up of overseas campuses, franchising by Indian institutions, eg. MAHE, BITS, Central Institute of English and Foreign Languages etc.

Mode 4: Indian teachers, lecturers teaching abroad in Middle East, Africa, researchers/scholars on visiting arrangements, especially in the subjects of Maths, Science, English.

It should be noted that exports may constrained by resource and capacity limitations, inadequate infrastructure and campus facilities, divergence of standards within country, lack of certification, recognition, equivalence, restrictive immigration and labour market policies, economic needs tests, technology and others.

IMPLICATIONS OF COMMITTING UNDER GATS

Without adequate domestic regulation and enforcement liberalisation of education services could adversely impact on quality, standards, equity, prices, up gradation of infrastructure and facilities of premier domestic institutions, and result in loss of competitiveness for domestic providers and possible diversion of faculty resources and students. Multilateral commitments in education services should be preceded by improved regulatory enforcement of provisions concerning accreditation, standards, registration, licensing requirements and improvements in educational infrastructure in domestic institutions.

CONCERNS ABOUT THE GATS

There are several criticisms that have been leveled at the GATS, mostly by non-governmental organisations and consumer and public-interest groups. These concerns are interrelated and mostly centre around issues of national autonomy and sovereignty, the likely adverse effects of liberalising services, and the trade-off between commercial interests and efficiency type considerations on one hand and social, developmental, and equity goals on the other. Some of the main criticisms are highlighted below. These are by no means exhaustive but are illustrative of the key issues and concerns raised about the GATS.

The Indian government has not made, as yet, any formal statement on GATS so far as Education Services are concerned. Being a member of WTO it is committed to progressive liberalisation but can take steps in this direction only after the economic, social and political ramifications are analyzed and understood. Keeping in mind the national needs and ethos, India is not likely to make any commitments in the Sub-sectors of primary education, secondary education, adult and continuing education and other education. However, it is possible that because of international compulsions some concessions may be made so far as higher education is concerned. If the country is obliged to do so it will be necessary, while framing responses, to take into consideration the following:

- The competitiveness of the Education Sector, in general, and of the Higher Education Sub-Sector, in particular.
- The present status and possibilities in the future for trade under different modes.
- Improve enforcement of standards and quality requirements in general.
- Improve coordination among and institutional capacity within domestic regulatory and professional bodies.
- Ensure academic considerations supersede commercial ones in provision of higher education services by private suppliers.
- Reduce number of unapproved institutions to reduce scope for substandard foreign and domestic partnership arrangements.
- Allow only genuine academic institutions approved by apex bodies to participate in twinning activities.
- Prevent selling/marketing of degrees of questionable standard by non-recognised institutions/even recognised institutions[1] .

- Exercise sufficient controls over franchising arrangements to ensure supervision by parent institutions, quality, appropriate financial arrangements, and genuine institutional link.
- Review, keeping in view the importance of higher education in the new knowledge era, the national policy relating to the funding of higher education. The urgency of this task has to be appreciated by our political leadership and bureaucracy, and every effort made to provide the long-promised 6 per cent of DNP to education. The allotment to higher education needs to be immediately raised to 1 percent against the present 0.4 per cent.
- Provide adequate financial support, at least to the leading research-oriented universities, for the modernization of infra-structural facilities, especially the laboratories, libraries and information technology systems and networks.
- Recognize the importance of the close relationship between teaching and research and promote quality research.
- Implement academic reforms that are so vital for Indian higher education to be brought in consonance with the higher education systems of the developed world.
- Develop a realistic policy towards the role of private enterprise in higher education and its internationalization.
- Recognize the role of good faculty in providing quality education and take steps to promote faculty development.
- Undertake innovative measures like the establishment of Free Education Zones, akin to the Free Economic Zones, at appropriate locations, like leading centres of learning (Delhi, Pune, Mumbai, Kolkata, Hyderabad and Bangalore), or within the Free Economic Zones.
- Examine, keeping in view the expertise available in the area of information and communication technology, the possibility of developing virtual operations and becoming a regional, if not global, provider of higher education.
- Take prompt punitive action where registration and other norms are violated.
- Provide comprehensive information to consumers on foreign courses and institutions to enable informed choice.
- Enforce international equivalence requirements in foreign courses and programmes.

- Upgrade infrastructure and campus facilities, increase autonomy in reputed public educational institutions to enable them to compete with foreign providers.
- Commitments in education services would subject India to domestic regulation disciplines under GATS and could affect regulatory autonomy.
- GATS disciplines on domestic regulation require that measures relating to qualification requirements and procedures, technical standards, and licensing requirements do not constitute unnecessary barriers to trade, be based on objective and transparent criteria and are not more burdensome than necessary to meet a legitimate objective.
- Legitimate objectives include protection of consumers, quality of service, professional competence, integrity of the profession.
- Conditions on transparency, administrative procedures.
- Specific elements of concern in GATS disciplines which could affect regulation of foreign education providers in India and autonomy over regulatory procedures and objectives include:

(a) Transparency and other administrative requirements.

(b) Procedures to determine competence, and equivalence.

(c) Scope for public provision and subsidization of education services.

(d) If India commits in education services, it must inscribe appropriate limitations and clearly specify conditions applicable to foreign education providers to ensure regulatory objectives met and autonomy retained.

Quality Assurance and Accreditation

The National Policy on Education, 1986 recognised the need to monitor and promote the quality of education through a process of assessment and accreditation (Government of India, 1986, 1992). Accordingly in the 1990s four major accreditation agencies were set up (see Powar, 2005, for a comprehensive description). These are:

- The National Assessment and Accreditation Council (NAAC) under the University Grants Commission, which undertakes institutional evaluation of all types of higher education institutions,

- The National Board of Accreditation (NBA) under the All India Council for Technical Education (AICTE), which undertakes programme evaluation in the disciplines of engineering and t3ecgnology, management and pharmacy,
- The Accreditation Board (AB) of the Indian Council for Agricultural Research (ICAR), which monitors the compliance with norms and standards set for agricultural education in India and
- The Distance Education Council (DEC) under the Indira Gandhi National Open University (IGNOU), which evaluates and accredits institutions offering distance education programmes.

These agencies have been able to inculcate a quality-culture in a large number of institutions. After a slow start, the different agencies are now operating at an optimum level, and NAAC and NBA have started the second cycle of accreditation.

The University Grants Commission, the All India Council for Technical Education and other Statutory Councils like the National Council for Teacher Education, Medical Council of India and Bar Council of India, have prescribed minimum standards as regards, infrastructure, faculty, duration of programme and eligibility criteria, and all institutions are expected to strictly comply with them.

Universities in India are entitled to determine equivalence of degrees and diplomas as thought fit. However, by a resolution of the Association of Indian Universities, passed in 1993, universities have generally agreed to grant equivalence on a reciprocal basis provided the eligibility conditions for admission, duration of programmes and course content are similar. The Association has been authorized by the Government of India to grant equivalence to foreign degrees with the degrees awarded by Indian universities.

Suggestions Regarding Entry of Foreign Institutions

The following guidelines were suggested for the entry of foreign institutions in India:

- While the foreign institutions may be allowed to set up their campuses in India, they should function under the control of the government or specialized bodies like the National Assessment and Accreditation Council (NAAC) set up by the Government for the purpose;

- The universities which want to function in India should have been accredited in their own countries;
- The foreign institutions should be subjected to pre-entry academic audit and accreditation norms devised by the designated government agencies;
- They should sign Memorandum of Understanding (MOU) with the government or a body designated by it. The Memorandum should give details of the courses of studies, infrastructural facilities–both academic and non-academic and the amount of expected cost recoveries from Indian students;
- The entry of foreign institutions should be allowed on the basis of reciprocity. The countries exporting education to India should also permit the opening of Indian university campuses in their countries. There should be provision for exchange of faculty among the various countries participating in the programme; and
- In the entire process of the entry of foreign institutions the paramount of national interests should be the crucial guiding factor.

CONCLUSION

As already stated, to most people GATS is a challenge to our existing education system and even a possible threat to the social/cultural fabric of the nation.[2] However, a pragmatic appraisal of available information suggests that cross-border education does not, at present, constitute a major problem. This is because first, for the average student cross-border education is neither accessible, nor affordable. Second, the foreign providers from the developed countries concentrate on the countries that rank high in the Human Development Index. Most of their students come from these countries and there are a very small number from countries like India that rank low in the HDI ranking (Daniel et. al., 2005). In order to make a significant incursion into India the foreign providers will have to cut costs dramatically, increase efficiency and offer programmes that are more relevant Till then the foreign providers can only reach the minuscule minority comprising the 'creamy layer'.

There are also those in India who look upon GATS and related developments as an opportunity to revamp our education system, enhance its quality, and take innovative steps that will be consistent with the process of globalisation and will, at the same time, generate significant revenue that could be ploughed back into higher education. In the scenario that has emerged in the GATS regime the option open to our administrators and academics is to act or to perish. As of today the situation is unclear. The government is looking into all aspects and will surely see that the interest of the country is protected.

In order to keep up with international developments in the Intellectual Property Rights (IPRs) regime, it is necessary to: (i) develop capacity-building forms of education for the New Millennium and (ii) develop tools and techniques of knowledge management. For a country like India which has a long tradition of oral education and an ancient and still valuable *guru-shishya parampara*, the viable approach to education development in the globalisation era is the evergreen philosophy of having "old roots and new shoots". That definitely helps sustainable development through education, education that is not only value-added but also value-based.

NOTES

1. Critics and knowledge experts feel that there is a trend of mushrooming of degree 'shops' today, besides the rising of the ugly heads of fake universities. Both have to be weeded out at the earliest and prevented in the future.
2. Some have reservations regarding socio-cultural impact of liberalisation of education service, particularly with regards to e-learning or IT-based education. The conventionists feel that man may change from God worshipper to gadget worshipper. So Norbert Weiner has this solution: "Render unto man the things which are man's and unto the computer the things which are the computers". We have to prove that being e-human is not being inhuman!

REFERENCES

Bhalla, V. (2003), "International Students in Indian Universities", 2001-02, *Higher Education Policy and Practices,* 1 (1-2): 71-72.

Carnoy, M. (1999), *Globalisation and Educational Reform: What Planners Need to Know*, Report No.63, International Institute of Educational Planning, Paris.

Daniel, J. Kanwar, A. and Uvallic-Trumbic, S. (2005), "Who's Afraid of Cross-Border Education?: A Developing World Perspective", *INQAAHE Annual Conference, Final Plenary Session: Quality Assurance in Transnational Issues,* Wellington, New Zealand.

GATS (1995), *General Agreement on Trade in Services*, WTO Document, Annex 1-B. *http://www.wto.org/english/docs_e/legal_e/final_e.htm#services.*

Geetha Rani, P. (2004), *http://www.ijeb.com/Issues/data/June04_6_erafheii.pdf.*

Government of India (1986), *National Policy on Education, 1986,* GOI, New Delhi/UGC, New Delhi.

Hans, V.B. (2000), *A Handbook of Economics of Development*, Mangala Publications, Mangalore.

Hurria, Charu (2003), "E-Human Resource Management". In P.P. Arya and Tandon (ed.), *Economic Reforms in India–From First Generation and Beyond*, Deep & Deep Publications, New Delhi.

Ilon, L. (1994), "Structural Adjustment and Education; Adapting to a Growing Global Market", *International Journal of Educational Development*, Vol. 14, No. 2, pp. 95-108.

Nimbur, B.N. and G.S. Hiremath (2006), "Intellectual Property Rights (IPRs): India is Chasing and World is Running–AN Unbridled Question", *The Journal of World Intellectual Property Rights*, 2 (1-2), pp. 1-14.

Powar, K.B. (2005), "Implications of WTO/GATS on Higher Education in India," Dr. D.Y. Patil. Deemed University, Pune, *http://wwwunesco.or. kr/kor/ activity, 2005.*

Rupa Chanda (2004), GATS, *Higher Education Services, and India http:// www.ficci.com/ficci/media-room/speeches-presentations/2004/dec/ rupa.ppt.*

Stewart, F. (1996), "Globalisation and Education", *International Journal of Educational Development*, Vol. 16, No.2, pp. 327-33.

Tilak, J.B.G. (2001), "Education and Globalisation: The Changing Concerns in Economics of Indian Education", Editorial, *Perspectives in Education*, Vol. 17, Special Issue, pp. 5-8.

——(2003), "Higher Education and Development. In J.P. Kleeves and Ryo Watanable (eds.), *Handbook on Educational Research in the Asia Pacific Region,* Kluwer Academic Publishers, Dordrecht, pp. 809-826.

Tilak, Jandhyala B.G. (2003), "Higher Education Between the State and the Market", UNESCO Forum on Higher Education, Research and Knowledge, 1-3 December, 2004, *http://portal.unesco.org/education/en/file.*

——(2004), "Higher Education and Development", International Seminar: University XXI, Brasilia, Brazil, 2-27 November, 2003, *http:// mescrv.04.mec.gov.br/univxxi/pdf/Jandhyala.pdf*

ANNUXURES

Annexure 1
Key Dates and Actions of GATS

Sl. No.	*Date*	*Action*	*Notes for Education Sector*
1.	1995.	GATS founded; initial commitments	44 countries (if you count the EU as one country) made commitments the Education. Of these 44 countries, 21 included commitments to higher education.
2.	End of June	Negotiating proposals due 2001	Four countries- USA, Australia, New Zealand and Japan submitted a proposal outlining their general positions related to commitments in the education sector. Japan's proposal was remarkably different as their statement highlighted quality assurance, recognition of credentials and distance education as key issues that required further considerations.
3.	June 2002	All requests for access to foreign markets due	To date, only 34 out of the 145 WTO members have tabled their requests. It is not mandatory for a country to publish their tabled requests for market access in other countries. However, there were leaks and it is known that the USA made substantial requests of other countries to remove barriers to enable greater access to higher, adult and other education services.
4.	March 2003	Offers fromeach country to provide access to their domestic market due	As of the end of April 2003, only 20 countries had submitted their offers. Argentina, Australia, Bahrain, Canada, European Union, Hong Kong, Iceland, Israel, Japan, Liechtenstein, New Zealand, Norway, Panama, Poland, Paraguay, South Korea, Switzerland, Taiwan, the United States and Uruguay. It is not necessary for a country to publish their offers and only 8 of the 20 countries have done so to date. These countries are Australia, Canada, European Union, Japan, Liechtenstein, New Zealand, Norway and the United States.
5.	Up to January 1, 2005	Countries could submit offers and requests until end of Doha round	The end date of this round may be extended given the significant delays in the tabling of both requests and offers. Further rounds will occur. It is important to note that offers made during the negotiation phase of the Doha round are conditional up to the conclusion of the negotiating round and at that time, final offers are included in a country's schedule of commitments.

Source: Jane Knight (2003): GATS, Trade and Higher Education Perspective 2003- Where are we? *http://www.obhe.ac.uk/products/reports/publicaccesspdf/May2003.pdf.*

Annexure 2
Examples of US Requests to Remove Barriers to Trade in Education Sector

Sl. No.	*Targeted Country*	*Request to Remove Barriers*
1.	Taiwan	Remove nationality requirements for certain executives and directors of educational institutions.
2.	Egypt, India, Mexico, Philippines, Thailand	Remove ownership limitations on joint ventures with local partners.
3.	El Salvador	Remove prohibition on joint ventures with local partners.
4.	Turkey	Remove requirement that foreign entities teach only non-national students.
5.	China	Remove ban one education services provided by foreign companies and organisations via satellite networksRemove requirements for foreign educational institutions to partner with Chinese universitiesRemove ban on for-profit operations in education and training servicesRelax other operational limits and restriction on geographic scope of activities.
6.	Israel, Japan	Recognize degrees issued by accredited institutions of higher education (including hos : issued by branch campuses of accredited institutions)Adopt a policy of transparency in government licensing and accrediting policy with respect to higher education and training.
7.	South Africa	Remove burdensome requirements, including non-transparent needs tests,applicable to foreign universities operating, or seeking to operate in South Africa.
8.	Greece	Remove restrictions that the granting of degrees is limited to Greek institutions only.
9.	Italy	Remove requirement that foreign entities teach only non-national students.
10.	Ireland	Remove quantitative limitation on education institutions.
11.	Spain Sweden	Adopt a policy of transparency in government licensing and accreditation with respect to higher education and training.

Source: Jane Knight (2003): GATS, Trade and Higher Education Perspective 2003-Where are we?_*http://www.obhe.ac.uk/products/reports/publicaccesspdf/May2003.pdf.*

Annexure 3
Education Framework for Cross-border Education

Category	*Model*	*Description*	*Arrangements*	*Notes*
1.People	Students/ Learners Trainees	-full academic programme -semester or year abroad -internship program -research/field work	-exchange agreements -scholarship/bursaries -govt/public/private sponsored -self-funded	-involves credit-based educational activities and programme
	Professors Instructors Scholars Experts	-teaching and/or research purposes -technical assistance/ consulting -sabbaticals/ professional development	-elf or institution funded -govt/public/private sponsored -contract/fee for service	—
2.Providers	Institutions, providers, organisations, companies	-foreign provider has academic responsibility for programs -foreign award granted -provider secures physical or virtual presence in receiving country	-academic/financial partner/s in receiving country possible but not required. -includes private, public, commercial & non-commercial providers	-branch campuses -franchises -stand alone foreign providers -some twinning arrangements
3.Programmes	Credit/ award based academic partnership programs	-involves domestic qualification awarded by receiving country or double/joint award -courses and programs move, not the student	based on academic linkages between sending and receiving institutions -can be commercial or non-commercial	-primarily involves institutional linkages -some twinning and franchise arrangements
4.Projects & Services	Wide range of education related projects and services	no award based program involved. -examples of projects include: research; curriculum design; professional development; capacity building, technical assistance and services	-includes development/ aid projects, partnership programs and commercial contracts	-involves all types of HEI institutions, providers and educational organisations/ companies

Source: Jane Knight (2003): GATS, Trade and Higher Education Perspective 2003-Where are we? *http://www.obhe.ac.uk/products/reports/publicaccesspdf/May2003.pdf.*

WATER–SHED DEVELOPMENT, AN EMERGING AREA OF VOLUNTARY WORK IN INDIA

*V.S. Adigal**

INTRODUCTION

Water is the source of life. Therefore, water sources development and management aims at meeting the basic needs of the people, starting with drinking water to developmental needs in various sectors of national life, such as agriculture, industry, rural and urban development, hydropower, and land management. Developments of inland navigation, fisheries and recreational activities are also of immense importance to any country. Thus, it is a multi-disciplinary pursuit and involves synchronization of diverse activities to enable optimum achievement.

As regards natural availability, India possesses 2 per cent of land area of the world, with 4 per cent of water resources, but has to sustain a comparatively larger, i.e. 16 per cent of world population. Therefore, the country is endowed with enough water resources from the general perspective. But when considered from the view point of per capita availability, the challenges for the water sector become very evident. Over and above, when the scenario of immediate future with a growing population requiring food security for the million, which, intern, largely depends on ensuring water for meeting irrigation requirement, is kept in mind by everyone, from planners, technologists, scientists and conscious stake holders who can not just feel comfortable in the way they could have been a few decades back. In more specific terms, the per capita annual water availability in the country is changing over the years. It was 5177 Cubic Meters Per Capita Water Availability as against 361 Million Population in 1951 which has reduced to 1820 with the Population of 1027 Million in 2001.

* Head Dept. of Economics, Kiriti College of Arts, Science & Commerce, Dadar (West), Mumbai-400028.

Water is the most important single requirement for the growth of plant, animal and human life. Water resources become a pre-requisite in all productive activities. The critical role of water for intensive agricultural production hardly needs to be emphasized. The scope for further increase in the area cultivation being limited, further growth in farm production has to be attained primarily through multiple cropping and higher yields per hectare controlled water supply becomes a pre-requisite for this.

WATER-SHED MANAGEMENT

About 65 per cent of the cropped area in India is rain fed; watershed management is regarded as a vital factor for improving for Rain fed Areas (NWDPRA) attempts a holistic approach to promote the development of integrated the forming system on watershed basis. During the Eights Five Year Plan an area of 28 lakh hectares was brought under this programme and for which an allocation of Rs. 1,100 Crores was made. "Application of Remote Sensing Technology for Soil Survey and Land Use Planning" technique was resorted during Eighth Plan. It was also proposed to actively involve the non-governmental agencies in the implementation of the soil and water conservation programme.

STRATEGY OF MINOR IRRIGATION

The strategy of minor irrigation development and optimum utilization of water sources irrigation works was adopted in India during the Ninth Plan. Its salient features are:

1. Restoration and improvement of existing minor irrigation tanks as well as the development of new works.
2. Priority to the on going schemes for early completion.
3. Census of ground water extraction structures once in five year.
4. Involvement of community organizations and NGOs in the management of ground water with active encouragement through legal financial and policy backups.
5. Conjunctive use of surface and ground water to be encouraged.
6. To create awareness on the judicious use of ground water and right type of cropping patterns for optimum utilization of water.
7. To complete on going major and medium irrigation projects which were in advance stage of completion, with financial assistance

under Accelerated Irrigation Benefit Programme (AIBP) and Rural Infrastructure Development Fund of NABARD.

The minor irrigation schemes consist of providing irrigation water through tanks, wells, tube wells, ponds etc. Minor irrigation schemes assure importance in the context of rural development. The advantages of the minor irrigation schemes are as follows:

1. The minor irrigation schemes required small investment which can be easily mobilized and the costs are borne by the individual farmers themselves.
2. The gestation period is short therefore the farmers can derive the benefits within a short period.
3. Irrigation facility can be decentralized, as they are not contingent upon any single major source of surface water.
4. In city areas, rainwater can be stored by minor projects works like small irrigation tanks etc., and farmers can be assured of irrigation water.
5. There is no drainage and water-logging problem in minor irrigation works.
6. Minor repairs or improvements of minor irrigation schemes are taken up by individual farmers themselves. Therefore the Government in the long run does not take the liability of direct expenses involved in minor irrigation.

ORIGIN OF GRAM GOURAV PRATISHTHAN

Substantial areas of country periodically experience drought leading to considerable loss of agricultural production and live stock wealth, besides causing untold misery to the people inhabiting these areas. In Maharashtra State, 7,000 villages in 87 Talukas or blocks in 12 Districts have been identified as drought prone by a Fact Finding Committee appointed by the State Government in the year 1973 and Purandhar block of Pune District is one of them.

Large sums have been spent by the Government for providing relief after occurrence of droughts. Such expenditure has not helped to the required extent to solve the basic problem of increasing the productivity of these areas and thereby reducing the severity of the impact of droughts on the human and cattle population. To develop these areas and thereby reduce the impact of the droughts is a challenging task.

Though the average rainfall of the Maharashtra State in 1070 mm, its pattern is not uniform; the average rainfall in the drought prone areas varies from 250 mm to 500 mm. Besides being inadequate it is very erratic, untimely and not assured every year. This area generally experiences drought once in three years and severe drought and acute scarcity once in ten year.

It is, therefore, not possible for marginal and small farmers, to sustain on the rainfed agriculture. This has forced a large number of them to migrate to cities like Pune and Mumbai, where conditions of life in the slums are hardly any better, or to become agricultural labourers or sharecroppers on the farmers or rich farmers, in areas where there is assured water.

In Maharashtra 33 per cent of total cultivable land is affected by drought. The population of the affected villages is about 150 lakhs, almost 1/3rd of the total population of the State. Only 12 per cent of the land is irrigated and only 15 per cent of the population is covered by it. Thus sectoral planning at the national level has resulted in socio-economic imbalances and patches of prosperity. It, therefore, poses a basic question of planning for the remaining 85 per cent of the population and their 88 per cent of dry land.

There was a severe drought and scarcity in 1971-72 in Purandhar block. There was no drinking water and fodder in a number of villages. The affected farmers not only sold their cattle at throw away prices but also gifted them to those who could look after them, instead of witnessing their slow death due to starvation and thirst. They also started migrating to nearby towns and cities.

Shri. V. B. Salunke, an engineer and the Managing Director of Accurate Engineering Company had an occasion to travel in the drought prone areas in Purandhar Taluka in the year 1972. The severity of drought and the plight of the people moved him. He decided to fight famine and thought of finding out permanent measures to face recurring droughts.

In 1972-73 Shri. Salunke approached the Collector of Pune for starting productive works in the scarcity area and helped the Government organization in preparation of plans and estimates of percolation tanks costing Rs. 5 lakhs in about two weeks. One such percolation tank was constructed near the village Naigaon Shri. Salunke selected Naigaon for further experiments in rural development and started working earnestly on soil and water conservation measures.

AIMS & OBJECTIVES OF GRAM GOURAV PRATISHTHAN

The aims and objectives of the Gram Gaurav Pratishtan are as follows:

1. To provide initially relief to the farmers of the Purandhar Taluka by improving their economic conditions and to remove the cause of recurring droughts.
2. To create facilities to raise their social and economic conditions to attain welfare of the people in this Taluka
3. To conduct research studies in socio-economic conditions, so that urban interests will be linked with the process of creating integrated rural development.
4. To do all such lawful things as are conducive or incidental to the attainment of all the above aims and objectives.

EXPERIMENT AT NAIGAON

For five long years from 1974 onwards Mr. Salunke and his wife Kalpana carried out experiments in water and soil conservation; designing of low–capital–cost community minor irrigation for eight months in a year (i.e. Lift Irrigation Schemes); possibilities of regenerating scarce water by building small check bunds on nullas below the main percolation tank, the theory that water in the tank above or used on the fields at higher elevations would percolation into the ground and raise the water table in lands at lower elevations; irrigation techniques and management; different cropping patterns, to see which would yield the optimum income and food; use of improved agricultural production.

The Naigaon experiment was carried out by Mr. Salunkhe in 16 hectares of land. The 16 hectare land is situated on micro–watershed. During the heavy rains a precipitation from about 200 acres run off from this watershed. To impound this water a percolation tank of the capacity of million cubic feet of water was constructed the fields were contour bonded, leveled, stones removed, ploughed and an open well dug at the base, on the downstream of the tank. A Pump of 7.5 H.P. was installed at the well to lift the water up to a height of 40 feet. (Say about 13 m). The rising main of R.C.C. Pipes about 300 meters was laid under ground by digging trenches to the distribution chambers. Out of the 16 hectares of land 9.60 hectares were brought under protective irrigation, 2.40 hectares under a forestation and the remaining 4 hectares came under the percolation tank, well, field bunds, tract and infrastructures.

When the above experiments were being carried out by the Trust on the barren land, the farmers of Naigaon Village showed little interest. They were not only skeptical but were sure, that it was a futile exercise. But soon the experiment proved a success. When the Villagers saw that 200 quintals of food grains were produced on 24 acres of land under experiment. Whereas 40 acres of their own hardly produced ten quintals, they flocked around Mr. Salunke, requesting him to start similar schemes for them.

Besides producing record food grains, the farm has generated full time employment for fifteen people and supports fifteen animals. 4000 trees on rocky rimland and 2000 fruits trees along field bunds are thriving. In addition, a three–quarter acre has been brought under Thomson Seedless grape vine. Some decades ago Purandhar Taluka was famous for horticulture. Today there are only a dozen of orchards that produce guavas and clustered apples.

The One Million Cft. of water stored in small percolation tank at Naigaon has proved quite sufficient to irrigate 2.43 hectares in the summer, or about 11.00 hectares in all.

The Trust has been supported, besides Mr. Salunke's Industry, by individual philanthropists, other industries in Pune and Mumbai and has received some donations from Novib, Netherlands; Church's Auxiliary for Social Action and Peoples Action for Developments (Maharashtra) all supporting voluntary rural development schemes.

PANI PANCHAYAT (WATER COUNCIL)

In 1980 Mr. Salunke decided that time had come to move forward for economic transformation of the villages. He first started with Naigaon by seeking the community minor lift irrigation schemes, building upon the experience he had acquired with the experimental farm.

The various experiments carried out at the experimental farm have conclusively proved that, with proper methods of water conservation and careful distribution, half an acre of irrigated land would reasons reasonably sustain one person. Thus, a family would have a maximum of 2 ½ acres of irrigated land. Here came one of the key ingredients in the rural transformation; the allocation of water not in proportion with land holdings but in proportion with the number of people in a family unit. This revolution concept is the key to altering the "refraction effect" of technological inputs.

Another key element in the plan was it's financing. When the lift irrigation programme started in Naigaon, a formula called 20/20/40 was followed, that is, the beneficiaries put in 20 per cent of the capital cost, the Government another 40 per cent as subsidy and the Trust the remaining 4 per cent. (Interest free loan, to be repaid in five years). The Government gave subsidy from a programme called Minor irrigation extension programme 2 to 4 hectares, which was later withdrawn in April, 1981.

This was another revolutionary approach of the scheme. When the Government sets up irrigation system, the beneficiaries do not contribute anything towards the capital cost. They pay water charges and in most cases, the water is misused and benefits reach only to a select few.

From the socio-economic consideration, the modalities of Pani Panchayat for sharing water, the scarcest resource in a drought prone area and the main input for increasing the agricultural production are, therefore, as follows:

1. Only group schemes are undertaken and not schemes for individuals. This fosters community spirit.
2. The sharing of water is on the basis of the number of members in the family and not in proportion with land holdings. Half an acre per capita, maximum of 2½ acres. The land in excess of 2½ acres is to remain under rain–fed condition. The principle of equity is thus incorporated and imbalance is avoided.
3. The rights of water do not go to the land, but to the individual beneficiaries for increasing their own agricultural income. If the land is sold, the rights of water revert to the Trust.
4. Beneficiaries share 20 per cent of the cost of the lift irrigation project, according to their share. Peoples' active participation and stakes are thus ensured. The balance of the 80 per cent will be given by the Trust, as an interest free loan to be repaid in five years, from the donations received. After the scheme becomes productive, the Government will be requested to reimburse the 80 per cent or part thereof, which may or may not be accepted.
5. The beneficiaries of the Project themselves are to administer, and operate all its aspects. The leadership, capability and skills of the rural people are thus recognized and enhanced.
6. Crop such as sugarcane requiring more frequent watering and consequently more quantity of water is not to be grown. This will enable to bring more area of seasonal crops under protective irrigation. Thereby more number of people will benefit than otherwise.

7. The landless can also share water, so that they gain full employment in the village itself by becoming share croppers to farmers having more land. This will check their migration to cities.

IMPLEMENTATION OF LIFT IRRIGATION SCHEMES

Initially the farmers were required to be motivated to accept the norms of Pani Panchayat, because of the revolutionary ideas of sharing water on per capita basis, i.e. ½ acre per person with a ceiling limit of 2½ acres and contribution of 20 per cent of the capital cost. These concepts were new to them. But, after a couple of schemes for the motivated groups were completed, the skeptical attitude of the people of Naigaon was soon dispelled and more and more groups of people came forward.

Farmers of the surrounding villages soon came to know of the most enviable transformation that was taking place in Naigaon. They started visiting Gram Gourav Pratishthan had the completed schemes at Naigaon. Some of them started asking enthusiastically if such a scheme would be taken up for them also. By now all those who came to Gram Gourav Pratishthan, and therefore on more explaining of the norms or motivating them was required.

Today there are 36 schemes in hand for which Government Subsidy was received. Out of these, 25 are operative, 11 schemes though almost completes, have not been commissioned for want of electric power connection. Two schemes are in various stages of completion. Even if they are completed they would not be commissioned, as getting power connection would be a problem.

Twelve fresh schemes are taken in hand for which the Government Subsidy is not available. Out of these, three are operational. The remaining is under various stages of completion and are going to meet the same fate as mentioned earlier is regards to power connection.

SOCIO-ECONOMIC CHANGES

In each village dry land cultivation is undertaken by the majority of the farmers. A community lift irrigation scheme is beyond the means of a dry land farmer. As mentioned earlier, in the schemes of Pani Panchayat a beneficiary has to contribute 20 per cent of the capital cost of a Project. He does not have the means to raise this amount. Therefore, most of them take a share of water much less than they are entitled to.

Many of the beneficiaries have raised their contribution of 20 per cent with great sacrifice. They had to part with whatever little valuable things they possessed. Some sold their cattle, some of their sheeps and goats, some utensils of the house and in a couple of cases they even sold a very meager quantity of gold from the "Mangalsutra" (a necklace worn by a married woman whose husband is alive), the only valuable possessed by the family.

It is just not possible for a family to subsist only on dry land agriculture. Many from Purandhar block had therefore to migrate to cities like Mumbai and Pune. The Shepherd community leads a nomadic life, returning to their fields only during the monsoon to produce whatever little grain they could. This has been the pattern of the dry land farmers for generations.

These circumstances are both a curse and blessing. A curse because of the hard conditions of life, which the lack of water imposes, but a blessing in that most of the families have some land. In order words, the critical constraint in this drought prone area is not land water.

The beneficiaries of the schemes comprise of all classes high and low. It has a blessing in a social change. They no more think in terms of individual gains but consider community or collective gains. There is an accommodating spirit in them. Some anti–social activities in which some people indulged have come to an end, as they have no idle time, because irrigation has given them full time occupation.

The beneficiary shepherds are no more leading a nomadic life. They have permanently settled on their lands. Those having their fields at distant places from their village are now living in their fields by constructing thatched huts, so that they can spend more time on agricultural work. This has forced the children to foot the distance to come to the village school, besides giving a helping hand to their parents in their spare time.

A couple of groups have even solved their drinking water problem, through the lift irrigation system. This has saved the womenfolk a lot of time and labour, which they can now devote to work on the fields.

Economic achievements are equally striking. An acre of land, which hardly produced 50 kg of grains, is now producing 400 kg to 500 kg of food grains.

Prior to the commencement of the Lift Irrigation Schemes, it appeared that the people had lost all the hopes about improvements in their conditions and feeling of helplessness had prevailed. But since the commencement of the schemes people have regained self-confidence. With assured supply of carefully rationed water, though only for eight months, the farmers have been able to raise fine crops of onions, cotton, vegetables, cereals and even fruits like grapes. This not only made a better life possible, but also brought it within their reach.

Water, which is a critical input in increasing the agricultural production, is a scarce resource in a drought prone area. The available quantum of water can be optimized to benefit a large number of farmers, provided the principles of Pani Panchayat are followed.

Crop planning assumes great importance in economic uplift of the poor farmers in a drought prone area. The farmar has to strike a balance between cash crops and other crops. When it comes to cash crops, there is tendency amongst the farmers to grow sugarcane, when some source of assured water is available. But they fail to appreciate that comparatively it requires more water, generates less employment, derives less income and benefits less number of farmers.

MANAGEMENT OF THE SCHEMES

It is comparatively easy to start a community minor lift irrigation scheme. But it is very difficult to manage it after completion. There is a number of minor irrigation co-operative societies operate in Maharashtra. But unfortunately many of them have come to standstill, mainly because of their mismanagement.

The Trust has already taken over an obsolete scheme at Akola in Sangola Tehsil of Solapur District, in which the Central Bank has already sunk more than Rs. 40 lakhs. The project has been made functional by the trust and is also being managed under its auspices. Similar requests have started coming in from some other obsolete co-operative society's lift irrigation schemes.

When Government subsidy under the defunct "Minor Irrigation Extention Programme 2-4 hectare" was granted, it was not laid down that each of these schemes should form a co-operative society. But now the Government insists on forming a co-operative society. But now the Government insists on forming a co-operative society in case a subsidy from IRDP can be obtained as each block or Taluka has been doted Rs. 6 lakhs to meet the requirement for its comprehensive development, which includes, beside minor irrigation schemes, dairy, afforestation; cottage industry, poultry, etc.

Pani Panchayat would like to administer these schemes itself, because the experience of the co-operative society is unsatisfactory. The wealthier and more important or influential members of the group get appointed to the key posts. The consequence is the usual "refraction effect" of magnifying economic and social disparities.

To provide management structure for each of these schemes, a manager or a group leader is elected by the beneficiaries of each scheme. A suitable "Parkari" or a water distributor trained for the duties is appointed by Pani Panchayat. He is usually from a neighbouring village, not directly involved in the scheme itself. This person is paid a modest stipend of 200 Rupees a month and assures day-to-day fair allocation of water to all its beneficiaries. In these bodies all the families participating in a particular scheme take part equally. Every Sunday group leaders participate in the meeting of Pani Panchayat.

LIMITATION

A voluntary agency working for the rural development, however dedicated it may be, cannot achieve much, unless it has got the banking of Government. Unfortunately the Pani Panchayat lacks it. The efforts of pani panchayat in getting the "community minor lift irrigation scheme" established has been quite frustrating and enervating. Some of the limitations from which the programme of pani panchayat suffers are as under:

1. The Government subsidy is available to marginal farmers (less than two hectares) and small farmers (less than four hectares). A farmer in most part of Maharashtra is a genuine small holder, but the land record prepared long ago do not reflect the actual present position. Many a time the lands are in the name of the eldest member in the family, whereas in actual practice the lands have been divided amongst sons and grandsons.
2. In case digging of an open well or bore well on Government land in involved, permission of the Revenue Department is required. Similarly for use of explosives to dig an open well license of the home branch of the collectors office is required, without which the explosive can not be procured. It is frustrating to obtain them. It takes months to complete these formalities and correspondingly the project is delayed.
3. For lifting water from reservoirs, the permission of the Irrigation Department is required. Normally permission to lift water is granted accordingly to the total area under command of the project, lifting of water to the extent of 1% from the reservoir,

5% between dam and pick up weir and 5% from the command area. In case of M. I. Scheme the Irrigation Department expects that there should be no water left in the reservoirs at the end of March. But in actual practice there is Abundance of water left, as possibly, it is not uses to its limit. Under such circumstances, there is need to relax the rule.

4. It is equally difficult to get electric power connection to the completed lift irrigation schemes. The M.S.E.B. applies a yardstick of revenue return for each scheme. That is, it must get a return of 20% on the capital investment. Otherwise it does not sanction a power connection. To improve the plight of the marginal and small farmers, this rule will also have to be relaxed.

Even where the condition has been met, it takes considerable time to get a power connection. There is a requirement not only to make a special allotment of funds for the provisions of power connections to the schemes of Pani Panchayat, but also to provide them within three months from the date of application.

In the new 20–point production oriented programme announced by the Prime Minister, top priority has not only been given for increasing irrigation of dry land agriculture, but it has also been mentioned that it would be carried out on the principles of Pani Panchayat. It was also mentioned by the Government that additional funds are being allotted to IRDP so that the states which are effectively implementing the schemes should not be starved of funds. This being so, there is no reason why the beneficiaries availing lift irrigation schemes through Pani Panchayat should not get subsidy. To bring early relief to poor dry land farmers, the Government should make a separate allocation to the schemes undertaken on the principles of Pani Panchayat.

FUTURE PLANS

Pani Panchayat aims at employment of 25,000 people who are struggling below the poverty line, in a period of ten years, in Purandhar Taluka. It has a proposal to cover all the hundred villages of the Taluka by undertaking 600 community minor lift irrigation schemes, which will bring under protective irrigation a land mass of 25000 acres at an outlay of Rs. 10 Crores. This target has been set on the basis of the result of the study of the on going schemes of Pani Panchayat. It is, therefore, not an unrealistic proposal.

Once the problem of the basic ingredient, that is, water is solved and the agricultural production of the beneficiaries is increased, other ancillary projects of rural development would be undertaken. There will be dairy, social forestry, horticulture, animal husbandry, health, adult education, marketing, etc.

When all the 50 projects taken in hand become productive, marketing of the produce on collective basis would be undertaken. It is proposed to sell the agricultural produce directly to large consumers such as canteens of industries in Pune.

As mentioned earlier, it is proposed to open a co-operative bank for the beneficiaries so that all the extension services would cater only for seeds, fertilizers and insecticides. Later, when the extension services provisions becomes self–sufficient it's scope will be enlarged into departmental stores the charter of demands of the Gram Gourav Pratishthan includes the following:

Acceptance of the Principles of Pani Panchayat by the Government

The Government should accept in principle their moral responsibility of making available irrigation facility of half an acre on per capita basis, to the maximum or two and half acres per family in consonance with the Government's family planning programme. This can be achieved by having community minor lift irrigation schemes on a large scale. Where the farmers avail of community minor lift irrigation schemes on the principles of Pani Panchayat, Government should provide 80 per cent of the capital outlay as a subsidy and the balance of the 20 per cent should come from the beneficiaries; crops requiring water more frequently such as sugarcane should be prohibited, water rights shall be to the individual family and not to the land brought under irrigation to avoid speculation.

Provision of Electric Power Connection

It is not possible to start agricultural production on the completed schemes, unless electric power connection is provided within a reasonable time. The Maharashtra State Electricity Board should, therefore, provide such connections within three months from the date of application. The formula of revenue return should not be made applicable to community schemes. It is estimated that the Electricity Board will have to meet, on an average, approximately 20 per cent of the capital cost of a scheme. The Government should, therefore, make a separate provision for the schemes of Pani Panchayat or for any other voluntary agency engaged in a similar programme.

Grant of 80 per cent Subsidy

Keeping in view the future plans of Pani Panchayat, the Government should sanction Rs. 50 lakhs (80 per cent) for 50 lift irrigation schemes each year. It is even accepted that the Government may carry out a comparative study of the programme of Pani Panchayat and then take a decision on the continuation of the aforesaid subsidy.

Flow Irrigation Tanks vis a vis Lift Irrigation Scheme

The Western part of Purandhar Block gets a good rainfall, whereas the Eastern part receives hardly 375 mm, as the area comes under rain shadow. In case a study of the rainfall and run off in the Purandhar block is carried out, it will reveal that there is still considerable scope to store water. Taking into consideration the large magnitude of future community lift irrigation schemes the maximum number of water storage tanks should be constructed by the Government. It should, therefore, reconsider its policy of having flow irrigation water tanks. The flow irrigation schemes may also be run on the basis of ½ acre per capita for social equity.

In Purandhar block average run-off from rain water is 820 lakhs Cubic Meters out of this, it is possible to utilize about 520 lakhs Cu. M. water for Lift Irrigation Schemes, on equitable share basis. The rest can be made available by flow canal.

The condition of allowing to lift only one per cent of stored water directly from the irrigation tank may be relaxed and if the records show that the balance of water at the end of March is sufficient to grant permissions to the extent of more than 1% such permissions may be granted.

According to the estimates of the Government about 500 lakhs of Cu. M. of water is available under ground. Taking into consideration the availability of water under ground and the run off, a master plan for all available supplies should be made. The Government should, therefore, direct the Irrigation Department to revise the Master Plans. The planning for the best utilization of water wealth, during the next ten years, capital investment and gestation period, should be determined after taking into consideration the experience of the people.

Re-charging of Water Tanks

There is an estimated run off of about 500 lakhs of Cu. M. of water from Nira river, which is yet to be harnessed. At present this quantity is drained to the sea. For the utilization of this water Government has set up "Nira Watershed Development Board". The board has planned on paper to make available 1500 lakhs of Cu. M. of water for irrigating 11,800 hectares of the block, through traditional flow can system. The Project is going to cost approximately Rs. 12 Crores. This is not going to solve the problem of even ten per cent of the people of Purandhar block. On the contrary, it will widen the disparities amongst the farmers. Instead of concentration of irrigation in a small patch, Government should consider diversion of this water into the neighbouring vallies. The conservation of water in projects of small magnitudes will benefit an area of 30,000 hectares on the basis of 20 hectares per 1 lakh Cubic Meters.

Re-orientation of Power Supply

At present 9 MW of Electricity is being produced at Veer Dam and it is even possible to increase this capacity. By using this electricity, if 100 lakhs of Cu. M. of water is lifted to a maximum height of 100 meters to re-charge the various water storage tanks, by linking them. It will irrigate 20,000 hectares for eight months. If ten per cent of this area, i.e. 200 hectares are brought under horticulture, it will aid in minimizing if not eradicating the drought conditions.

In case the above proposal is accepted by the Government, the beneficiary farmers are even prepared to bear 30 per cent of the capital cost, that the Government would incur to lift run off water as a "Development Cess". And when the scheme is completed they are also prepared to defray the expenses that will be required to operate and maintain it, along with the electricity bills, under the guidance of Pani Panchayat.

CONCLUSION

The watershed-based technology gives importance to post-harvest cultivation following the post-rainy season crop before the soil hardens; land leveling and shaping, dry-seeding before the monsoon; use of improved seeds and optimum fertilizer doses and timely plant protection. The watershed based technology has ensured some social benefits also, for instance, reducing the loss of top soil and deep infiltration of water to recharge ground water. Also, farm labour employment is substantially high (and more stable) under the watershed based technology than under traditional technology).

Pani Panchayat is not just for irrigation and equitable distribution of water. It is a philosophy that can bring about a complete socio–economic change among the poor farmers. It has a tremendous potential for rural re-construction and can prevent the migration of young men and women from rural areas to urban centers.

REFERENCES

Dr. I. Satya Sundaram (2002), "*Rural Development*", p. 97-105 Himalaya Publishing House.

V.K. Sarma (1985), "*Water Resource Planning & Management*", Himalaya Publishing House, Mumbai-400 004.

Bandhudas Sen (1974), "The Green Revolution in India", A Perspective–Wiley Eastern Pvt. Ltd., New Delhi, p. 26-27.

Jain Ashok (2001), "*Political Process in Maharashtra*", Sheth Publisher, Mumbai.

Dr. K. Venkata Reddy (2001), "*Agriculture & Rural Development (A Gandhian Perspective)*", Himalaya Publishing House, Mumbai.

Mr. Vilasrao Salunke (1983), "Pani Panchayat (Dividing Line Between Poverty & Prosperity)", Gram Gaurav Pratishthan, Maharashtra (India).

B.L. Patil (Irrigation Constraints & Efficiency Measures), *Yojana*, Feb. 16-28.

Bharat Singh (1992), "Water Resources Development & Environment", *The Hindu*, July 21, p.17.

A. Vaidyanathan (1993), "Proper Pricing of Irrigation Water", *The Hindu*, March 21, p. 12.

M. Venkata Reddy (1988), "Irrigation Water Rates Need Increase", *The Economic Times*, July 7.

APPLICATION AND PROCEDURE UNDER THE PATENT ACT

*Kuljit Kaur**

"The work of founder of states, law givers, tyrants, destroyers and heroes cover narrow spaces, and endure but for a little time, while the work of the inventor though of less pomp is felt everywhere and lasts forever".[1]

INTRODUCTION

The word 'patent' has originated from the Latin word 'Patenti' which means to open.[2] In some European languages the word 'Patent' has been used in two sense: one is to mean a 'document' which is called 'Patent', the other is the "Letters of Patent" implying the content of the protection which is provided by the patent to the concerned person or individual private or corporate.

A patent is a monopoly right granted to a person who has invented a new and useful article or an improvement of an existing article or a new process of making an article. It consists of an exclusive right of manufacturer of new article invented or manufactured according to the invented process for a limited period. After the expiry of the duration of patent, anybody can make use of the invention. A patent is a form of industrial property or as it is now called intellectual property.[3] The owner of the patent can also sell this property or he can also grant licences to others to exploit the patent. A patent being a creation of statute is territorial in extent. A patent granted in one state cannot be enforced in another state unless the invention concerned is also patented in that state. The object of Patent law is to encourage and develop new technology and industry. An inventor may disclose the new invention only if he is

* Head, Department of Laws, Guru Nanak Dev University, Amritsar.
Article presented in the One-day National Seminar on Intellectual Property Rights held at Khalsa College for Women, Amritsar under the auspices of HRD Ministry of Govt. of India on 28th October, 2006.

rewarded; otherwise he may work it secretly. The main object of Patent law is that Firstly, it encourages research and invention, Secondly, it induces an inventor to disclose his discoveries instead of keeping them as a trade secret, Thirdly, it offers a reward for the expenses of developing invention to the stage at which they are commercially practicable and Fourthly, it provides an inducement to invest capital in new lines of production which might not appear profitable if many competing producers embarked on them simultaneously.[4]

APPLICATION TO OBTAIN A PATENT

There is a proper procedure for a person who is applying for the Patent right. The patentee has to go through from different stages to apply for the Patent right. These different stages are:

Who May Apply: An application for a patent may be made by the actual inventor of the invention, or an assignee of the right or legal representative of either. The right to apply for a patent is assignable. Though an oral assignment is not precluded, for establishing title to apply an assignment in writing is preferable. The right to apply, on the death of the owner of the right, devolves to his legal representatives.[5]

Form of Application: An application for a patent in a prescribed form alongwith the prescribed fee, must be filed in the appropriate patent office. The application should be accompanied by a provisional specification. A complete specification should be filed within twelve months from the date of filing an application. The specification should relate to single invention.

Examination of Application: The application is examined by examiners of patents to see whether it complies with the requirements of the Act, and to check that whether the invention has already been published or claimed by any other person. After examination of the application, the patent office will communicate to the applicant, and if there is any objection than the ground of objection is also conveyed to the applicant.[6]

Term of Patent: Subject to the provisions of this Act the term of every patent granted after the commencement of the Patents (Amendment) Act, 2002 and the term of every patent which has not expired and has not caused to have effect, on the date of such commencement, under this Act, shall be twenty years from the date of filing of the application for the patent.

Register of Patents: The Register of patents is Prima Facie evidence of any matter entered therein. A copy of any entry in the register certified by the Controller and sealed with the patent office will be admitted in evidence in all courts and in all proceedings without further proof or procedure of original.[7] The Controller has power to correct any clerical error in any matter entered in the register on a request made by any person interested or without such a request. The Register of Patents have the following particulars:

(a) The name, address, etc. of the grantee, the title of the invention, the date of the patent, the date of sealing and the official number of the patent;

(b) Notification of assignments, transmissions, licences, amendments, and revocation of patents, and;

(c) Particulars of such other matters affecting the validity or proprietorship of patents. No notice of any trust, whether express, implied or constructive, will be entered in the register.[8]

Where any person is aggrieved by:

(a) The absence or omission from the register of any entry;

(b) An entry made in the register without sufficient cause;

(c) Any entry wrongly remaining on the register or;

(d) Any error or defect in the entry in the register

He may make an application to the High Court for rectification of the register. Any order of the High Court for rectification of the register will be notified to the Controller who will than rectify the register accordingly.

Patent Office: Its head office is at Calcutta. There are branch of offices at Bombay, Delhi and Madras. The patent office is the office established for the purpose of administering the various provisions relating to grant of patents and maintenance of Register of patents. The Controller General of Patents, Designs and Trade Marks are the Controller of Patents. To assist the Controller there are examines of patents and other officers. These officers perform their functions under the superintendence and direction of the Controller.[9]

Powers of Controller: The Controller of Patents is conferred with various powers and functions. He has the following powers:

- To Review his own decision
- To Correct clerical errors in Patents, document or any matter in Register, either Suo Moto or on request made by the person interested.

- To permit amendment of any document for which no provision is made in the Act.
- To give secrecy directions to an applicant for patent relating to invention which is relevant for defence purposes.
- To Correct irregularity in procedure etc.[10]

PROCEDURE FOR ACCEPTANCE AND DISPOSAL OF APPLICATION[11]

An application for a patent shall be deemed to have been abandoned unless within 12 months from the date on which the first statement of objections to the application or complete specifications or other documents related thereto is forwarded to the applicant by the Controller that the applicant has complied with all the requirements whether in connection with the complete specification or otherwise in relation to the application.

Oppositions to application and their disposal:[12] At any time within four months from the date of advertisement of the acceptance of a complete specification or within such further period not exceeding one month in the aggregate as the Controller may allow on application made to him in the prescribed manner before the expiry of the 4 months aforesaid, any person interested may give notice to the Controller of opposition to the grant of the patent on any of the following grounds–

(a) That the applicant for the patent or the person under or through whom he claims wrongfully obtained the invention or any part thereof from him or from a person, under or through whom he claims.

(b) That the invention so far as claimed in any claim of the complete specification has been published before the priority date of the claim–

(i) In any specification filed in pursuance of an application for the patent made on or after the Ist day of January 1912 or;

(ii) In India or elsewhere in any other document;

But the ground specified in sub clause (ii) shall not be available where such publication does not constitute an anticipation of the invention.

Where any such notice of opposition is duly given, the Controller shall notify the applicant and may, if so desired to the applicant and the opponent an opportunity to be heard before deciding the case.

Grant and sealing of Patent: Where a complete specification in pursuance of an application for a patent has been accepted and either–

(a) The application has not been opposed under Section 25 and the time for the filing of the opposition has expired; or

(b) The application has been opposed and the opposition has been finally decided in favour of the applicant; or

(c) The application has not been refused by the Controller by virtue of any power vested in him by this Act; or

(d) The application has not been found to be in contravention of any of the provisions of this Act, the patent shall on request made by the applicant in the prescribed form, be granted to the applicant or, in the case of a joint application to the applicants jointly, and the Controller shall cause the patent to be sealed with the seal of the patent office and the date on which the patent is sealed shall be entered in the register.[13]

Right to secrecy of certain inventions:[14] Where in respect of an application made before or after the commencement of the Act for a Patent, it appears to the Controller that the invention is one of a class notified to him by the Central Government as relevant for defence purpose, or where otherwise the invention appears to him to be so relevant, he may give directions for prohibiting or restricting the publication of information with respect to the invention or the communication of such information. The question in respect of which directions have been given, continues to be relevant for defences, shall be considered by the Central Government for intervals of 12 months or on a request made by the applicant which is found to be reasonable by the Controller and if on such reconsideration it appears to the Central Government that the publication of the invention would no longer be prejudicial to the defence of India or in case of an application filed by a foreign applicant, if it is found that the invention is published outside India, it shall forwith give notice to the Controller to revoke the directions and the Controller shall then revoke the directions previously given by him. The result of every such re-consideration shall be communicated to the applicant within such time and in such manner as may be prescribed.

Patents of addition:[15] Where an application is made for a Patent in respect of any improvement in or modification of an invention described or disclosed in the complete specification filed thereof and the applicant also applies or has applied for a patent for that invention or is the patentee in respect of it, the Controller may, if the applicant so requests, grant the patent for the improvement or modification as a patent of addition. Where an invention is an improvement in or modification of another invention, is the subject of an independent patent and the patentee in respect of that patent is also the patentee in respect of the patent for the main invention, the Controller may, if the patentee so requests by order revoke the patent for the improvement or modification and grant to the patentee a patent of addition in respect thereof, bearing the same date of the patent so revoked. But a patent shall not be granted as a patent of addition unless the date of filing of the complete specification was the same as or later than the date of filing the complete specification in respect of the main invention.

PROCEDURE

The procedure for obtaining a patent and matters connected therewith are detailed in the Patents Act 1970 and Patent Rules framed thereunder.[16] Time limits are prescribed within which parties to the proceedings before the Controller have to comply with certain requirements at various stages through which an application for a patent has to pass. These time limits are designed to facilitate quick disposal of the applications well within the monopoly period of the patent when ultimately granted.

An application for a patent in the prescribed form alongwith the prescribed fee should be filed in the appropriate patent office.[17] The application should be accompanied by a provisional or complete specification. A provisional specification needs to describe the invention only briefly and need not contain the claims. Where the application is accompanied by a provisional specification, a complete specification should be filed within 12 months from the date of filing the application. If this is not done, the application will deemed to be abandoned. The complete specification should fully and particularly describe the invention and the method by which it is to be carried out. The claims should relate to a single invention. They should be clear and should be fairly based on the matter disclosed in the specification. The specification should be accompanied by drawings where appropriate and necessary. The specification should relate to a single invention.

The application is examined by examiners of patents to see whether it complies with the requirements of the Act and the Rules, whether there is any lawful ground of objection to the grant of the patent, and whether the invention has already been published or claimed by any other person.[18] The examiner makes a search in the publications available in the patent office and specifications of prior applications and patents to see whether the same invention has already been published or claimed or is the subject matter of existing or expired patents.[19]

After examination of the application, the patent office will communicate to the applicant, the objections, if any, to the grant of a patent. The objections generally relate to the drafting of the specification and claims, anticipation of any of the claims in prior publication of any specification or claims or documents. In many cases these objections can be overcome by suitably amending the description of the invention and the claims and in some cases by insertion of a reference to the prior specification number. If the objections are not satisfactorily met, the Controller of patents after giving an opportunity of hearing to the applicant will refuse the application.

Where the applicant has satisfactorily removed the official objections the Controller will accept the complete specification and advertise it in the official gazette.

CONCLUSION

From the above discussion, it is clear that the procedure for obtaining a patent and matter connected therewith are detailed in Patent Act 1970 as amended by Patent Act, of 2002 and Rules Framed thereunder. But the applicant has to fulfill all the procedural requirements and that too within the time limits prescribed for obtaining patent under the Patent Act. Invention may be made by two persons, but both will not be entitled to a patent right. The person who first applies for the patent right in the invention will be holder of the patent registered under the law. Therefore, an inventor should obtain patent for his invention at the earliest to get the benefit under the Act.

NOTES AND REFERENCES

Francis Bacon, Quoted in mainly on patents at page 1, edited by Felix Liebesny, Butterworths.

R.K. Nagarajan (2003), "Intellectual Property Law", Allahabad Law Agency, Allahabad.

Ashok Soni (2003), "Complete References of Intellectual Property Rights Laws", Delhi Law House, New Delhi.

Acharya, N.K. (2004), "Text Book on Intellectual Property", Delhi Law House, New Delhi.

Chowdhury Salil K. Roy (1999), "Law of Trade Marks, Copyright, Patents and Designs", Kamal Law House, Calcutta.

Myneni, S.S. (2003), "Law relating to Intellectual Property", Delhi Law House, New Delhi.

Myneni, S.S. (2003), "Law of Intellectual Property", Delhi Law House, New Delhi.

Shiv Sahai Singh (2004), "The Law of Intellectual Property Rights", Deep & Deep Publication, New Delhi.

Vikas Vashishth (2002), "Law and Practice of Intellectual Property in India", Delhi Law House, New Delhi.

Jayashree Watal (2001), "Intellectual Property Rights in WTO and Developing Countries", Oxford University Press, New Delhi.

R.K. Nagarajan (2003), "Intellectual Property Law", Allahabad Law Agency, Allahabad, p. 147.

Ibid., p. 151.

Sec. 43 (1), Patents Act, 1970.

Ibid., p. 153.

Ibid., p. 154.

P. Narayan (2002), "Intellectual Property Law", Eastern Law House, New Delhi, 23.

Robert R. (1976), "European Patents at the cross roads", Oyiz Publishers, London, p. 126.

Ibid., p. 130.

Ibid., p. 132.